PRYOR LIVES!

HOW RICHARD PRYOR BECAME RICHARD PRYOR

OR

KISS MY RICH, HAPPY BLACK...ASS!

A MEMOIR

BY

CECIL BROWN

DEDICATION

F or Randi, of course; thanks for your patience, inspiration, and love.

But also,

For Paul Rucker, and his wife, Jessica, and Dexter and Dash— Thanks for your support and putting "fun" back into family.

And also for my nieces: Ingrid Brown, Yuri Brown, Dawn Brown, Patrice (Bookey) Brown, Winter Brown, Fifi Brown, and Trina Brown: I love you and will always be with you.

ACKNOWLEDGMENTS

I WANT TO THANK my friends who helped me and who also gave me insight into the writing of the book: David Peeples, Phil Kaufman, David Foster, Taj Mahal, Ray Holbert, Alex Dilone, Bob Zagone, Al Young, Billy Woodberry, and Ishmael Reed.

A special gratitude goes out to my students at Santa Barbara who took my Richard Pryor class (2005). The grades have long been turned in, but the class continues. Thanks for the experience of teaching you and learning from you.

Social Drama Number One *141*

Social Drama Number Two *195*

Social Drama Number Three *213*

Social Drama Number Four *223*

Social Drama Number Five *243*

Social Drama Number Six *249*

Social Drama Number Seven *269*

Social Drama Number Eight *275*

CONTENTS

Part One: The King of Comedy 1

Chapter One: Introduction 3

Part Two: Working the Small Room (Berkeley Days) 21

Chapter Two: Threshold 23

Chapter Three: Mandrake's 27

Chapter Four: Live Stand-up Performance! 33

Chapter Five: Third World Strike 45

Chapter Six: The Black Stranger 51

Chapter Seven: People's Park 55

Chapter Eight: Chez Panisse 63

Chapter Nine: Bill Cosby 75

Chapter Ten: Hi, I'm a Nigger! 81

Chapter Eleven: His First Pad 83

Chapter Twelve: A Literary Party 87

Chapter Thirteen: El Topo 89

Chapter Fourteen: Warren Beatty 99

Chapter Fifteen: KPFA 103

Chapter Sixteen: Super Nigger 111

Laney College Auditorium 111

Chapter Seventeen: Mudbone 119

Chapter Eighteen: The Mack 125

Chapter Nineteen: "The New Pryor" 135

Part Three: Working the Big Room (Hollywood) 139

Chapter Twenty: The Comedy Store 141

Chapter Twenty One: Franklin 155

Chapter Twenty Two: The Sunset Marquis 159

Chapter Twenty Three: Rosalind Cash 169

Chapter Twenty Four: Greased Lightning 177

Chapter Twenty Five: Black Hollywood 183

Chapter Twenty Six: The Richard Pryor Show 189

Chapter Twenty Seven: The Hollywood Bowl 195

Chapter Twenty Eight: This Is The Way Up!....... 205

Chapter Twenty Nine: Blue Collar 213

Chapter Thirty: How to Shoot a Car 223

Chapter Thirty One: Liminality................. 229

Chapter Thirty Two: Albert Goldman............ 239

Chapter Thirty Three: California Suite 243

Chapter Thirty Four: Richard Pryor:
Live in Concert 249

Chapter Thirty Five: At Home with the Pryors 255

Chapter Thirty Six: Stir Crazy 269

Chapter Thirty Seven: Freebase Inferno 275

Chapter Thirty Eight: Controlling the Crisis 279

Chapter Thirty Nine: Star-Groupers 283

Chapter Thirty Forty: Recuperation in Maui 291

Chapter Forty One: The New Pryor
Returns to Northridge......................... 295

Chapter Forty Two: The Law Suit................ 307

Part Four: Which Way Is Down? 313

Chapter Forty Three: Jo Jo Dancer,
Your Life Is Calling You 315

Chapter Forty Four: Richard's Last
Performance - 1994........................... 323

Chapter Forty Five: No Longer The Fool – 1995.... 329

Chapter Forty Six: Teaching
Richard- Pryor Lives!......................... 335

Chapter Forty Seven: Richard Pryor
and Misogyny 345

Chapter Forty Eight: Epilogue 351

POSTSCRIPT: 355

SCREENING OF RICHARD PRYOR:
OMIT LOGIC 355

Appendix.................................. 359

Note on Sources 361

Bibliography 363

✖

PART ONE:

THE KING OF COMEDY

Life imitates Art far more than Art imitates Life.
—Oscar Wilde, *The Decay of Lying*

CHAPTER ONE

INTRODUCTION

I T IS A SUNNY MIDDAY, ON Sunset Boulevard, Hollywood California, spring in 1995. As you entered the café, you passed a line of limousines. You could tell you were about to enter a celebrity party. The waiters wore tuxedos, the waitresses wore stockings and white aprons, and the guests wore the most expensive casual clothing. The sound of laughter mingled with the clanging of wine glasses. Now the only question was, whose party was it?

*Quincy Jones, Robin Williams, and Pryor at
Richard's book signing party in 1995.*

Seated at a round table was Richard Pryor scribbling in a hard-back book. It was his autobiography, *Pryor Convictions*, published by Random House in 1995. Enfeebled by disease and drugs, here was one of America's greatest comedians, if not the greatest—"The Picasso of our profession," Jerry Seinfeld once said. Come to pay homage were friends and Hollywood legends. Hovering over Richard's table were Paul Mooney, Quincy Jones, Bill Cosby, George Wallace, and Sandra B. Bernhard.

Robin Williams leaned over Pryor's shoulder, looking at what he had written to him as a dedication. Richard's thin, frail hand shook—he suffered from the late stages of multiple sclerosis—as he handed the book to Williams and said, "This is for the night we spent together!" The other celebrities cracked up.

When he opened the book to read what Pryor had written, Williams, playing his role well, said, "Thank you, Richard, for that wonderful night, I'm still sore!" Again the two great comics sent the room roaring with laughter.

"I can't read this in public!" Robin added, extending the gag and laughter.

The book signing celebrated not just Richard's career, but also the huge, incalculable influence he had on comedians. Every comedian who wanted to succeed treated the occasion as if it were a holy shrine. They all stooped down over Richard and got their pictures taken with the stricken master.

Born in Peoria, Illinois, in 1940, Richard Franklin Lennox Thomas Pryor grew up in a bordello. He joined the army and later went to New York as a teenager, competed in and won an amateur contest at the Apollo Theater in Harlem in 1959. He was nineteen.

By the time he was 26, he had been on "Kraft Music Hall," "Merv Griffin Show," and had a part in the film *Carter's Army*. Modeling himself on Bill Cosby, he began his career in 1963 in the coffee houses of the Greenwich Village. In 1967, he had a breakdown on stage in Las Vegas. Until this breakdown (the rumor spread quickly that he was crazy), he was just a good comic who imitated Cosby. After the Las Vegas meltdown, dying horribly on stage, his life changed; he claimed his material was letting him down.

Later that year, April 1967, he was arrested in San Diego for bringing an ounce of marijuana into the country. In July, at the desk of the Sunset Tower motel in Hollywood, he hit the clerk, broke his glasses—and was convicted for assault and placed on probation. He did not contest to the lawsuit filed by his wife for $1,000 a month child support.

He decided he would entirely remake his career, so in 1969 he hitched a ride from a fan to Berkeley and performed at a small club, Mandrake's, down in the Berkeley flatlands, near the old industrial zone. Throwing out the entertainer role, he became an artist—Richard Pryor. It was this change that would not only transform his act, but would also transform the role of stand-up comedy forever. Pryor was possibly the only nightclub entertainer in America who would have thought to remake himself by moving to Berkeley, the capital of the counterculture. Because of this single act he changed himself and twentieth century American culture, too.

A few years after I met him, Richard told an interviewer from the *Washington Post* that he wanted to become so famous that he could be recognized from a "nameless caricature," like Bob Hope and Muhammad Ali. He said: "When everybody can look at my caricature and say, 'That's him! That's Richard Pryor!' then I'll be great. I had doubts before but I don't have those doubts any more." As Leo Braudy points out in his history of fame and celebrity, *The Frenzy of Renown*, Richard's ambition for "immediate visual recognition" goes back to the heroic statues of antiquity – and at the height of his fame he got what he wished for.

The 70s belonged to Richard Pryor. He dominated the first half of this decade with his standup comedy, just as he dominated the last half with his films. During the late seventies, he was the biggest star of Hollywood, *Which Way Is Up?* and a long comedy tour. The year 1979 was a particularly potent with such films as *Which Way Is Up?*, *Greased Lightning*, and *Silver Streak*, with Gene Wilder. However, this new change had brought its price. He was jailed for not paying $250,000 that he owed in back taxes. "I was involved in leading a new life and old shit didn't matter," he said. What mattered was the new form of expression, not taxes.

It was in 1977 that Richard began to have real trouble with his audiences. At the Hollywood Bowl benefit, September 18, he told an audience of 17,000, mostly white gays, to "kiss my rich, happy, black ass." But after this disaster, he bounced right back with a hit movie, year for Pryor; it was also perhaps the toughest year of his life. In the middle of that year, he collapsed from two heart attacks. On New Year's Eve, a few months later, he emptied his magnum into his fourth wife Deboragh McGuire's Buick. He was arrested, fined for a misdemeanor, and put on probation.

Quincy Jones, author, and Pryor.

By the end of the year, he picked himself up and produced a masterpiece entitled *Richard Pryor Live in Concert* (1979). Regarded by the critics as a low budget comedy achievement, this film connected Pryor's humor, enjoyed by counterculture audiences for years, to a wider audience including the Hollywood elites like Neil Simon, who was inspired to write films for him (*California Suite*). "Granted that Pryor is a victim of racism, of family troubles, of drugs, fame, and illness, still he impresses as someone who might have found a way of liberating self-destructiveness even if circumstances had stayed tidy and nurturing," the film scholar David Thomson writes of Pryor, whose "raw wildness" he finds "close to genius." Surely, Richard's work passed over into it.

But in 1980, disaster struck again, this time leaving half of his body burned. In a "suicide attempt," Richard soaked his polyester shirt with rum and lit it with a cigarette lighter. With his clothes aflame, he ran down the street. When the police tried to stop him, he screamed, "If I stop, I'll die!"

When they did stop him, he was crying and pleading, "Lord, give me another chance!" As had happened before, the Lord did gave him another chance—although many of his friends and critics did not. Many people, including his friend Jim Brown, thought that his suicide attempt was a result of "bad karma."

There was speculation that he might not survive the skin graft operations. Once again, however, Pryor not only survived, but also was inspired by his own failure to be creative again. Using his life experience with death, he produced another outstanding video concert film, Richard Pryor Live on Sunset Strip (1982). After making a string of films like *Superman III* and *The Toy* (1982) he decided to make a film of his life, *Jo Jo Dancer, Your Life Is Calling You* (1986). He was on top again after finishing the film, when another irrecoverable disaster struck.

While driving across country with his new girlfriend, he fell ill and was diagnosed with multiple sclerosis. The year was 1986; he was forty-six years old. At first, he was still able to work, despite the disease. He worked with Eddie Murphy and Red Foxx on the film *Harlem Nights*. But in 1991, the disease had taken away his ability to stand. So, he did a film in a wheelchair called *Another You*, with Gene Wilder. He made his last appearance in 1997 in a small role in David Lynch's *Lost Highway*.

Back at the book party, I watched him as he signed his last book. As I watched, he began fumbling with a cigarette. Just then, when he looked up and saw me, an old friend from Berkeley, he started to smile. The cigarette slipped out of his fingers.

His wife, Jennifer Leeo—who was always at his side—had not seen the cigarette fall. She didn't see it fall, because she was talking to the Random House editor. Jennifer Lee met Richard in 1979 while she was working as an interior decorator in his house. They had married in 1981, and then divorced a year later. In 1992, they reunited for business reasons and remarried for the same reasons. Part of her new job was to bring out his autobiography, and that is why she is celebrating with the Random House editor.

Random House editor (on the left) Errol McDonald, Jennifer Lee (center), and a friend of Jennifer's.

Nobody else had noticed the cigarette fall. I went over and picked it up from the floor and handed it to him. Grasping the cigarette, he thanked me and smiled. I had not seen him for a few years. I drove down from Berkeley to attend his book party. I was probably one of the few people who had known him since the Berkeley days, back in 1969, before his Hollywood fame.

"Come by the house later," he whispered in a low, hoarse voice.

After the party had exhausted itself with food, drink, and conversation, we all stood on the curbside of Sunset Boulevard as Richard in his motorized chair was hoisted into a van. We stood there watching Jennifer as she helped Richard in his wheelchair. After we all had exchanged numbers and congratulations, I went for a walk, during which I remembered a film that Richard and I had seen in Berkeley. It was called *Belle de Jour*. In the end, Catherine Deneuve pushes her husband around in a wheelchair. At the time, the ending of that film shocked Richard and I. Now, he was in the same situation. How strange that was.

As I drove out to see Richard in his home in Sherman Oaks, I reflected on the more than twenty-five years I had known him. I thought about the first time I saw him in Berkeley, the many years that had passed, and how he had changed and yet remained the same person that I met so many years ago.

I walked up a poinsettia-laden brick path to the front door. A few years back, in 1992, Richard sold his Bel-air mansion for 3.5 million and moved to Sherman Oaks, to reduced quarters. One of his five assistants, Marilyn Staley, opened the door and greeted me with a pleasant smile.

When you stepped inside Richard's newest place, you felt like you were in a hospital or a nursing home. There was the quiet humming of a ventilator and the room temperature was always kept at 68. It's white and clean, like a medical facility. There are spacious rooms that overlook a large garden. Outside the back window is a medium sized swimming pool. Nothing compared to the one he had out in El Encino at the big ranch-like spread he had out there. This setting was also a long way from that one-room apartment Richard had when I first met him in Berkeley, in 1970.

Richard's staff consists of an executive assistant and a live-in nurse, Marilyn Staley as well as his personal trainer, cook and maid. Marilyn led me to the next room, where Richard was seated in his motorized chair. When I came around and sat next to him, I saw he had a 50-inch TV on and had the TV Guide on his lap.

A fresh pack of Marlboros sat on the table near him. He had always been a heavy smoker, and had not been able to give it up. He smiled.

"Sit down, partner." I sat down.

"What you want to drink?" Marilyn asked.

"Just juice."

"Can I have some water, please, and a Pepsi?" Richard was very polite.

He was always courteous to the people helping him. This was a trait I noticed when I first met him in Berkeley, when he was sleeping on a friend's couch. He was grateful for those who helped him.

He ruffled the papers, nodded, and took a long time to speak. Even so, I could still see that spark of light in his eyes when he laughed.

The symptoms of M.S.—drifting eyes, tremors, vertigo, muscle weakness, chronic fatigue and impotence—are cruel and unpredictable. At this point, Richard's career was obviously over with. He was finished now for good, and there were no more comebacks.

Now he rattled the newspaper and looked up at me.

"I just saw Paul Schrader's movie, about Patty Hearst. Have you seen it?" Richard asked me.

I had seen it. Not only had I seen it, I had worked on it. Paul Schrader came to Berkeley to make the movie, and the producer Tom Luddy, who was a friend of mine, asked me to help Schrader. I met with Schrader and his crew in San Francisco in an apartment he had rented. For taking him around and showing him a few places, like the Starry Plough, where the SLA hung out, Schrader offered to give me an interview. In the interview, he talked about how difficult it was to work with Richard on *Blue Collar*, because Richard often showed up for script readings with a pistol.

In 1974, during the early days of the Patty Hearst's kidnapping, I was walking on Telegraph Avenue with Richard who was visiting from Los Angeles.

I had picked up the *San Francisco Chronicle* that day, and Richard and I were walking across the street. As we stood on the corner, I opened the paper and as I did, Richard looked over my shoulder at the headline.

"Look," I had said, commenting on the police photo of the suspects who might have kidnapped the Hearst heiress.

Richard and I looked at the picture of a black man in the newspaper. The composite looked like not a particular Black man, but like every black man. Now twenty-eight years later, he looked at me from the motorized wheelchair.

"That picture in the newspaper looked like everybody," Richard grinned.

Pryor had woven the bit into his act, exploiting the news and my comment. Twenty-four years later, we were seated in his Hollywood home.

I broke the silence. "So what did you think of Schrader's movie?" I asked.

"I wanted to apologize to Patty after seeing that movie," he said, "She had to sleep with every nigger in the SLA gang."

"I didn't know that. She came out okay, though," I said. Richard said, "She must have had some good and beautiful pussy, though."

"Why do you say that?"

"To make a motherfucker like Cinque go crazy and get burned up in the basement!"

We also talked about the revolution that we used to hope for. I reminded Richard of a comment he once made.

"'I'm not afraid of The Bank of America, The FBI, the CIA, but I am scared of the moment my son will ask me, 'What was you doing during the revolution?'"

Richard nodded, acknowledging the moment in the 70s that seemed so important to us, to Black people especially, in America.

"The Revolution never really happened," I said, because I remember that's all we talked about in those days.

"No," Richard said, "it didn't. But Cinque had them scared!" After a little chuckle and a grin, Richard changed the subject slightly.

"You remember Santa Barbara?" he asked.

Santa Barbara! I thought. Why was he bringing that up? Santa Barbara was the summer of 1971.

"Yeah, man," I said. "I remember."

Richard, myself, and Ishmael Reed flew from San Francisco to Santa Barbara to give support for a black man who was being railroaded to prison. The political battle turned out to be an adventure of comedy and realizations that the sixties were over.

"I met your friend Claude Brown," he said.

Claude Brown, one of the most celebrated black authors of the sixties, wrote the best seller *Man-Child In the Promised Land* (1965). He was teaching in the English Department at UC Santa Barbara. He arranged to fly the three of us down to be in a benefit performance for a friend of his who was accused of killing a white man. Claude and Richard became really good friends, both impressed by the other's talent and personality. Whenever I talked to Claude, he'd always ask about Richard. When the evidence came out that the black man had been killed in the bedroom, and that his affair with the man's wife had nothing to do with racial politics, we were disappointed. The article about our concert appeared in the Celebrity column, which described what we were wearing, but nothing about our politics. Richard announced to all of us, "That was the end of the Sixties for me!"

"We had our hearts in the right place," Richard said, commenting on those events that shaped our experience.

We turned our attention to his book that we had just celebrated. After he signed my copy of the autobiography, I mentioned that Jennifer had a stamp made for him.

"Yeah, I got tired. I don't write that well, even before M.S. I never could spell. You know, it's embarrassing. How to spell names. How to spell 'sincerely.' Fuck that!"

We had often talked about writing such a book together. His book was a great disappointment for me. I was there in the Berkeley years, egging him on about black creative writings. But Tom Gold was the editor of *People Magazine*, so he had the advantage on me. The book was organized from top down, not the other way: the way we learned in Berkeley.

Richard was never much of a writer, not in the traditional sense. He didn't have the patience to sit behind a typewriter or computer screen. His genius was telling the story through gestures and mimicry. When the publicity describes him as a "writer," they are referring to his dictated verbal performances.

In 1971, the *Rolling Stone* writer David Felton asked him if he had been doing any writing. Richard got very excited. He answered, "I want to write, but it's hard when you have to travel." For Richard, performing bits on a tape was just as good, if not better, than actually putting it on page. It was better, too, because you didn't have to do the drudgework. Performing didn't require the discipline of sitting down and staring into the abyss of a blank page.

Richard credits his trip to Berkeley as being the most important transformation in his comedy, because it was in Berkeley that he had found his unique style. Yet in his book, he left out the circumstances that brought him to Berkeley. He didn't mention the man on whose couch he was sleeping, nor the Richard Pryor that I met in Berkeley. He zonked it! How could he leave out the core of his art, the moments when he went from being a "white bread" comedian molded on Bill Cosby to being the inimical word artist?

There was a long silence as Richard and I just sat there. As I listened to the humming of air conditioner, I looked over at him and saw that he was thinking about something in the past—something that disturbed him.

Suddenly, he interrupted the silence and spoke.

"There was a young girl who loved Janis Joplin," he said. He glances over my shoulder to the green lawn behind me.

"She had some shoes that Janice Joplin gave her. In a fit of downright cruelty," he recalled, "I threw those shoes in the Bay." I remembered the scene from the autobiography. In this book, the ghostwriter, Gold called her "Geena, this hippie chick."

He remembered the scene, and felt sorry about the selfish act he had done over twenty-five years ago.

"She came in the house wearing these Janice Joplin shoes and I threw them into the bay. I wish I'd not done that. She jumped in after them an hour later looking for her shoes. I had no right to do that."

There was a moment of silence. After this moment of sadness and catharsis, I steered the conversation back to the style of the book.

"I like the way that Gold weaves your comic style into the narration. Did you put that in the book? Or did but Gold put it in the book?"

"He did," he confessed, "He got it off a record."

"Which one?"

"He listened to them and where he got it, don't make me lie, but I don't know."

He looked in the paper and shook his head. What's this about? He was referring to the movie advertisement in the paper he was looking at.

"*Braveheart?* What's it about?"

Then he saw a film with Clint Eastwood in it.

"Did you meet Clint Eastwood?"

"Clint Eastwood. Yeah."

"What was he like?"

"I met him at the race track. He seemed like a nice guy. He had that bitch with him. The one who is now suing for palimony?"

I nodded.

"You can't win with a woman. You ain't gone get it from a woman," Richard said. Sandra Locke, who had lived with Clint Eastwood for 14 years, sued him for "palimony." I could see why Richard would side with Clint Eastwood on this issue. Jennifer had once contacted Marvin Michelson, Richard once told me, the famous divorce lawyer.

I decided to change the subject. I could see he was getting tired.

"What would you say is your comic genius?" I asked the question because at that moment I felt I would not have another opportunity to ask it.

He looked at me and laughed.

"Damn if I know and I couldn't tell you, if you paid me cash money."

I reminded him of those times we used to hang out with Cosby. "Cosby said you could take pain and make it funny," I said.

He paused for a long time. Then he raised his finger, and shook it. "Don't begrudge me that. 'Cause I'm not on a rooftop trying to kill some motherfucker," he laughed.

There was another long pause, and I waited as he tried to clear his throat.

"Were you influenced by Lenny Bruce?" I asked.

"I would say that." Richard said. Then he started talking about the first time he heard Bruce. I already knew the answer to that question, but when we first met in Berkeley, he would often play Bruce. We'd had this conversation before.

"I ain't never heard nothing like that in my life. Ever! A lady played it for me. I sat straight up in my chair. What the fuck am I doing if that's comedy?"

"At what part in your life did you hear him?"

"In the early 60s. When I did, I shot straight up. I listened to him over and over. Funny records. Some were green and some were red. I got a bunch and listened to them. Now they are on CD."

"Satire?"

"Yeah—satire."

"What did you learn in Berkeley?"

"That I could get a room and be by myself. That was my first place, but it was all mine. A little furniture. Maybe a chair. That record player. I put it all together."

"I remember that leather hat," I said. Back in the Berkeley days, he always wore a leather hat with a straight brim. That hat made me think of our passions. We had a passion for Bert Williams. We were going to make a film about Bert Williams called *Nobody*. I wrote the script for him to play Bert Williams.

"Bert Williams—we didn't do that."

He smiled a bit. "We tried."

I introduced him to Bert Williams in the Berkeley days. I ordered the 16-millimeter film that shows Bert playing cards and passing the card to his partner under the table with his toes. Richard liked the scene when Bert Williams put his white-gloved hand out and made the audience laugh. I thought that other early records were characters in a film, and that you could listen to them and make up pictures. In Berkeley, I was listening to all of the old records.

"I saw your daughter in the Panther film," I said. The film was by Melvin Van Peebles.

"Which daughter?" Richard asked.

"Rain—"

"I didn't know she was in that."

"Did you see it?" I asked.

"No."

"White people hated the Black Panthers then."

The maid brought his soda.

He flipped through the newspaper. There was a picture of the SLA when the police in Los Angeles attacked them.

"Something happened, I didn't see it coming. They blew up that building. They went crazy. He didn't mean to do that to the kids." He was talking about the police that burned up the SLA house in their final raid on it.

Flipping the paper again, he came to an article on the OJ trial.

"They have some shit going on, I don't understand. That OJ shit. If he did, he has to sit down and get to see the lives everyday."

"Yeah and you get to listen to the motherfuckers who's lying for you and it ain't going so well." Richard referred to OJ's ten million dollars he was reputed to have had.

One passage in *Pryor Convictions* described Richard's early childhood sexual abuse. The entire child abuse thing was revealed in the book. He devoted three pages to a graphic description of being raped by an older boy. From the descriptions that he dictated to his biographer, he was obviously upset about the experience.

In that autobiography, his name was Hoss. Hoss threw the six-year-old Pryor against a wall in an alley and said, "Suck it." The child did as he was told.

According to the book's version of the incident, "Afterward, Hoss walked off happy and left me trembling in the chilly darkness. I cried and shook and tried to make sense of what had happened," he told Todd Gold, the ghostwriter. "I felt violated, humiliated, dirty, fearful, and, most of all, ashamed. But I couldn't sort that shit out. Fuck. I carried that secret around for most of my life. I told no one. Ever." Yet in his comedy routines, one can sometimes hear references to this incident.

"What was his name?"

"I don't know what his name is in the book, but his real name was Bubba. People don't know the pain," Richard said, barely audible. He stared ahead, looking out to the swimming pool as if he were remembering the scene.

Again, he paused.

"They don't care," he said finally. "My dad would sit at the kitchen table and sing a song. 'You are forever blowing Bubbles!' He knew this was going on. Why didn't he do something? I think he did. I think he said, see my kid out there, make him suck your dick!"

I was embarrassed to hear this, because it was obvious that he was taking it seriously. Why hadn't he spoken of it before? Or, had he? Wasn't it in his comedy? Or, was it?

"Our people were sexually abused in slavery," I said.

"I would think so."

"Some of them were pimps," I said, "The white man was a pimp!" Richard keeps laughing.

"No, it seems silly, but outré' on – on point, as they say."

"Good book title," I said.

"Thanks."

For some reason I thought of Ray Stark, Richard's producer. "Where's Ray Stark now?" I asked him.

"He's being rich somewhere."

One of Richard's nurses brought him his late lunch.

I said, "Go on and eat, don't notice me."

"How can I not?"

I got up to go. I told him I'd come down and see him as often as I could. On my way out of the house, I reflected on the twenty-six years I had known Richard. What would I say in my book about him? How would I explain the people and the incidents he left out? I would write that book, I decided, as I drove down the hill. That book that he and I always said we would write. The book he never got around to writing. A book that didn't have to pass through the mind of a white man. That would be a book that started at the beginning-the beginning that was in Berkeley.

As I drove out of Sherman Oaks onto the freeway, I thought about Richard as the Perfect Fool. The term came from an article I'd read. This article traced the art of the American standup to the lost art of the court jesters. Frank McConnell said the court jesters had a magical function. They could say things that nobody else would dare utter to the King. They had license, but sometimes they went too far. Not only would they expose the disease of the society, but also often they embodied the disease and acted out the ritual. "The standup lineage is of the Court Fool," Frank McConnell wrote in *Commonwealth*, the leading Catholic intellectual journal. "The Fool is officially sanctioned chaos. As the shaman, he is the holy madman of archaic religion." He claims you could still see this in the comedy of Robin Williams and Richard Pryor. But, it becomes scary when these comedians become self-destructive by making themselves into the Perfect Fool.

What is the Perfect Fool? I wondered.

The fool reincarnates the foibles and sickness of society, going so far out that he cannot come back in. We, the society, pay him well to become a train wreck so that we can be warned. But sometimes, he goes too far and cannot return to normalcy. "The Fool," as McConnell says, "is the one who just might not be able to come back from his incarnation of disorder." Richard was the Perfect Fool: the Negative Exemplar. The Perfect Example of WHAT NOT TO DO!

But how did he get that way? In the following chapters, we will revise all of these themes, but this time, more in depth, filtered through the eyes and ears and heart of one who was there.

Part Two:

Working the Small Room (Berkeley Days)

You taught me language; and my profit on't
Is, I know how to curse: the red plague rid you,
For learning me your language!

Caliban, *The Tempest* by William Shakespeare

CHAPTER TWO

THRESHOLD

I DROVE OUT TO the freeway, heading up north, up to Berkeley. How many times had I done this over the past thirty years, leaving Richard's place and pulling out to Interstate 5? I-Five, as it is known by us Californians. I had a long time to think, about six hours. I reflected on the many different inaccuracies in the book that we had just been celebrating. In fact, I read the galleys a few weeks earlier, noticing that the editor left out a lot of material on Berkeley, including only a half page on Pryor's experience in Berkeley out of a 300-page book.

Then and there, I began imagining my own book, because the exclusion of these experiences would disable the reader from understanding the influence Richard had on the politics and culture of the 60's and 70's.

I hope that, in revisiting my personal experience with him, I can recall the vital connection between the culture of the 60s and the evolution of his comedy from Bill Cosby-type imitation to a unique creation that transformed many of the comedians who attended the Sunset celebration. I wanted to show how the Berkeley experience changed Richard from an ordinary comedian to a brilliant spokesman and anatomist for black—and white—society.

McConnell was right about fools having licenses. Richard certainly had license. His license implied a marginality that he shared with millions of Black people.

Furthermore, the kind of license he had made sense given the history of Blacks. "The standup lineage is of the Court Fool," as Frank McConnell puts it, "as the shaman, he is the holy madman of archaic religion."

My personal experience with Richard bears this out. I don't believe everything in the comparison between the Jesters and contemporary comedians, but McConnell is up to something solid when it comes to Richard. Not only would jesters expose the disease of the society, but often they would embody the disease and act out the ritual. Richard certainly embodied many of our society's unconscious maladies.

In Berkeley, a reporter commented that Pryor had his own Black language to express himself and that whites do not have that. "But they do," Richard argued. "They know that I'm speaking for them. My voice is their voice. They are glad to hear my voice, because what I'm saying is what they are saying."

Like a shaman, Richard brought out the demons in society; and by purging the society of those demons, he helped maintain some measure of sanity in society. But in his life, he often took on the demons not of society, but of himself. As Richard suffered from the abuse of drugs, society slipped by unnoticed—its demons were never expelled.

In his early comedy, Richard was able to use spoken comedy effectively to purge his audience. Like the old Native American shaman Mudbone of the Hopi, he is the one who exorcizes our public demons as a nation. Such a status reveals the meaning of Richard's act. Also central to Richard's development was his spiritual journey with Jodorowski's film *El Topo*. From this single film, Richard constructed his own personal view of cinema.

It is a mistake to see Richard as just a neurotic who was addicted to drugs who happened to be a funny man, as some people do. This view leaves out the Richard Pryor that I knew personally. Emotionally, he was as stable or unstable as most people. It is important to emphasize drugs, but we should not loose sight of his real concern: his audience. It was his own attitude toward his audience that is so significant in understanding his humor and comedy.

He wanted to coax his audience—that shy, inhibited representation of society—out of its shell, making people face up to their own dishonesty and hypocrisy. Not surprisingly, there were always people who would walk out on his routine. But the ones who stayed often went through some cathartic changes. Like the primitive, Richard had a social role to play for our society at large. To play that role required that he was "either neurotic or psychotic." Whether he was or not, in any case, Richard's art was based on the same mechanism as the primitive shaman.

Richard was a lightening rod for the "common anxieties" of the American public. Like all primitive shamans, he fought the demons for us. He fought the demons so that we can "hunt the prey and in general fight reality."

The first critic who ever wrote about Richard was a writer for the *San Francisco Chronicle*. Phil Elwood wrote about him as early as 1966. He thought Pryor "exaggerated" his background stories. He didn't like him and he certainly didn't think he was charming.

Elwood saw Richard in 1966 in Enrico Banducci's nightclub Hungry i. In his review, he gave an example of Pryor's vacuous non-sequiturs: "On the subway, you either can watch the junkies or read the ads." Even worse, Elwood thought that Pryor was not authentic, claiming he "exaggerated" his accounts of his upbringing. He did find some of it funny, but most of it "distasteful." Richard ended the act with a bit about "Mankind, beginning with Adam and Eve..."The act, Elwood concluded, was "neither original, nor funny."

But in 1971 – just a few years after Richard arrived in Berkeley - Elwood changed his mind about him. He thought Pryor's background stories were "pure theater."[1]. Pure Theater! He went on to write that: "In the vernacular Pryor is one of the 'baddest niggers' around. He is exceptionally bright. He works easily and smoothly on stage." How had Pryor gone from being a bad comic to a brilliant one? What had happened to him between 1966 and 1970 that changed his comedy? I hope to find answers to this question in this book.

Chapter Three

Mandrake's

ABOUT SIX HOURS later, I pulled into Berkeley. I drove up University Avenue that leads right into the University about three miles east. I passed the Cat and Dog Hospital at Tenth Street and University. Back in 1969, this Cat and Dog Hospital was Mandrake's—a rock and roll club and a hangout for hippies. It was also the place where I first saw Richard. How different Berkeley was in 1969 from what it is now in 2013!

Mandrake's was on the corner that catered to a rock and roll crowd. White rock was a popular music, especially in Berkeley. There was a freedom from cultural restraints, but the real focus was on national events like the death of Martin Luther King, the rise of the Black Panther party, and the antiwar movement. My then girlfriend, Marianne, and I had to stand in a long line that snaked around the block. We were waiting to see Richard Pryor, who was to appear any minute. Mandrake's, the space that Richard performed in, was a cool spot in those days. The counterculture had reached its peak. With the deaths of Jimi Hendrix and Janis Joplin, it was also beginning to wane. "Counterculture is largely anti-culture," the great critic and biographer Albert Goldman, my professor at Columbia University, observed at the time, "one step more and it becomes non-culture."

Richard arrived in Berkeley at the tail end of the countercul-ture revolution, just at the point when the youth culture was about to take that "one step more." If he had been here six months later, he would have missed it entirely.

Marianne was the one that hipped me to Richard. In those days, Marianne was typical of a whole cadre of white women who were "hip." She mentioned to me that Richard Pryor was a satirist, and that he was trying to do the same thing I was doing. I was curious that somebody was trying to do satire, which was my thing. She gave me his album—his only one. On the album cover, he is squatted, dressed in a loincloth, with a bow and arrow—a parody of a *National Geographic* photograph. His image was that of the fool who had a message.

She had said that there was a guy who is a satirist, "like you." It was the "like you" part that got me to go see Richard. Who was it that was like me?

We were finally allowed to go inside. As we were waiting, a medium-built, middle-aged white woman guided us to a seat between couples not far from the stage. Her name was Mary. She owned Mandrake's.

The year 1969, when Richard came to Berkeley, was the tipping point. The decade had begun with the A & T College Woolworth sit-in in Greensboro, North Carolina. The sit-in was the event that would ignite the fire of student movements in the country. This decade—the revolutionary 60s—would end with the Rolling Stone's concert in Altamont, California, where members of the Hell's Angels sacrificed the life of a young black man.

In the beginning of the 60s, the nation was optimistic because segregation was finally ending. With the exorcism of this demon, the country could finally release some of its stored up energy. With the integration of schools and universities, it was commonly be-lieved: blacks would find the future promising. For the first time, they would have the same access to education, health and business opportunities that their white counterparts had been enjoying since the beginning of the nation. These opportunities had been kept from them because they were Negroes.

For some Blacks, the future was brighter. But by the end of the decade, many people began to see that the future was not that bright for the majority of Black people. After the assassination of Martin Luther King, Jr., it soon became clear that not everybody welcomed the demise of segregation and the rise of the New Negro. In fact, the nation witnessed the assassinations of the great heroes who championed Black progress: J. F. Kennedy, Robert Kennedy, Malcolm X, and Martin Luther King. By the end of the decade, the music had gone from "We Shall Overcome" to the militant "Fight the Power!" People had gone from a hopeful beginning of the civil rights movement to the disappointment of the Black power movement.

According to some scholars, after the failure of Dr. Martin Luther King Jr.'s non-violence movement, many young black Americans moved to the philosophy of Black power. This new interest ushered in a host of young black leaders like Stokley Carmichael, Huey P. Newton, and Eldridge Cleaver. These new charismatic leaders replaced the moderate leaders of non-violence. When Richard came to Berkeley, he became saturated in the rhetoric, poetry, and vision of these leaders; some of whom he would meet in Berkeley.

Students from prestigious colleges like Harvard and Columbia protested against the police on campus, the war in Vietnam, and the disrespect that administrations showed to Black Americans. In many of these colleges, students held administrations and faculty hostage. They took over universities, and often closed them down. When Richard arrived in Berkeley, Reagan had just been reelected for the second time as Governor of California.

During that spring when I saw Richard at Mandrake's, Berkeley's social culture was reeling from one catastrophic event to another one. The first was the Third World Liberation Front strike that had closed down the UC campus. Reagan had ordered 2,700 National Guard troops to manage the students.

Then, on April 18, came People's Park. In this incident, the UC Berkeley Chancellor and Governor Ronald Reagan sent troops to beat back students and "street people" from occupying a university-owned parking lot. As in the other disaster, the police and national guards opposed the students. Many people were beaten and hospitalized. The police brutally murdered James Rector, an onlooker.

The audience that came to see Richard that night were kids who had seen a dreadful downturn in the local optimism. Just a few months ago, in January 1969, they had seen Nixon inaugurated as the 39th president. The first thing Nixon did was to escalate the war in Vietnam by bombing Hanoi. They would be further disappointed when on May 8, Nixon unleashed B52 air strikes just inside and around the Cambodian border. Anti-war rallies were growing by the weeks, culminating in the biggest anti-war march of all times: in November, 250,000 young people marched on Washington. It was larger than the 1963 civil rights march.

The white youth who lined up to see Richard that night were from this generation. They had witnessed many "free love" concerts in the Golden Gate Park by now. They formed the core of the counter culture. They had been lied to by the leaders of the nation, by the leaders of their local towns, by the Oakland Police, and by the Berkeley Police. When somebody conducted a Gallup poll about how well Nixon was doing with the Vietnam War, about 53% of voters approved of his performance and of his escalation of the war. But the whites that were waiting with me in line were not represented in that percentage. They were not included with the majority of whites that Nixon addressed in his famous speech "the silent majority."

Richard arrived at a time when the Berkeley counterculture would respect a funny guy who had a hipster's take on everything. His reputation as a satirist and as an "interesting" person had traveled through hearsay. He was already known to be a social miscreant, a screw up. When you came through the door, you saw a line of folding chairs all in a row, with little rickety tables in front of them. To your left was a cork-board pasted with notices of rock bands to appear. In the center of the room was a tiny stage for the performer. The owner, Mary, ran back and forth frantically. We were greeted by the news that Pryor was going to be late.

Seeing that Country Joe McDonald, the singer and guitarist for "Country Joe and the Fish," was in the audience, Mary asked him if he would entertain us until Pryor showed up. Country Joe, a white dude with long, blonde hair and an apache headband, didn't want to oblige Mary. He said he didn't have a guitar. A few years earlier, at Woodstock, he had been asked to fill in after Richie Haven. He was so scared that he complained that he didn't have a guitar. The next thing he knew somebody handed him a Yamaha FG 150, and so that he would remember to return it, the owner had tied a rope to it. Reluctantly, Country Joe got up and began playing an Erik Satie song. When the audience didn't respond to that, he started with "Louie, Louie."

"Louie, Louie" just happened to be the worst song he could think of to entertain us with. It had been a doo-wop song when Richard Berry, a Black singer first created it back in 1955. Then, Led Zeppelin recorded a beautiful version of it. But it was left to Paul Revere and the Raiders to turn it into a frat party song. Country Joe slung the incomprehensible lyrics out at the audience to get their attention. About another thirty minutes later, Mary came out on the stage and, pushing Country Joe off the stage, announced, "Richard Pryor's here!" The beginning of the rite of passage for the new Richard had just begun "On Stage."

CHAPTER FOUR

LIVE STAND-UP PERFORMANCE!

THE AUDIENCE BROKE into a large applause. A slim shadow lurched behind Mary, and we took this to be Richard. "Ladies and Gentlemen, the crown prince of comedy, his highness, Richard Pryor!" Mary had the good sense to get off the stage as soon as possible so we could have a glimpse of what we had been waiting for.

This was my first time seeing Richard. I had never seen him on the television programs he had been on, "Merv Griffin" and the "Johnny Carson Show." Before he walked across the stage to the mike I could see him standing behind Mary in the shadow.

In the light, he was tall, almost skinny. He wore a green sweater, grinning, holding a cigarette. His face was open, sincere, and genuine. He was a hip brother, and looked streetwise.

He stood, looking out, his eyes moving over the audience, then to me, nodding, then past me, refocusing.

"Thank you...Thank you, and good evenin'..."

His voice was deferential, relaxed, and anxious.

"Thank you...for waitin'...Hi..." he says to somebody in the audience. I am aware that he senses how white this crowd is when he turns and notices me. I'm one of the few blacks present.

"...I would like to take you back to my childhood..."

The audience reacts happily. Childhood was a good choice, considering how adults were getting their tooshes kicked by revolutionary reality. Good choice. Let's go back to innocence and bliss. But it wasn't the childhood that they had in mind!

"I liked being a kid very much," he says in a childish whine. "I like being a kid very much."

Long pause.

"You don't have to be anything else. I was a kid until I was eight. Then I became a *Negro*..."

In the singsong way he says it, he cracks us up.

"They made me do it at school. The teacher said, 'Say, Negro!' I said, 'Negro!' 'Negro!' 'Negro!' The teacher said, 'Very good. I will give you an A!' I used to go home and tell my Daddy that I was a Negro. My father said, 'Really? I thought you were Polish!'"

The audience burst with giggles, because Richard had fooled them. They were waiting for one thing, and he had slipped past them with a joke about race.

"We used to play this game called 'The Last-One-To-the-Store–is—a—Nigger Baby, right? It was called The Nigger Baby game. That's right." He stopped as we burst into laughter. "You played it, too?" He directed his question to this one woman who is laughing the hardest. Then there was a white dude sitting next to her. Richard pinned him with a stare. "I know, *you* played it!"

The guy cracked up. If he did have any racist feelings left, Richard exorcised them with a single word, as if he was some evangelist burning demons out of sinners. "Yeah, you played it!" he jeered. This was his method—get the audience involved with the unfolding of the humor. Bring out their demons.

Now we were all laughing—from ear to ear.

"I used to run like hell myself...I didn't want to be it! I didn't want to be the damn Nigger Baby...But I didn't know that I had lost before the race started." The audience loved it, because the comic's image of himself as a schmuck was worse than their own self-images.

"Remember how we used to go to the confectionary store and ask for a dime of Nigger Babies?"

They laughed from recognition.

"But nowadays this don't happen because the kids are very progressive, right?" By using the word "progressive" he meant the audience in front of him.

"Now, the progressive kids go in and ask for a dime worth of Negro Babies." When they have stopped laughing, he adds: "They say, 'Charge it!'"

For having brought out some of their buried prejudices and for having snapped their venom right in front of everybody, for this public service, the audience rewarded him with a very big laugh. Very big. In the middle of this routine, he paused and introduced himself, as if he had forgotten to do it when he first came on.

"I'm from Peoria. Where is that? Good question! It's a city in Illinois. Oh, in my town Peoria…"

A white female laughs. She is an attractive young woman and Richard is drawn to her.

"…You from there? From Peoria? You are? Really? Well, if you're from there… What did you do there, in Peoria? What is there to do there? Good question!"

He has the audience in his palm now and they playfully love it.

"…You lived on Washington Street?"

He was actually talking to a member of the audience.

"…Oh, you were there?"

We all turned to look at the young woman. Nobody talked to audiences in those days, not even comedians.

"…That's where the whorehouses are!" He looked deeper into her young, white face as it blushed red with embarrassment.

There were bigger laughs now from the audience.

"…Funny, you don't look like a whore!"

Talk about being spontaneous! He was so spontaneous that it's like he hadn't prepared anything to say. He is ad-libbing like a jazz musician—shooting off whatever comes to his mind! Richard had an immediate power to soothe the audience, to work the room, and to make us one family. We were a family – one big family enjoying the communal laughter. He established this kind of rapport with the audience by asking them questions.

He warmed them up to each other, so that when they laugh, they laugh as a group with shared values. Often this interaction between the audience and the comic, as it was that night, might include some ritual insults, like suggesting that the white girl was a whore.

"I was born there, in Peoria, and got my start in show business there. I started out in the play Rumplestiltskin. Maybe some of you read about it? I was in a play called Rumplestiltskin. My mother made me a costume. I played the wind. Whee! [He imitates the sound of the wind]. I did a little encore."

He makes a childish, foolish noise like the wind, and we just crack up. "When I came up, I only went to a storefront church. We were told Black people didn't have a god. We worshipped things like Air, Water, and Trees, each other. And white people considered it pretty savage. So the white man said, why worship those silly things when you can worship me, White Man! 'Here take these beads and cool it.' When I say 'white man' I don't mean everybody," he warns. They find that funny, too.

From the back of the room comes this voice of a white dude who wasn't going for it. "You're lucky I have a sense of humor!" the guy says.

There is a slight chill in this tight space. Then Richard comes back with a zinger.

"Yes," he says slowly, deliberately, without a trace of intimidation. "Yes, I'm lucky you have a sense of humor, 'cause I know what you white folks do to us Negroes!"

The audience lets out the loudest laughter of approval and does everything but jump to its feet. They love Richard for doing what they want to do—shut the guy up and put him out of the club.

"Can I ask ya'll something?" he says. "Why are you afraid of Black Power? Why?"

Then he looks over to the guy and asks him. "You seem to be the spokesman for the bigot group." He moves in on the guy. "You seem to be the spokesman for the bigot group from Bigotville." The crowd applauds and laughs. "Black power is just a word...

but if you hear it on television, 'Black Power is coming!' everybody gets uptight. But if the White Knight come stickin' people, that's alright!"

For that, he got another shower of applause." Anyway, you have nothing to fear from the black man, except his thoughts." His riff on "Black Power" was appropriate, since at the time, it was difficult for anybody to escape the impact of the news of the rise of the Black Panther Party. That year saw the police murder 27 black panthers, as well as the arrest of the founder, Huey P. Newton for the murder of police officer John Frey.

I was one of the few blacks in the crowded room, and Richard seemed to be glancing over at me through his entire routine, as if I were a witness to what he was telling this white audience.

"There was a time only a few years ago," he said, "when Black was not beautiful." He paused and took me in again. "There was this guy who used to come through our neighborhood. He was dressed like you!"

Like me? I was wearing a black leather jacket and I had a Free Huey button on it. I had been at a Free Huey rally with 5,000 others. After everybody had an eyeful of my outfit, he went on.

"And he used to come by our house and tell people, 'be black and proud.' My parents say, 'That nigger's crazy!' Back before Black was Beautiful, the wino's just a wino. Now..." He glared out at the audience. "Now...them motherfuckers want more than wine now—they want justice! You used to give them wine. But now you have to give them some bullets – and a target!"

*Teaching at UC Berkeley,
when I met Richard.*

Tooting and hollering, these white kids wanted everybody to know whose side they are on. And they were not on the side of this nut in the back of the room! Richard helped make their burden lighter with joke after joke.

The next routine that he brought to us was a gem of pure sexual and racial fantasy. He started off by pretending that he was reporting on a skit about a play that is performed in a prison. But this façade barely disguised a fantasy about sex and sexual jealousy. The dramatis personae were hilarious. First, we met the Warden Tucker ("And now I'd like to put on a play for ya! This play is called 'Black Ben the Blacksmith' and it's produced by some nice folks from Joplin…"). Next, he used a fake British accent to introduce the play director Ben Dodge ("The play is about a young white girl, who has fallen in love "with a Black.") Next, we met Ben the Blacksmith (who sees the white girl and says, 'Gee, is that yo' body?'). Then, he brought on his verbal stage, the "White Girl." He had us laughing as he pulled the White Girl Voice out of his hat. Her voice was feminine, liberal, and naïve. The white girl met Ben the Blacksmith. She had something else on her mind, and it wasn't the horse.

In his monologue, Richard had The White Girl In Love With Ben, say, "My, you have some handsome biceps!" Ben replied, "Thank you, mama. Would you like to feel my *ass?*"

There was a loud outburst from the white women around me. Undaunted, The White Girl In Love With Ben replied, "I'd love to! *Should I pinch or squeeze it?*" When the white girl admitted her "love of the Black," the Warden threatened to stop the production. "Just a minute here! The play is closed. Okay, start loading up the prisoners and take them back. Oh, we ain't having this play!" But the director reassured him that the Black gets killed in the end. He said, "Oh, that's different," and allowed the play to continue.

In this way, Richard had the license to speak about the system of sexual fantasy that seems to undergird everybody's secret life.

"I like big-titted white girls," he said now in his real voice, "The kind that you know. You just want to rip their blouses off and the titties just fall out…" The excitement for the audience was in hearing jokes that were forbidden to be told in public; again, this was a way to expose publicly some private demons.

Richard switched his voice, transforming into a British twit. I began to notice that he had a special talent of finding the "key" to a character. He found the *one thing* that made you imagine that he's nailed the character. This "key" could be in the voice, the way he said a particular word, or the way he delivered an intonation. Whatever it was, it worked.

The kicker that ended the verbal skit was when the Warden insisted on the promised ending: "Just a damn minute! You said the nigger gets killed! If we don't get a dead nigger, we gonna hang one of these homosexuals!"

Applause! Whoa! I thought. What better way was there to expose the private demons publicly? His approach to politics, however, was indirect. A good example was his attitude toward Nixon. Most of his audience was against Nixon because of his escalation of the Vietnam War. Therefore, Richard could have gone on record with a statement about his disagreement. Instead, what did he say about Nixon to them? Just this one quip:

"Nixon is a lesbian!"

That was enough to send the audience off. Such howling!

This was what many people had thought—not that he is a man pretending to be a woman, but a politician pretending to be honest, that the entire Nixon Administration was absurd.

"—And Agnew is his woman!"

That was the punch line—that the vice-president was the President's woman! That implication addressed our deepest moral recesses. But it wasn't that much different from what Stokley Carmichael, the black power leader had said a few weeks earlier at the Free Huey Rally when he shouted to the crowd, "President Johnson is Hitler's illegitimate child and J. Edgar Hoover is his half sister!"

Judging from their closely cut haircuts and polyester shirts, some members of the audience were from the suburbs, like Orinda. However, most of them were white students who were active in Berkeley's politics. They were, as he had intimated, the progressives, the Yippies, and the anti-war protesters. But everybody thought they were hip, because they were not prejudiced and could laugh at a racist joke.

I had my Nikon camera with me. Why shouldn't I get a picture of him? I'd never get this chance again. I stood up from my chair to take a picture, but Richard, seeing the camera out of the corner of his eye, turned. Just as I was about to snap the picture again, he beamed his big black eyes on me. The audience had noticed me standing up to take the picture. I felt I was in the joke with Richard.

"Damn, nigger," he said to me, amidst great laughter. "Take the damn picture!"

While we laughed, he said, quietly, "Goodnight."

He walked off stage. The audience jumped to its feet. Hands clapped, jaws slackened, and lips curled. I looked at my friend, Marianne. We were both blown away. We weren't the only ones blown away either. I crossed the stage and followed Richard out of the back door. The door led outside the club into a parking lot.

I had heard this kind of humor all my life, but never in public. Just hearing him talk to an audience in public—especially a white audience—made me especially proud to come from that black oral culture. The door opens to a parking lot, where Richard was standing, smoking a cigarette.

"Hey! —"

He turned. I felt we have already met, especially since he called me out in the audience.

"That was fantastic!" I extend my hand.

"Glad you liked it. Who are you?" He shook my hand, giving me the Black Power handshake. Then, he shielded his hands over his eyes to kill the glare from the light shining through the door.

"My name is Cecil. I wrote the book *Life and Loves of Mr. Jiveass Nigger.*"

"Oh, I read about that." He laughs. "I like it that you called it Mister. Not just any jiveass nigger, but Mister Jiveass Nigger." I laughed, too. I was delighted that he knew my book.

Before the evening was over, Richard bragged about my book, again saying how much he liked the title. "Mister Nigger," he laughed.

"How long are you going to be performing in Berkeley?" I asked him.

"I live here now." He said it like it was something to celebrate.

"Oh," I said. "Then we can see you perform again?"

"Yeah," he said, "Alan, give him my address. You can come by and hang out with me. I live about three blocks away." The white boy called Alan writes the address 1505 Berkeley Way, about ten blocks north, and telephone number down for me on a piece of paper.

"Come by around two o'clock," Richard said. "I want to talk to you."

What I saw that night was definitely satire, it was unique, and Richard was an incredible character. Although I had not given much thought to stand-up comedy before this time, I was to learn that it is the most universal of all forms of human expression. Through Richard, I would begin to see the connection between the trickster slave humor and the public exorcism.

CHAPTER FIVE

THIRD WORLD STRIKE

MARYANNE WAS UP already when I came into the kitchen that morning. It was about ten and I had a class at eleven. I drank some coffee and reviewed my lecture notes for class. It was not just that I was excited to have met Richard. I wanted to know and read everything I could about him.

I was living in the Berkeley Hills, at 2700 Virginia Street. From my living room, I had a view of the Bay Bridge, the cityscape of San Francisco, and the Golden Gate Bridge. I liked getting up in the early morning and stand up at a podium and write while looking at the view.

In the living room, I had put in big green plants and upholstered pillows. Out in the yard, I had a glass-top table and a lounge chair. I shared the back yard with my neighbor, Adam Hochshild, his wife, Arlie, and their baby boy David. Adam spent time at home taking care of David and working on his novel. Arlie taught sociology at UC Berkeley. Adam and I often talked about writing. His novel was eventually finished and rejected, but he later had great success by founding the *Mother Jones* magazine.

I left Maryanne and drove to Campus in my red Jaguar XK150. At the corner of Telegraph and Bancroft, a large group of students held signs and blocked the entrance to campus.

"Third World College!" the protesters cried.

"Hey, man! You livin' a contradiction!" somebody yelled at me because they saw I was driving a Jaguar. This was Berkeley after the Chicago Seven trial, after the rise of the Black Panthers, and after the bombing. The fever of protest was subsiding, but you could still see plenty of protest as you walked across campus through Sather Gate.

As I passed through the student protesters, I realized that, although I supported the cause of the Third World College, my real thoughts were elsewhere. I had to get to my class in Wheeler Hall. As I strolled across Sproul Plaza, I was haunted by the voices that Richard had created. There were so many voices!

When I got to the classroom, Peter, my teaching assistant, met me at the door. His dark, bushy hair was unusually messy, as if he had not slept well that night.

"We've got another problem," he said. "We have too many students now. Ten more showed up. But we can't have any more students."

"How many students are we over?" I had to find out how many we had already. I was thinking that I could ask the chair to open up another session of my class.

"Ten already," he replied. I took a deep breath. I didn't really care. I wanted to talk about Zora Neale Hurston and Richard Pryor. I wanted to talk about Black humor and folk speech.

"Let them all stay."

When I said it, it was more of a bluff. Peter's eyes got wide with agreement, and I felt encouraged.

"You mean...let them all stay?" he asked me, not sure that he had heard me right.

"Yeah."

"Okay." He gave me a look. "Okay, but..."

I walked into the class. There were about sixty students. This was a big class for freshman English. My other class was African American Literature, and it had about two hundred.

In 1967, I received my master's degree in English Literature from the University of Chicago. Armed with a letter of recommendation from Charles Van Doren for a teaching position at Fresno Junior College, I took off with a rented Cadillac for Berkeley. I had been teaching for about a year when the publication of my first novel gave me a lot of recognition. I was already teaching before the book came out, but after the publication I received national attention. After I drove out to Berkeley in the summer of 1968, I got a job teaching at Merritt College. After joining the Black Students Department, headed by Huey P. Newton's brother, I wrote and installed a play on the stage. Professor Larry Ziff, from the UC Berkeley department of English, saw one of my plays and invited me to teach a class at Berkeley. When I applied for the job, the college paper published a headline: Black Lecturer Denied Job at Berkeley.

For the position, a room full of Black students interviewed me. They wanted to know what I thought of Fanon's *Wretched of the Earth* and Leroi Jones' *Blues People* and Malcolm X's *The Autobiography of Malcolm X*. I didn't dare tell them that my real preoccupation was Spencer's *Faire Queene* and William Faulkner's *The Bear*.

When I did begin in the English department in the fall of 1969, I was assigned three classes—African American, Creative Writing, and English. I was teaching Zora Neale Hurston's *Their Eyes were Watching God* and Charles Chestnut's *The Conjure Woman*.

Now as I walked into my Afro-American literature class, I reflected as I looked at the faces. They were mostly black, with many white students, too.

"Today, we will discuss the first chapter in Their Eyes Were Watching God. That afternoon, I talked to them about oral literature, of which I saw Zora Neale Hurston as an example. But I could have added Richard Pryor. Alfred Lord's *The Singer of Tales* had inspired me to think about the traditional oral tale and African American folk culture. Lord had talked about Homer and Shakespeare as oral poets. Weren't Richard Pryor and Zora Neale Hurston also oral poets?

"The oral voice is the essence of African American writers like Zora Neale Hurston," I said to the class. I wanted to tell them about Richard Pryor and his voices that I had heard that evening in Mandrake's. Richard's voices were portraits of black people who belong in the novels and short stories. Whereas black authors wrote their stories, Richard delivered his stories out loud.

In one story, there was the voice of Richard himself, as hip, black Narrator. There was also the Racist Cop, Pryor's Father, and the Black Policeman Who Has to Tom to Impress His White Partner. When he came to the "line up," he described all the suspects with a different voice. There was Allen T. Johnson; Bundy T. Wilson, the anti-government agitator; and Arnold T. Perkins, the child molester. He spoke in the voice of a Black Preacher, who knows God personally, the Wino who knew Jesus Christ, as well as his mom and whole family. Richard had voices of women, too. Of girls who masturbate, but claim they don't and girls who will give you some but make you swear you won't tell about. There are also dudes, too. Dudes who fight and talk to you at the same time, and then Dudes who argue before they fight you.

"Voices create pictures," I told my students. But, as they gathered their belongings at the period's end, I was never sure how many of them understood what I was driving at.

After class I went to pick up my mail in the faculty department. There, I ran into Mark Shorer, the most well known professor in our department.

"We want to invite you to a party," he said, "Ruth wants to have a party for the incoming writers." I had been to the faculty parties and loved them. I was so proud to be on the same faculty with Mark Shorer, because I admired him so much. "Literature is the world we dreamed," he often said. "Writers use technique," he wrote, "to discover their subject."

"Mark," I told him. "I'll have to cancel."

"That's too bad."

I couldn't explain to him about meeting Richard Pryor and wanting to hang out with him.

What I saw in Richard was an artist, a satirist, whose work was related to the classic Greek and Roman writers, especially Juvenal, the urban wit that left brilliant pictures of everyday Roman life. At

Columbia University, Professor Albert Goldman had introduced his literature classes to the great Roman writers, and his affection for Juvenal rubbed off on me. When I witnessed Richard's show that night at Mandrake's, Juvenal's art sprung to mind. A more direct influence on Richard during his stay in Berkeley was Lenny Bruce.

CHAPTER SIX

THE BLACK STRANGER

TODAY, THIRTY-NINE YEARS later, 1505 Berkeley Way has not changed in appearance. It is still the same white-shaded and wooden nondescript bungalow set off from a driveway. It squats on the corner of Sacramento Street and Berkeley Way. Just as you enter the driveway, you turn left onto the small porch that sticks out from the house.

Thirty-nine years ago, I knocked on the door. There was a patch over the small window so that I couldn't look inside. The door opens to the living room.

*This is where I found Richard was staying, sleeping
on Alan Farlan's sofa.*

"Come in," he said. I walked in and saw Richard lying on the sofa with a blanket pulled up around him, as if he had been using the sofa for a bed.

"Sit down," he said. I sat in the chair opposite him.

How could the who had been on the "Merv Griffin" and "Tonight Show" be living like this? I wondered.

He was smoking a cigarette. Alan was bringing him some food on a platter. He acted like his servant. Having a white guy working for him gave Richard a sense of being different, of still being in show business.

It was the first act I saw him in that would have produced a fool-making situation to somebody else. But Richard took his circumstance as an opportunity to find his identity, his voice in his act. For him, it was a period of wood-shedding, a term used by Black Jazz musicians like Charlie Parker that refers to a period of time in which one goes into a woodshed to practice, to explore, to find something "new."

Richard laughed. He was really glad to see me.

"He's my friend," said Richard, referring to Alan. I later learned that Alan worked at the independent radio station KPFA and that Richard was staying with him until he could get his own place. A few weeks before this, Richard had left Los Angeles, sleeping in the backseat of Alan's car.

Alan took away a plate that Richard had just finished. I took a seat and said hello. I saw a review on the table, picked it up, and read it.

Richard was watching television, a show about the battle between the British and the African king, Shaku Zulu.

"The white man is going to win," I commented. Richard burst out laughing.

"You're right!" he said. "Unless we write our own films, they will always win!"

We shared a mutual understanding of how racist white society had been to our people. When I told him how much I liked his show, he said, "It'll get better." I was surprised that he thought it *could* get better.

"How?"

"Well, I'm not satisfied with it. I want to get, you know, better." We complemented each other, respectful but not standoffish. Richard got dressed and we headed up to Telegraph Avenue where all the action was in Berkeley. That day Richard wore a leather hat with a wide brim, shielding his eyes. He had a turquoise Sagittarius symbol hanging around his neck. I didn't know at the time, but in the next four months I would witness the birth of Richard's comic genius.

CHAPTER SEVEN

PEOPLE'S PARK

WE DROVE UP to Telegraph Avenue and walked over to Haste, where a throng of people was gathered. The day before, May 15, people had clashed with the police over the question of occupying the parking lot- the parking lot in front of us.

The helmeted cops with rifles in their outreached arms stood around the eight feet tall chain-mail fence. In front of the cops milled hundreds of people. Some were yelling at them, and others were just staring.

"What happened?" Richard wanted to know. We could smell the stench of tear gas that lingered in the air, see the broken glass in the street, and hear the gushing of a broken water hydrant.

"I saw something on television," he said.

I had seen the same images, too. No doubt half the world had gazed at the television screens showing the police as they chased the demonstrators and beat some slow or unlucky ones with billy clubs. There were trashcans afire and a police car overturned and torched. Everywhere, people were running.

I explained that until a year ago, lovely old brown-shingle houses had occupied the block just above Telegraph between Haste and Dwight Way, with rooms rented out to students. The University of California invoked eminent domain to buy the three acres for $1.3 million, and having evicted all the tenants and torn down the existing housing, announced that the lot would be used for dormitories. Then for a year the property sat vacant and derelict as the University failed to come up with the money it needed to build; the lot became a muddy, rutted parking lot, and the homeless were camped nearby. At a town meeting convened by Telegraph Avenue merchants in mid-April, 1969, a local activist named Michael Delacour proposed that the lot be cleaned up and converted into a park.

In his mind the most important thing was that it would be a liberated zone in which speech would be freer than it was in Sproul Plaza, four years after the Free Speech Movement led by Mario Savio.

Stew Alpert, co-founder of the Yippies, wrote a manifesto proclaiming People's Park that was published in the *Berkeley Barb*, the "underground" newspaper that was required reading in Berkeley for anyone who was not actually a registered Republican (there were a few of them). As he had explained it, "The people who lived in the abandoned lot realized that if they were going to survive, and not get kicked out by the University, they had to reclaim the park."

Stew implored people to show up to help reclaim the site. With a few hundred dollars contributed by the Telegraph merchants, like Moe's Books and Cody's, the street people got some shovels and began planting trees, grass, and flowerbeds.

The first weekend, only a hundred people showed up, but by the end of the third weekend, there were three thousand people from all walks of life building a children's playground, complete with wading pool, and adding to the foliage with advice from University landscape architects. "There were old people, young people, straights, gays, blacks, revolutionaries," Alpert wrote.

In the meantime, the university had announced a new plan; this time, it was to build a sports facility in the contested space. Violating his promise not to move into the park without further discussions with the activists, Chancellor Roger Heyns ordered a paramilitary predawn raid on May 15, in which construction workers under police guard razed the park and installed the fence. The students at Berkeley responded with a rally at Sproul Plaza, where 3,000 people debated what to do "about the fence."

I told Richard what I knew. I had been at that rally, and I described for him the people chanting, "We Want The Park!" At Channing Way the Berkeley police blocked the way to the park, and when the crowd kept going toward Dwight Way on the Avenue the Alameda Sheriff's deputies met them with batons and rifles.

Chancellor Heyns had acted under pressure from Governor Ronald Reagan, I told Richard. In his 1966 race for the office, Reagan had largely run against UC Berkeley, which he denounced as "a haven for communist sympathizers, protesters, and sex deviants." Although he started out as an ardent New Dealer with a reputation in Hollywood as a left-winger, Ronald Reagan became a passionate anti-Communist and an informant for the FBI in the 1940s. In 1947 he was elected for the first of many terms as the president of the Screen Actors Guild. According to some scholars, I went on, Reagan had enjoyed a special relationship with the FBI chief, J. Edgar Hoover.

Having often used the term and practice of seeking out communists, and being rewarded politically for it, he now turned his attention to UC Berkeley. You have to imagine that when Richard arrived in Berkeley, he was well aware of the political scene, and what a hassle it was going to be. He even joked about it in his first routines.

The Alameda County sheriff's deputies, familiarly known as the "Blue Meanies," for their azure-blue jumpsuits, were the deadliest antagonists of the protesters. Tear gas filled the air. Students threw bottles, and the guards shot back. They started shooting the resisters with birdshot.

It was soon discovered when the victims were taken to the Highland Hospital, that "double 00," lethal ammunition, had replaced the birdshot. That night, indeed, a man named James Rector, was shot by a policeman. He died later that night. An artist, Alan Blanchard, was blinded.

When I finished telling Richard the story of People's Park, he just shook his head. We continued walking up the street. Coughing from the tear gas, we found a marble-topped table at the Forum on the corner of Haste and Telegraph.

Out of the blue, he changed the subject. "I want a whole new act."

"But you are good... as you are!"

"No, I don't have a style yet. You know, something special, something every good comic has. I don't have a tone. I can blow well. But the best I can do now is getting compared to Lenny Bruce. I mean, they ain't seen me yet."

I ordered beer from a longhaired blonde. As I took in the green plants hanging from the center of the cafe and the aroma of weed being smoked somewhere, I longed to hear why Richard had come to Berkeley. But now he made no bones about it. He wanted a new show. He didn't want to continue being a parody of Bill Cosby.

"Last year, I was working in Las Vegas at the Aladdin." He was completely fucked up, he said. What he told me was more hilarious than his own act. Richard was funny to be with, because he kept me in stitches.

Anytime he told a story about himself, it was hilarious. He would treat you like a member of his audience—a special audience of one.

They had put him between the headliner, Pat the "hip Hypnotist" Collins and the Brasilia Jazz Review. It was the opening night. When he came out he got applause—nice and warm.

Then he looked at the audience, and sitting there was Dean Martin. The famous Dean Martin. The real one. Sitting right there. Dean Martin stared at him. Then he noticed something else: the whole audience was starring at him, too.

They were all waiting for that first joke. He began to imagine what he looked like to them. What they saw was a freak, a pervert. A silly nigger jokester, the ridiculous fool!

"They were lookin' at me, like. Fuck this nigger."

He had been acting the part of a fool, but for some reason, he didn't want to be their fool any longer. He became so disgusted with seeing himself through the eyes of these white, fat, rich entertainers that he walked off the stage. The only thing was, he walked off in the wrong direction!

Inspired by his own self-disgust, he realized that he was locked in their image of him. We are other people, Sartre said. "Hell is other people." He couldn't take it any longer, and shouted out at them, "What the fuck am I doing here?" (Whenever he described this scene, he might add or subtract a detail, but this trope, "What the fuck am I doing here," was invariable.)

In his confusion, he had walked to the wrong side of the stage, opposite the exit.

"They said, 'you can't come through here!' I said, 'Fuck you! I ain't going back across that stage!'" He ended up forcing his way through, and didn't have to go across the stage again. He didn't say to me that he took off his pants and walked naked across the stage, shouting "Black jack!" as some rumors have it.

When he was finished, I said, "So now what is it you want to do in Berkeley?"

I'm sure I took a good swig of beer and waited for his reply.

"Find my new act."

"But you are so brilliant. I'm still laughing." I simply could not understand where the problem was: who wouldn't be satisfied with the howling laughter that he got? How could he get better?

"That act was what I'm working on, but it's not where I want to go."

"So that's why you left LA?"

"Yes, and also my personal life is fucked up."

Again, he told me a story of being made the butt of a joke.

His ex-wife Maxine was suing him for child support checks—1,000 a month—and his then-current wife was a bitch, too. He often talked, as he did that day, about his ex-wives. At that time, he had been married three times. First, in 1961 to the mother of his son, Richard Jr. Then he got married again in New

York in 1964 to Maxine and had a daughter Elizabeth. When I met him, he was married to Shelley and had a daughter Rain.

Shelley, his eventual ex-wife, was even worse than that, according to Richard. Besides being a terrible wife like Maxine, she was a comedian, too! She had a way of getting under his skin. Richard heard that she was hanging out with Miles Davis. He thought that she might be sleeping with him. He got so crazy that he bought a trumpet, and tried to play it.

Later that summer, we would go to Enrico's café in crowded streets of Broadway, and Richard would take out his trumpet and play it in the street.

He couldn't live with Shelley and their daughter, Rain. Shelley was like an incredible drag. She was reviewed in the *San Francisco Chronicle* and the reviewer said she was a terrible comedian and that she was trying to tell his jokes!

Then he went on to tell me about another subject that was tangential to his marriages an ex-wives, his legal hassles.

He said his first legal hassle started back in April 1967 when he was busted with an ounce of marijuana at the San Diego border. He was convicted of possession and placed on probation.

I said, "I have heard your stories. They are truly amazing."

He would get dark and silent, as if he was threatening not to speak. His face changed color like a cloud darkening the ground as it passed over the sun.

"Hey, man, I am going to introduce you to some of my friends," I said. "They're all writers."

"Okay."

The writers I was to introduce him to were starting a revolution in Black American literature—Ishmael Reed, Claude Brown, David Henderson, and others. At that time, Richard was not well-known to the art scene in the Bay Area. He had appeared at clubs like the Hungry i and Basin Street West, but he had no major write-ups. There were no critics who paid attention to him at all.

The one exception was the reviewer Phil Elwood, who gave Pryor a single paragraph or two of praise, and got shot down for his effort. After reading his meager appreciation of Richard's talent, one reader wrote the following:

"Dear Philip Elwood:

Your reviews on the gutter people who frequent such dives, as Basin Street is vomit provoking. These people are degenerates. You idolize a mulatto like Richard Pryor—yes he has white blood—which you admit talks shocking & dirty. We have enough dirty [sic] niggus over in the Fillmore District whose every 2nd word is "mother f... even the black children screech out this foul word & other disgusting obscenities.

How can these degenerate people ever hope to mix with a white nation? And to think we are busing our little white children into this horrible neighborhood where they will be utterly destroyed – staggers the imagination & fills us with killer rage.

Mrs. John McCormick – Millbrae"

Mrs. McCormick saw Elwood's mere mentioning Pryor as a promotion of "gutter people," particularly ones who use profanity. How can such "degenerate people" ever hope to be a part of a "white nation," she wanted to know. Phil Elwood's never saw fit to publish such a letter because it represented a large majority of white people who resented performers like Pryor. His fame was yet to come because he had not found the key to unlock its door.

CHAPTER EIGHT

CHEZ PANISSE

A FEW DAYS LATER, I took Richard to a French restaurant called Chez Panisse, on Shattuck Avenue. Today Chez is a destination, even a cult—one of the most famous restaurants in the world. Back then, it was just a French-provincial venture, only a few months old. I knew Paul Aratow, a lecturer in Comparative Literature at Berkeley, who started it with Alice Waters. Tom Luddy, then the curator at the Pacific Film Archive, later a well-known film producer, was another one of my friends, and was living with Alice at the time.

As we came into the door, Paul, in those days the "chef de cuisine," rushed over and gave us the best table, which was to the front near the sidewalk. After ordering some French food and wine, we talked about our upbringings.

I felt like King Alcinous in Homer's epic, *The Odyssey*, greeting Odysseus, who had washed up on the shores of his land. Like Odysseus, Richard had washed up on the shores naked, having suffered a lot. It was not the beginning of his journey, but the middle. I wanted to offer him the proper zenia—the correct welcoming. His was a trip home, his Greek nostos.

As we savored the wine that noon in Berkeley, Richard talked about himself and his childhood. I had grown up on a farm in North Carolina. He had grown up in whorehouses in Peoria, Illinois.

Journalists often complained about Richard's shyness about his family background. One *Rolling Stone* journalist, David Felton, accused Richard of being ashamed of his birth in a whorehouse. "It took many years," he noted, "before he would talk about it openly." But Richard was always upfront and open with me about his background. He told me that his mother and father were a part of the trade. Perhaps his candor with me had to do with the fact that we were both black men.

When he talked about being raised in a whorehouse it was a way of sharing the stories with someone he trusted, just as I shared with him my stories of growing up on a farm. In the dead of winter, he was born on December 1, 1940, in Peoria. His birthplace was a part of the town called the "Washington district," which meant the red light district. On the other hand, I was born on July 3, 1943, in the height of summer. Both his mother and his fraternal grandmother were prostitutes and he was an only child; I grew up the eldest of seven on a tobacco farm.

His grandmother's house was at 313, between their house and China Bee's—where the pretty whores lived. In the stories that he told me, Richard pictured himself in the role of a fool. It was the role he loved to play and retell. He said he was getting A's in school, until the teacher found out he was raised in a whorehouse. In almost every instance, he is put in the position of a fool, one who is assigned negative qualities.

When he was four years old, his father came back from the war. This was the first time he saw his father. His father opened a bar called The Famous Door.

He touched the wine to his lips.

"It was a colorful place," he acknowledged. "As a comedian, I couldn't have asked for better material."

He soon discovered that the news he heard there in his father's bar was more sensational and reportable than the news in the papers. One night he heard Uncle Dickie tell about his friend

Shoeshine who had killed both of his women when he discovered they were cheating on him with each other.

Many of the characters that showed up in the bar and pool hall—the junkie, the policemen, the hillbillies, all looking for black girls—he reproduced in his second album, *Craps*. He had another version of it, "Hank's Place", a posthumous release. In both of these sketches, the characters depicted are modeled after his memories from his father's bar. I don't believe that he copied those people and incidents, but that he re-created them. He never copied ghetto life; he always *re*-created it.

According to a 1999 profile about Pryor in *The New Yorker*, Pryor's first professional job as a comic was the Harold's Club in Peoria, when he was twenty. He jived Harold Parker, the owner, into believing that he could sing and play piano. Between the terrible songs, he told some jokes. The jokes got more of a positive response than the singing. Harold came to him and said, "Man, you have a lot of nerve!" He also told him if he wanted to continue, he would let him. Richard agreed.

As he continued, Richard got better. He used the comedy to build up his confidence of going on stage. When he was on stage, he was never afraid. It was like that from the beginning. At this point, his comedy was "not that honed," as he put it.

"But, you know, it was funny," he reminisced. "I'm a funny motherfucker. I was always funny. I enjoyed the stage and having command; I've never been afraid once I was out there."

As I listened to him, it was as if he were telling me about his adventures so that he could prepare himself for his final trip back home, to his success that awaited him in the future.

"What kind of jokes would you be telling back then?" I asked.

"I'd do a lot of TV commercial jokes," he laughed.

One of them was a take-off on the Edward R. Murrow show, "Person to Person" in which the host goes to interview sophisticated people in exotic places. In Richard's bit, the whole thing is reversed. Instead of sophisticated people, you had these black sharecroppers. Instead of some exotic place like Paris, you got the Mississippi Delta.

Mr. Marrow is commenting on the nice place the black man has.

Black Man: "Mistuh, Murrow, this heah is mah chair. My son made dat chair…Heah my boy now, he goin' to college. Come here, boy!"

The son comes out, looks around at the television equipment. "Mistuh Murrow, we are on TV!"

Even just telling me about these routines then was funny. "I came up in an era where there weren't ever gonna be no niggers on television." He was stuck to working the black comedy circuit. His ambition was limited. He could hope to work these black clubs, and perhaps get to MC a rock and roll show.

One of these clubs was called the Collin's Corner, a black and tan club. He would get $70 to $100 a week. He said his father kicked him out of the house, when a whore his father had given to him asked him to beat her up. "Hit me," she would say. So he beat her up. When his father saw how badly he had beaten her, he kicked him out of the house. "You don't know how to beat a whore?" Obviously he didn't.

Then he was invited down to East St. Louis to perform in the Faust Club. At the Faust club, his material was too raw. One of the comics gave him some advice he never forgot: "Your routine isn't bad, but your delivery is wrong. You've got to talk to the people," he said, "You always look like you want to kill them. Persuade 'em." For the next ten years, he traveled from Cleveland, Buffalo, and Chicago doing these same jokes.

In each of these towns, he would have adventures. It was like hearing Odysseus telling Alcinous about the adventures he had as he went from island to island in the Odyssey. Along the way, he got married to his first wife and had a son, Richard Jr. In Pittsburgh, he met a singer. He told everybody she was giving him money. She got angry and came after him for revenge. Ended up that she didn't kick his ass, but he kicked hers. She got the police and they took him to jail. The judge sentenced him to 90 days, but he got out in 35 days. How was he able to do that? He gambled and placed a dime on a 313 (which happens to be the address of the whore house he grew up in) and won 70 dollars, which he used to bail himself out of jail.

Through a juggler, Donnie Simpson, he went to Windsor, Canada, and from there to Toronto. After Toronto, in 1963, he ran out of clubs. He opened the *Newsweek* magazine and saw an article on Bill Cosby.

He said the *Newsweek* magazine article killed him.

"Here was this nigger [Bill Cosby]. He is doing what I'm fixing to do. I want to be the only nigger. There ain't no room for two niggers."

His friend told him, "You've got to go to New York. That's where all them big cats are." He headed to New York City.

During the summer of 1963, we both went to New York, both for the first time. This was a big year for the country, too. Martin Luther King marched on Washington. For me, it was a big year: I was enrolling into Columbia University to study comparative Literature, and Richard went to the village to continue his career as a stand-up comic. While I enjoyed the structure of the university, Richard was making his way into the structure of popular entertainment.

He told me how he stood at the train station with only ten dollars in his pocket.

He had only heard of the Apollo Theater in Harlem, when he met the guy who was the booking agent. The booking agent looked at him funny and said, "Go down to the village." He didn't know what village he was talking about. Then the man told him that he meant downtown. He took the bus downtown, and went to Café Wha? Somebody introduced him to Manny Roth, the owner of the venue.

"Before long," he said, "I was opening for Superman Victor Brady and his Trinidadian steel band." He said that soon he was running into one comedian after the other—Ron Carey, Martin Harvey Freeberg—even Dylan and Bill Cosby!

Yes, he had actually met Bill Cosby, his idol. He knew that Cosby was going to make it, he said, and even still he had such admiration for Cosby's act that he had a lot of bits based around his Cosby persona.

Before long, he was a regular at the Bitter End, the Living Room, and Papa Hud's. But it wasn't until a year later, on August 31, 1964, that he made his TV debut on Rudy Vallee's "On Broadway Tonight," a summer variety show. When I was still an undergraduate college student at Columbia University, Richard was making his first appearance in New York at the Living Room, 915 2nd Adenine and 49th street. During this time, from 1965 to 1967, I was hibernating at Columbia University and the University of Chicago. I was reading John Milton, Sir Spenser's Faerie Queene, and Shakespeare.

So now he had finished his tale. The sun was going down as we sipped wine.

"Well," I said, "Where are you now? In your journey to fame and success? What are you going to do?"

"If this film comes through, I'm doing that. I'd like to do that more than stand-up." He was referring to an independent film that he was going to make as soon as his manager got the money together.

"Do you think film is more where it's at?" I asked.

"I love film making," Richard said, "Yeah. I like films—being in them, putting them together, doing things, and seeing them. Yeah. I'd rather do that than anything."

"Did you see *Sweet Sweetback's Badasss Song*?" I asked.

"Yeah, I really dug it," he said. "I envied the people who were in it. It was as exciting to me as it must have been to Walter Cronkite when the man went to the moon," he joked. "I took people to see it, and I went several times. That's the way I felt about it. I think Black people should make their own films," he said.

We both laughed at that. He lit up a cigarette. I waited.

"But you know what? In my film," he said, seriously then, "I want to show that these people have dignity, and are not just a bunch of fall down people."

"Can't you do that in your comedy, too?"

He dragged on the cigarette.

"It's not that I don't want to help people with my comedy. I do. But helping people with my comedy is not why I do comedy."

"No? Why then?"

"I do comedy because it makes me feel good." He laughed and I laughed with him.

"So why do they laugh at you?"

"They understand something," he claimed. "I really have fun at it. And if they don't laugh, I still like it. When they laugh at what I intend them to, that's an extra bonus."

"Did you see *Putney Swope*?" I asked.

"I loved that film. I wish I had been in it."

"It's a great satire." I had seen it, too. The film showed black people as satirists of the American advertising dream. Richard and I saw eye to eye on this kind of new emerging black cinema.

"I did a few movies back in L. A.," he said. He had already been in several movies—*Carter's War, Bon Appetite*, (which he had produced himself), and *Wild In The Street*. Only *Carter's War* had a major release. The *Bon Appetite* film was so bad that he canned it and didn't want to see it again. Wild in the Street was released but it was not successful either as box-office or art. Still, he was excited about filmmaking.

"You like Dick Gregory?" I asked.

"Hell, yeah. He's great. I've met him."

Dick Gregory had a style that allowed the comedian to have a license to speak about serious issues like politics. "I called LBJ, and talked with him on the phone," he would tell his audience, as he did in Berkeley. "And I talks to the president of the United States. I ask him. I say, 'Mr. President, why do you say the Chinese have a primitive weapon, when they got the H-bomb!' He would take the license of a simple-minded black man, uneducated yet blessed with common sense as his mask. "If you call me a communist," he'd tease, "then, you should call Tom Paine one, 'cause he the one that said let's work together for peace!"

Richard admired the skillful way Dick Gregory used humor and satire to get his point across.

"What about Sammy?" I asked.

"Yeah, I met him. Matter of fact, I camped outside his hotel room just to meet him."

He told me about how he was too nervous to knock on Sammy's hotel door, so he just sat outside waiting for him to come out or in. "The next day," he told his biographer, "Sammy finally came out of the room. I stood up, grinned like a fool with nothing to say. Sammy asked him what was happening and he stammered that he was in town and was just wondering if Sammy would give him a job, or something. Sammy nodded hopefully, and then let him bum a cigarette.

"But he was so jive," Richard said, laughing as he recalled the incident a few years back. Sammy was very proud of being a star. It made Richard envious.

Richard's conversations about Sammy Davis revealed his attitude toward show business. It was a game and there were people like Sammy who wouldn't admit that it was a game.

Had he heard about how Sammy had hugged Nixon? I asked him. We both had seen it and now Richard laughed. Being sensitive to the role of the fool in society, Richard doesn't like the fact that Sammy hugged Nixon when he visited him in the White House. It made Blacks look as if they have to kiss the white man's ass to get equality.

"Sammy's a whore."

"You think he knows it?" I asked.

"I think so," he said. "He would have to know it." Then, he continued: "I'm a whore, too," he said, "I know when I'm up on the stage that I'm a whore. I know how to make the audience come, right? Just like a whore? Right? But just like a whore, I'm holding out for the big money. Everybody knows the game. What I don't dig is that they don't want to 'fess up about it. I don't mind saying that for my part, I'm a whore. You dig?"

Afterwards we ate the lunch, paid the bill, and started driving down University Avenue. Richard pointed to the International Pancake House across the street.

"Pull in there, and park."

Inside, we had hardly slid into our booth before Richard had ordered a stack of pancakes and an eight-ounce steak. Over the steak, he chewed and smiled.

"That French food was okay," he said, "but this shit here is serious!"

As I got to know more about Richard and saw the progress he was making with his show, I began to give the idea of comedian a lot of thought. If I considered that the fool has a special status and function in the group, and how he represents a departure from the group norms of propriety, of what is right and what is wrong, which are subject to the sanction of ridicule, then it is easy to see why he plays the fool.

As a comic spokesperson, he has a license to deviate from the norm status quo; because he is not expected to have normal behavior, he can raise questions that nobody else can ask. As a comic, his strength is in being a negative exemplar. By deviating from the norm, he has a freedom. Despite these shortcomings, he is distinguished from the villain because he is harmless. As a fool, he is tolerated with amusement rather than being punished.

There are several different types of fools, and Richard had a handle on all of them. The types of fools are distinguished by the particular way in which they depart from group norms, whether by an excess or by a deficiency in respect to some virtue. Richard, I sensed, was conscious of all of these distinctions too.

But Richard would eventually go beyond the role of comic spokesman and enter the realm of shamanism. He would be the shaman for the anxieties of the American public and its repressed desires. He would cull them to give up their most hidden and repressed demons, and once he had them exposed on the table of the nightclub space, he would exorcise them with a laser wit and humor—like a surgeon on the operating table—the demons would explode into thin air. Once the audience had been expunged of its demons, it could return across the marquee to the real world, better equipped to deal with reality.

This would come, this transformation from the small room in Berkeley to the Big Room in Hollywood at the Comedy Store on Sunset.

We started hanging out at my pad. We would have our sessions, shooting the breeze about this or that. But each of them was highly charged with slang and cussing and booze and weed. Identifying it as "The Spritz," Albert Goldman, the culture critic, described a similar ritual among Jewish comedians in Brooklyn with himself and Lenny Bruce.

"My own experience with this Jewish hipster is intensely personal," he wrote. "For seven years I lived in Brooklyn and the Bronx, which have produced as many Jewish comedians as Vienna Jewish analysts or Odessa Jewish fiddlers."

He met with these Jewish comedians every Saturday. They got together and indulged in a kind of verbal conversations they called "the Spritz."

Black men had a similar form of discourse. But there was a big difference here. Jewish people were known to be literate. But Black people are not. During slavery, the slave masters discouraged blacks from literacy with the threat of death. If a Black person was trying to learn to read or write, the practice was to cut off their middle finger. If the slave persisted in trying to learn literacy, he could (and was often) put to death.

The only way Blacks could archive their history was through the oral tradition. For that reason black men valued oral transmission and verbal dueling. This tradition of preservation of identity through speech forms was called snagging, rhyming, cutting, signifying, marking, ranking, shucking, sounding, joning, and screaming, to name a few.

For middle classed, highly literate people this kind of nonstandard English was obscene and therefore offensive. But for, Richard, a man who was going to change comic history, it was essential. One of these bits that Richard especially loved was "super man" that went:

I fucked yo' mamma on the top of a can
The baby came out and hollered, Superman!

Sometimes you could do the same rhyme as a riddle. *What's black and wears a cape? Super Nigger!* Later in his career, Richard used both "Super Man" and "Super Nigger" in his comic routine and in the movie with Christopher Reeves.

As with The Spritz, we staged ritual sessions inspired by anger at the world we lived in. We used sexual fantasies, political figures, black humor, and tall tales—anything we could get our imagination around. We liked poking fun at pomposity of people and language. But more than that, we permitted ourselves to laugh out about the unconscious that ruled our daily lives.

For Richard, these cutting contests became a form of "rehearsal process," to use a term from Victor Turner. He would bounce jokes on the rest of his cut-buddies and see what stuck.

CHAPTER NINE

BILL COSBY

THE DAVID FOSTER Production company called and told me that Cosby was going to be in San Francisco, and that he wanted to meet me at Enrico's. Bill Cosby was one of my earliest fans for *The Life and Loves of Mr. Jiveass Nigger*. When he hosted the *Tonight Show*, he had me come on the show. Behind the scenes, he met with me in his office and personally expressed his admiration for my novel. I met him in LA, both at his house and at several parties he threw for Black dignitaries like Andrew Young and Julian Bond.

I immediately went down to Richard and invited him. I knew that he admired Cosby, and I was right.

We took off in my XKE for the City.

As we drove across the Bay Bridge, Richard was excited about reading the novel, *Being There*.

Had I read it? He wanted to know. I had read it, and was as excited about talking about it as he was about Black films.

As we got closer to Enrico's and to Bill Cosby, he started talking about how much he was not like Cosby.

I parked the car and we got out and approached the sidewalk cafe. Richard and I strolled down Broadway, passed the Hungry i, where he had performed about a couple years ago, in February, 1966

"I did my bit I call 'Mankind,'" he said, as we passed the Hungry i, "I sound just like Bill."

It's true, too; he sounded like Bill Cosby in the urbanity of his voice.

It was high noon, a sunny day as we came within sight of Enrico's, we could see Bill Cosby holding court.

White people surrounded him. Enrico and Bill sat facing each other across the white tablecloth.

Herb Caen occupied the third chair, facing the sidewalk. Seated next to Cosby was a beautiful blonde woman.

When he saw us coming, Cosby leapt to his feat.

"My man!" He said, greeting me. *"The Life and Loves of Mister Jiveass Nigger.* "Hey, you gotta read his book! He's a funny writer. That's right! That's the name of the novel! And Richard! My man! Richard! This guy...this guy is funny! Sit down!"

We sat down and the beautiful girl, whose name was Billy, was introduced.

"Hello, everybody," Richard said, quietly, and took a seat.

First Cosby went after me.

"Have you ever read his book?" he said to Billy.

Billy shook her pretty blonde head.

"Well, you gotta read him!"

"Herb, you know, Cecil's book?"

"Didn't I blurb your book?"

"Yes."

Herb Caen had written a few lines about my having lunch at Enrico's, some months ago. David Foster, who bought the rights to my novel, had arranged for me to have lunch with Herb Caen.

"Yeah that's right!"

"Hey, go across the street and buy a copy of your book for me." He reached into his pocket and took out a wad.

"No, I just don't—"

"Go ahead, man!"

Still I was reluctant to go. I didn't want to be away from the action, from what Richard was going to say.

"I want you to get the book, because the way the book opens, it's marvelous. I want to give a copy to Billy."

"I'll bring you a copy tomorrow."

"If you can write me a page, just like that first page of your book, I'll give up a thousand dollars."

Billy said, "Wow!"

"A thousand dollars?" I repeated it again.

"Yeah, just the first page."

I shot across the street and bought a copy of my novel. When I got back to the table, I gave the book to Cosby.

"Where's Richard?"

They were looking out at the street. Richard was clowning on the sidewalk like a Junkie. He liked playing the role of the schlemiel, a fool in the Jewish culture. That Richard would love the role of schlemiel was no surprise to me. Albert Goldman had hipped the reading public to the influence of Jewish comedy to the contemporary hipster culture of the 1960s. A schlemiel was "a symbol which stimulates not only sympathy but also empathy."

Everybody was watching Richard in the street and laughing. He was pretending to play a trumpet. Cosby, who knew exactly what Richard was doing, cracked up and used a line that Richard would use himself. "Get out of the street, fool!"

When he got back to the table, everybody was applauding him.

"Fuck, I thought I was Miles Davis."

"That was great," Cosby said, clapping his hands in a polite gesture.

Then the jokes swapping session started.

Cosby would tell a joke. Then, I would tell a joke.

"We can't laugh at that," Richard said, "You ain't a professional comedian." Then, Richard would tell a joke.

"How's Roy?"

Bill looked puzzled. "Roy?"

"Roy Silver, your manager. Roy Silver."

"He told me," Richard recalled for us, "Bill Cosby is the kind of colored guy I'd introduce to my sister, but a guy like you...'"

Pausing, he let us have a chance to finish laughing. Cosby's mouth was yapped wide open.

"…'A guy like you. I wouldn't introduce you to my sister!' So I told him, 'Your sister is ugly! Why do I want to meet her?"

"I don't know nothin' about it," Cosby said, pulling on his cigar. "Why would you want to meet his sister?"

"Yeah, that's what I'm thinking. Bitch is ugly, anyway." We laughed. But it was clear that Bill Cosby was America's ideal of a successful Black man. Richard was at the opposite end of the spectrum and Richard was clear about that, because the managers who ran the business made sure that he knew that.

"You know, and I was buying this shit," Richard said, cursing at his own stupidity. "'Don't mention the fact that you're a nigger.' he told me, 'Don't go into such bad taste.'"

We were cracking up.

"They were gonna try to help me be nothin' as best they could," he concluded.

Cosby would laugh at Richard's dirty joke, but he wouldn't tell one himself. Maybe that was the reason he liked my novel so much. He could use the word "Nigger" and not be responsible for using it, because it belonged to my book title.

Whatever the reason, Cosby was the essence of a clean comic, what Richard thought of as "white bread" jokes. Yet it was obvious to both of us and especially to Richard that Cosby was a super star.

He was the black figure in the media that the white liberal power structure in entertainment wanted to push. As an example on our way back to Berkeley, Richard talked about how he wanted to be better than Cosby.

"I bet you he can't say the word 'motherfucker,'" Richard said. "He gave me 1,500 hundred dollars not to screw Billy."

"No?"

"Yeah, when you were not there, you went to the book store."

I found it hard to believe, but then, years later, I've changed my mind.

"Man, I ain't giving up my style for him! Fuck him!"

"What you gonna do?"

"I'm going to work harder."

"Satire is where it's at, man." I told him this and I believed it myself.

I got it. Race is beyond Richard, I kept thinking, and he never mentions it. Didn't he have the attitude that Cosby was the famous star—and he was because he was still on television's ISPY—and treated him with great respect? Yes. And wasn't Bill equally respectful of Richard? Yes. They were comfortable with the knowledge that they were so different in their approach to comedy that there was no rivalry. In fact, Richard's album, *Evolution* (1968-1971) maps that journey, as he intended it to by calling it "evolution." Most of the cuts on that record do not even have curse words on them, as critic David Felton pointed out in his record notes. Wasn't that true? Yes. We were driving back across the Bay Bridge.

CHAPTER TEN

HI, I'M A NIGGER!

A FEW DAYS LATER, he walked onto the stage at Mandrake's.

"Hi, I'm Richard Pryor," he said, took a drag of his Marlboro, and announced, "I'm a nigger." This was a big step he was making, a big step from Cosby's influence.

The audience broke.

"I've long suspected it."

The premise was so ludicrous. He took an old routine and changed it accordingly. When in the routine, he came home and told his father he was a Negro, now he came home and told his father he was a "nigger."

Instead of being inspired to be more like Cosby, Richard after meeting the great comic turned around and did the opposite.

He wanted to pull all of his characters from the ghetto. "I have these ghetto characters, these voices, in me. Now, I'm gradually letting them come out."

I helped Richard move from Alan's apartment to his own apartment at 1988 California Street, a few blocks away. The building was a cheap place to live, even back in 1969 when Richard moved in with his newly purchased hi-fi and recording equipment upstairs. When we pushed open the door, I saw that he had just a bed, a table, and a couple chairs.

"This is the first place I've ever had to myself," he said.

As we assembled his hi-fi set, he exuded with pride at how he enjoyed having an apartment to himself. This was the first time in his life that he was living independently.

"Every other place, I had to share with somebody. That's why I left L A."

That evening he launched into a routine that painted a large canvas of different characters from the ghetto.

In ten minutes, Pryor had introduced his audience to Mr. Perkins, Hank, Big Black Irma, and Lester, The Policeman, Jesse, and Young Richard. He was using characters that tied the routine together, creating the illusion of a neighborhood. He put his voice into other characters. Even though Richard created the voices, he gave the illusions that these characters were independent of his wishes. Sometimes, the characters said outrageous things that even seemed to surprise Richard.

The characters were snapshots of a larger environment. They were only a part of the picture, and as such, they spur our imagination to create more than was presented.

His voice was always that of the writer, disinterested yet engaged, observing and relishing the slangy and the precise nomenclature of the low life. In the way he preserved the technical details that Mr. Perkins has for making a cushion on a pool table is artfully observed. He has the writer's eye for detail. He wanted the audience to appreciate the small world of these characters.

His love for nuance in ghetto speak was well appreciated by the audience, too. The characters were created out of words, voices, gestures, and facial expressions. This is accomplished with no help from stagecraft, costumes, or even other actors.

He used the "silent auditor" very effectively. In one scene, he joked about the person who never says a word. "You never say nothin'!" this is a self-conscious wink at his own technique.

Everybody was blown away, and the reputation that a new guy was in town spread fast. Soon the line for Richard's performances was all around the block. Going to see Richard quickly became the thing to do for the smart set in Berkeley in the late Sixties.

CHAPTER ELEVEN

HIS FIRST PAD

VISITING RICHARD SOON after he moved into his new apartment, I watched him take out a stack of records from a box. He took out one record. When he put it on, Marvin Gaye's "What's Going On!" filled the room. "I got some of Malcolm X's speeches, too!" he said, taking out another record.

Richard sprawled out on a chair, picking up the *Autobiography of Malcolm X*. He read a few sentences, and looked around himself.

"Man, I got myself a little apartment," he would say.

He played the record over and over again.

One afternoon, we were listening to Bobby Seale on the radio. He was having an argument with another Black Panther back on the East coast. Their telephone conversation was being broadcast over the radio.

"...Sister, listen," Seale went on, "We tried to make that point. Do you recall the shootout at the Marine County courthouse? Yea...well...no, no, listen. We killed a whole judge just to make that point..."

*Here I am standing in the entrance to
Richard's first pad.*

When he said "whole judge," Richard and I cracked up. A whole judge—as opposed to a half judge? We would get into a laughing jag over such malapropism of language. We supported the Black Panther Party, as we did any positive Black organization. But as artists, with a sensitive ear to the aesthetics and justice, we were quick to target black people, too.

He would talk about having a love affair with his audience. Long before anybody had discovered that all an artist needed to be successful was a thousand "true fans," as Kevin Kelly, one of the founders of *Wired* magazine, maintained, Richard had made the discovery himself.

He would often talk about having the same audience that a writer has. You don't need that many people, he would often say, to get over. All you need was the ones who really are into your stuff.

Mandrake's was a perfect place for his new audience. The place was small, but that was okay, because it cemented the audience together, gave them more of a core "us against the world" feeling.

Yet there was another element, too. By reenacting our negative failings, we elicit sympathy. By playing the fool, the classic schlemiel he was discovering the psychological dynamics underlying the schlemiel pose. "It is safer to attack ourselves or to laugh at ourselves before others do, because in this way we gain the offensive," Albert Goldman wrote in his essay, "Sick Jew Black Humor."[2]

"By controlling the reenactment, we also have the psychological satisfaction of enlisting sympathetic laughter. As Freud has shown, people side with you when they laugh at something with us; and this solidarity exists even when we encourage them to laugh with us *at us*."[3]

For Richard, all the stories about how messed up his family life was came to the same thing as that of the schlemiel. Typically, in Mandrake's, after he had shared a good laugh with them, he would say: "Isn't it nice that we can all sit in the same club together—and not understand each other!"

Then in a satiric voice, he shared another insight: "Amazing. It could only happen in America!" Perhaps he should have added that it only could happen in Berkeley!

CHAPTER TWELVE

A LITERARY PARTY

I DECIDED TO INVITE some professors and students from the English department to a party to celebrate Richard at my apartment on Virginia Street, in the Berkeley Hills.

1969 was a turbulent time for UC Berkeley faculty. Most of the time, faculty met off campus. As a member of the English department, I was told that I could have classes off campus to show solidarity for the striking students.

Among the other writers I invited to meet Richard were Richard Brautigan, Victor Cruz, Barbara Christian, and Leonard Michaels, who had just published *Going Places*; Ishmael Reed, author of *Mumbo Jumbo*; Al Young, author of *Sitting Pretty*; and David Henderson, poet, author of *Felix of the Silent Forest*.

They were all living in Berkeley at the time, and I saw them frequently. I thought it would be good for Richard to meet some black writers other than me.

The person I was most proud of introducing Richard to was Claude Brown. Richard and Claude had a mutual admiration for each other. In many respects they were very similar, both had been brought up in the inner city—Richard in the Midwest and Claude in the East. Claude described his life as a violent boy growing up in Harlem, New York in *Man-child in the Promised Land*, which had been published in 1965. Close to what Richard would provoke in his monologues about the Peoria whorehouses, Claude's book became an instant bestseller, giving readers a rare view of the ghetto life of the early 1950s.

In Claude's books the same kind of violent existence plagued the youth everywhere. Poverty shaped the future of all of Claude's young people. Like the narrator, Sonny, who is expelled from school at age 8, joins a street gang at age 9, is shot in the leg at 13 while admitting a burglary and sent to a reform school at 14.

It was the kind of life that Richard understood so well because it closely paralleled his own. Both Claude and Richard shared another passion: they both loved to get high and "play the dozens."

Often after these kinds of parties, after we all had danced to James Brown and exhausted ourselves, the main party would break up. (The whites would finally leave.) Often, four or five of us Black men would be left. I had a party with the gang. We would get into these sessions. Richard called them "jive parties." What would happen is that all of our demons would come out verbally, that is. The whole fantasy level went up. Much of what we call the "dozens" and "signifying" were the weapon and the tools.

As Claude and Richard got to know each other better, we would gather a large amount of liquor and weed and start to tease each other. Sometimes the skits would be so creative, that Richard would find something that he wanted to use in his act. If Richard found a fantasy so incredibly funny, he might ask permission later to use it. "I like that, man, do you mind if I use it?" The next night, you would hear your comment again in Richard's show.

Steve Treadway, a friend of ours, was telling us a story about his father. His father said to him, "Nigger, take that bass out of your voice!" That evening we all went down to Mandrake's to catch Richard's show. Soon he had built up a following of Berkeley fans. In his skit about his father, Richard had his father say that he was going to take that bass out of his voice, echoing and weaving in what Steve had said. Steve, who was sitting in the audience, grinned when Richard did that.

CHAPTER THIRTEEN

EL TOPO

O NE DAY AFTER eating again at the International Pancake house, Richard looked at me and asked, "Did you see *El Topo?*"

"Naw."

"Let's go see it." Richard wanted to hang out."*El Topo* is playing right down here on University." I was down for it.

"When you see *El Topo*," he said, "you'll know what I'm talking about. They have this scene where El Topo throws his hat and cuts this dude's head off."

"No shit."

Richard and I sat in the darkened theater, and waited for *El Topo* to begin. "You gonna love this!"

John Lennon had introduced El Topo and its director, a Chilean Jewish immigrant, Alejandro Jodorowsky, to the counterculture in 1970. Everybody who was hip, Richard told me, had already seen it a couple times.

One of the things Richard liked about Berkeley was the movie theaters. In Berkeley, he recalled many years later, you could see movies you can't see anywhere else in the world! I saw the *Hellstrom Chronicles* (1971), the Swedish documentary about the insects that take over the world, with him a couple times. (The producer of Hellstrom Chronicles was David Wolper, a man Richard would later work with. Wolper produced *Roots* and was introduced to me by Richard later.)

But that afternoon, I sat with Richard for the first time in the theater, and watched his face as the scene came into view. He had seen the film before and was excited to share it with me. The lights went dark and then the scene came into view. From the upper left corner, a man on a horse comes across the screen. He is riding with a small boy on the horse and carrying an umbrella.

In a medium shot, the man—El Topo—gets down from the horse on the desert and helps the boy down. We see now that the young boy is naked, except for a man's wide brimmed hat on his head. In his hands he has a teddy bear and a framed picture.

"Today you are seven years old," he says to the boy, "You are a man. Bury your toy and your mother's picture." El Topo plays a sad tune on his flute, as the boy, presumably his son buries the teddy bear and a picture of a woman in the sand. This ritual of manhood appealed to Richard, and he glared at me. I was to later understand from Richard's own childhood why this scene impressed him.

As the credits came up, a picture of a mole was on the screen. The title said, "The mole is an animal that digs a tunnel under the ground to get to the sun. When he gets to the sun, he is blinded."

In the next scene, El Topo and his naked son arrive in a town. All they see are dead people—some scattered in the street, and others hanging by their necks from trees. An old dying man begs them to shoot him to put him out of his misery. El Topo hands the gun to his son, who shoots the man.

Richard laughed. "Now watch this." In the next sequence, bandit #1 is kissing a pair of women's shoes. Then, he sets the shoes up as targets and shoots at them. Bandit #2 uses a machete to cut a banana into slices and then takes a toothpick and eats them off. Bandit #3 draws a picture of a woman on the ground and lies on it and makes love.

These three bandits then chase El Topo and catch him, and finally surround him. One of them puts an inflated balloon in front of El Topo. When the balloon is finally out of air, the bandits will draw and kill El Topo.

Just as the balloon is deflated, the bandits reach for their pistols. The one in the middle notices that his partners are falling from their horses. El Topo is so fast that the guy in the middle doesn't even see his hand move (neither do we the audience). We realized seconds later that El Topo shot them. He is just that fast.

"Wow!" Richard shouted. "Ain't that something? El Topo is bad!" He watched El Topo as he chases down the third bandit shooting him in the knees, chest, as he sadistically demands he tells him who killed all the people in the town.

In a subsequent sequence, some other bandits break into a church, read the Bible and put on a classical record. They dance a waltz with the six priests, disrobe them, and rape them. This was done in the style of a Brunel film, with bits of Fellini's surrealism.

In one scene, El Topo meets a woman. He takes the woman with him, leaving his son behind. Then, another woman challenges him for the woman. She takes the woman from El Topo and seduces her. Both women leave El Topo.

At the end of the film, El Topo is killed. He goes to hell and meets a performing clown. The trip he has to make around the countryside with the dwarf (a woman) reminded me of Fellini's *La Strada*, in which a big man abuses and exploits his female partner.

We came out of the theater. He was laconic about the film. "That's real." He saw this as a really honest film. Now as we walked to my car, he was interested in what I thought.

I thought it was an incredible film. I had never seen anything like it, and I told him that. When I got to know Richard better, I could see a parallel between El Topo and his son and Richard's father and Richard as a boy growing up. Richard admired and hated his father; simultaneously he both emulated him and distanced himself from him.

Richard and I would sit at the Forum Cafe and drink beer all afternoon and talk. Richard was getting more into writing now. He was working on two projects, both screenplays. His first one was called *This Can't Be Happenin' to Me*.

It was a screenplay about a young black man, also called Richard, like the author, who is killed by his grandmother in an accident. The screenplay opens in a typical whorehouse environment. The mother and the grandmother are prostitutes, just like the mother and grandmother of the author.

After I had seen *El Topo*, I could understand Richard's screenplays better. He would use the same motif over and over again, but from different angles. He was impressed by the last moments of death, and so most of his screenplays had the same pattern. They were always about somebody dying, who saw their whole life flash before them.

That was the case with *This Can't Be Happenin To Me*. This is the excerpt he showed me:

```
FADE TO:
INT.ROOM IN A WHOREHOUSE
Richard, His Mother, and Trick.
This is a hallucination of Richard as he is lying. He
goes to see his mother, who is a prostitute, in her
room while she is turning a trick. A white dude is
on top of her.
MOTHER AND TRICK—ANGLE FROM CORNER OF ROOM -HIGH
          RICHARD (OS)
     Why is it happening to me?
          MOTHER
     Life is like that, Richard.
     That's the way life is.
     Sometimes things just go down that way.
The Trick is fucking her, and asking:
          TRICK
Is it really good?
          MOTHER (nonchalantly)
Oh honey, there ain't a white man in the world can
fuck good as you!
```

Other character indicates by her voice and face that she means just the opposite. She turns her head to Richard and continues talking to him.
OUTSIDE DOOR TO ROOM - RICHARD'S FATHER
RICHARD'S FATHER is watching through the keyhole.

As Richard opens the door to leave, he saw his father. Did growing up in a whorehouse affect Richard? Why did he write about it so early in his life? The *Rolling Stone* reporter David Felton thought that Richard took his background lightly until he read the screenplay. "Typically he would relate such tales of injustice without noticeable regret. 'Wasn't a big thing? Well fuck them, that's all you could say' but later when he gave me a copy of his screenplay, I got an idea of how strongly his childhood turmoil remained in his memory. The screen play, which he wrote in Berkley round 1970 following his mother's death is a surreal but extremely auto-biographical comedy about a teenager named Richard who gets shot accidentally by his grandmother in a whorehouse and sees his absurd life flashing by before him."

Some of the scenes show their influence of *El Topo*:

PRIEST'S OFFICE—PRIEST—CLOSE UP—PRIEST—DRAW BACK TO MEDIUM SHOT
As the camera draws back, we see the PRIEST is in the process of jacking off in a vat marked HOLY WATER.
RICHARD leaves the PRIEST'S office, and walks into the cathedral, which is very large.
INT. CATHEDRAL - RICHARD - LONG SHOT
Richard decides to pray, since he doesn't want to die. He kneels down to pray. He hears a voice.
                    VOICE (o.s.)
Psst…Psst!
RICHARD looks around to see who is trying to get his attention.
                    VOICE

```
That ain't going to help. Praying ain't going to help
you.
RICHARD looks up and the Crucifix is whispering to
him.
CRUCIFIX - RICHARD'S POV - MEDIUM
        JESUS
Help get me off this cross and out of this church!
(Beat)
I've been hanging around here for 2000 years, and
they ain't buried me yet, and I'm tired.
RICHARD pulls the spike out of JESUS' hands and feet,
and helps him down. They talk for a while.
        JESUS
Man, I can't wear this shit. Get me into the streets.
RICHARD
No problem, man, just come with me.
EXT CATHEDRAL -FRONT DOOR—RICHARD AND JESUS
As they are about to leave, all kinds of sirens and
bells go off, like it was a prison break. Monks come
out from everywhere and jump JESUS and RICHARD as they
fight back. It looks for a while like they might win,
but eventually the monks overpower them. They put JESUS
back on the cross; he's screaming, but they nail him
on the cross again. They toss RICHARD into the street.
        MONK
Who's going to believe you, Nigger?
        Richard (to himself)
Somebody'll believe me.
```

Such scenes showed the influence the El Topo film had on him. But what Richard added was that your life flashes before you just at the moment of death. Richard took this popular notion and structured nearly everything he wrote around it. It became the structure he used years later for the *Jo Jo Dancer, Your Life is Calling You* (1986).

But he had another topic: The Vietnam War.

"Since I been here I been writing scripts. I just finished one about Vietnam," he told me.

"Can I read it?"

"Oh, yeah. I'd love for you to read it. Alan has just sent it to PBS. I hope they take it."

"What's your script about?"

"It's called 'The Assassins.' It's about this brother that's drafted to Vietnam, and in the end he realizes that this was just Nixon's way of gettin' rid of niggers."

We laughed at that—black people had their own view of the man called Nixon.

"I have something I want to show you." I gave him a copy of my short story, "I Never Raped One Either, But It Never Bothered Me," which had been published in the *Evergreen Review*.

He took it and put it aside.

"I have a story for you, too."

He gave me a copy of his story in *The Realist*. It was called "Uncle Sam Wants You Dead, Nigger." He had written a script for PBS, as he had already told me, but he later told me how PBS had rejected it. Officials at PBS sent Barbara Gordon out to Berkeley to talk with Richard about writing a screenplay for a possible production.

Richard was excited about the prospect of writing a television show based on his own view of life. It was here in Berkeley that Richard made his first attempt at writing a screenplay. As he dictated his story into a tape recorder, Alan typed it into the screenplay format. When they were finished with the script, they sent it in. PBS rejected it and never explained why. Maybe it was the title. The title was, "Uncle Sam Wants You Dead, Nigger." Maybe it was the way the young black hero soldier protested against the Vietnam War.

Whatever it was, they didn't want to make a movie from it. Undaunted, Alan and Richard turned to a friend of Alan's, Paul Krassner.

Paul Krassner, who owned and edited *The Realist*, knew of Richard Pryor's satire and agreed to publish the manuscript. So in

1971, Richard Pryor saw himself for the first time, an author with a story in print.

"I'll read it right away."

"Read it now." I started reading it and Richard watched me out of the corner of his eye.

"What you think?" he asked after I had just finished the first page.

I was surprised that his writing and the characters were so different from the characters in his stand-up. In the play, his father would say, "Son, why don't you stop hanging out with those Black Panthers. You should get a job, Son." All of his characters talked like that, in Standard English. Making no attempt to capture the slang and ghetto speech that was making his stage characters inimitable characters, he created characters that were wooden and pedestrian. Perhaps it was because he dictated his screenplays to Alan, who had no acquaintance or ability to notice the difference.

During his stay in Berkeley, Richard had plans to make his own film. I remember once when I went by Alan's house, Richard was there with a couple of white reporters from the San Francisco magazine *Good Times.*

The interview started out rough, with Richard reluctant and uncooperative. The reporter didn't know how to get into the interview, to get Richard on his side. So he just asked Richard about sharing the same name with the President Richard Nixon. "How do you feel about having the same name as Nixon?"

Richard dragged on his cigarette. "Nothing."

The interviewer had to pull the answers out of him. Stingy with his answers and resenting even the presence of the interviewer, Richard acted like he was being attacked. I sensed that any moment, he was going to run the poor guy out of the apartment. Then, after nearly an hour of short spurting of "yes," "no," he opened up and began elaborating on his ambition to make an independent film.

"I hear you are going to make a film?" the reporter said to Richard. "Yeah." He looked surprised by the question.

"Is this a feature length film?"

"Yeah."

"Who's producing it?"

"My manager, Don Pruitt."

"Gonna be filmed locally?"

"Yeah."

"Getting nationally distribution?"

"I don't know about that. All I want to do is make it. I think all that shit falls into place. You know, like left and right."

"So it's all ready to go, huh?"

"As soon as he gets it back from the people who gonna get the money. It's 90% there. It's a comedy, but not a – if you can dig it..." He never finished the sentence.

Now that I thought about it, Richard had indeed been getting the money together for a film, but the manager never showed up with the money, so vague dreams of using film to tell his story was replaced by concrete reality. The film never got made.

Another reason Richard liked film was that filmmaking seemed like an escape from the pitfalls of nightclub entertainment.

"So what was so wrong with being an entertainer?" the reporter asked him.

"I'm fortunate to be an entertainer," he muttered. "I make big bread. Things just come to me. Improvise, that's how I get changes. I get the shit, try it out, weave it up, so it'll work. "

"What do you like about being an entertainer," he asked.

"I enjoy it," Richard said, "I feel important when I read about myself. Being interviewed and reading about what I said. It makes me feel important."

"What else do you get out it besides reading the reviews?"

Richard sensed that the reporter was trying to get cute and answered, "Pussy..."

The reporter disguised his shock, Richard went on, "... Good dope...Good friends," he said. "Peace of mind, understanding, confusion. Respect. Not necessarily in that order."

"What is your message when you go on stage?"

"When I go up on stage, I want people to enjoy themselves, I really do."

"You talk about being black…a lot," the young reporter asked.

"I *am* black…a lot." Richard replied. The white girl who had come with the reporter and I laughed.

"What would you do if you were President?" he asked, glaring down at the notebook he scribbled on. He looked down at his notes.

"Bring the troops home. Build factory jobs for people out of work."

"What could be done to improve the status of the black man in America?

"Educate him," Richard answered, "Every man scratches his own ass. Look at the economics of it. Everybody doesn't have to be a gangster to work the earth." He was talking about ecology a long time before many politicians even gave it much weight. "So people no longer have an interest in the earth. They want to have their Rolls Royce, if that's your choice; you must pay those dues. Everybody has to find his own light that moves, find out who you are." Putting emphasis as he did on the environment, Richard was, indeed, ahead of his time.

CHAPTER FOURTEEN

WARREN BEATTY

I N 1993, WARREN Beatty made "a reverent pilgrimage," according to *New York Times* critic Craig Wolff.

This was the last time Warren Beatty saw Richard Pryor in person. Pryor was seated in the backseat of his limousine. Suffering from MS, he could hardly move to put his hand out of the window and touch Beatty's hand.

The first time Beatty saw Pryor was in 1970 in San Francisco. I arranged for them to meet.

The film producer David Foster had bought an option for my novel. He hired Norman Jewison to direct the screenplay. I went to Vancouver to meet with Foster who was producing *McCabe and Mrs. Miller.*

When Foster called me to join him and his wife up in Vancouver, I left Richard in Berkeley and flew up to Vancouver.

It was brutally cold and white everywhere. After breakfast, we were driven up to the set, which was built up in the mountains.

There on the set I met the director Robert Altman and the star of the film Warren Beatty. At that time, no one could predict that this film would become an American classic, even though it was directed by one of the most controversial directors Bob Altman and was starring the hottest young movie stars in Hollywood.

When Warren heard that I knew Richard Pryor, he told me he wanted to meet him. He was coming to San Francisco and wanted us all to meet.

After I got back to Berkeley, I called Richard and told him that we were going to lunch with Warren Beatty. That was great with Richard, so I got ready and went by to pick him up.

Richard and I then left for San Francisco where we had lunch with Warren Beatty at the Mark Hopkins hotel. I was afraid to be late, but as it turned out, we were right on time.

At the lunch, Warren and Richard both tried to outdo each other with jokes about sexual escapades. They were delightful in each other's company. I had also invited a woman who had been Beatty's date for their senior prom, but as soon as she had her moment with Warren, she took off and left the table to the three of us.

Warren must have felt competitive with Richard because he started telling us a story about a sexual escapade involving a three-speed vibrator he had picked up in Copenhagen. "And then, I switched on the second speed…" Such an idea of a three-speed vibrator impressed us in 1970. I had vaguely heard of vibrators, and knew nothing about ones with gearshifts. Richard commented on the fact that he only knew about the one speed vibrator.

In any case, it was enough of an introduction for Richard to segue into a discussion of Julie Christie and Warren's sex life together.

In 2008, at the San Francisco Film Festival, Warren Beatty appeared to receive an award for the film *McCabe and Mrs. Miller.* "When I had a problem with the character," he told the audience, "Altman would just say, 'Remember that he will do anything for Mrs. Miller.'"

If the character of Julie Christie could be the trick that made Beatty's character understandable to him, it was because he was so much in love with Julie Christie. The whole world was in love with Julie Christie at that time, including most Black men. "Warren, tell us about Julie Christie?" Richard joked at one point. "What's it like to F…her?"

Beatty roared with laughter. Crazy Richard! He would have to ask that! He had the license to ask Warren if Julie Christie had some good nookie.

I knew that he was going to come up with some off the wall shit. But I just didn't know what. But to ask Warren Beatty if Julie Christie had some good p....y knocked me out. Did Warren throw down his white napkin and walk out? I don't think so.

Richard and Warren became great pals and playboys in Hollywood.

This incident with Beatty characterizes what I will call Richard's unique brand of craziness.

In Zen philosophy, there are "Koans." The purpose of a Koan is to open the mind and perception to the truth. Koans are questions or riddles designed as instruments by the Zen Master to aid the student in finding the truth behind the everyday images of reality.

This is the effect of Richard's shocking craziness. Immediately after he asked Warren about his sex life with Julie Christie, Warren opened up.

In the language of the anthropologist, Richard had found the way to reverse the situation with Warren, the more famous hero of Hollywood. He had found the symbolic structure to invert. Turning the social situation on its head, he took control of the situation.

As it turned out, Richard's question was the appropriate thing at the time.

One of the sad results was that Warren caused Richard great pain, although he may not have been aware of it. Years later, Richard met Jennifer Lee whom he married twice. Some of Richard's grief came from the fact that Richard really respected Beatty. Richard would say to me, "Jennifer slept with Warren Beatty!" I always thought that was an exaggeration until I read Jennifer Lee's book, *Tarnished Angel* (1993), in which she described in detail her ménage à *trois* with Beatty and another woman.

Richard did not meet Jennifer until the late seventies, about ten years later, but as with many people in his life, he had already planted the seeds for his future encounters in the Berkeley days.

He respected Beatty so much that he refused Beatty's offer to make a film with him. He felt that if he made a film with Beatty, they would end up enemies. Richard thought that the film business always made enemies of people who had begun as friends. (Even when I was about to write *Which Way Is Up*, Richard would say, "It's going to destroy our friendship." It didn't, but he always felt that if you respected somebody, you should never make films with them).

The lunch with Warren lasted so long that when we left, it was getting on into the evening. Warren wanted to go the movies to see a porno film starring Chuck O'Connor from *The Rifleman.*

Richard thought it was an incredible idea. Was it a homosexual role, too? We took Warren's limousine and went to the Mitchell Bros on Broadway. I can't remember the Chuck O'Connor film, but we did see a hot short with a girl called "Mona," who gave a lively oral sex scene. After that Richard and I would use "Mona" as a keyword to refer to a juicy, attractive woman.

After he went to Hollywood a few years later, he called me on the phone and told me that he and Warren had met "Mona" in person.

When we were in the movie theater, somebody recognized Warren Beatty. "Look, there's Warren Beatty! And Richard Pryor with him."

Out of that incident, Richard developed a comic bit. "I can't go to porno movies any more," he would say in the bit, "People recognize me!" He was careful enough not mention that they recognized Warren Beatty, too.

There was a limit to his craziness, especially when he respected someone as much as he did Warren. The feeling was mutual, which is why when Richard was really sick, Warren's appearance to shake his hand as Richard sat in the back of his limousine carries with it a special poignancy.

After partying with Warren Beatty, Richard and I made it back to Berkeley. He was still wood shedding and he knew that when the time was ripe, he would pick up on Warren again. It was still 1970 and there was plenty to do in Berkeley.

Chapter Fifteen

KPFA

"**O**PENING UP: RICHARD'S First Public Image"
One day I came by Richard's apartment where he
was talking with David Reverend Banks, one of
the brothers that began to hang out with him. For some reason,
Richard called him "Reverend Banks."

Reverend Banks was older than Richard. Having been in the
army, he had graduated from UC Berkeley in 1955 under the G.I.
bill. He had majored in Psychology and Religion, but he had a
street-smart education that made Richard refer to him as "jive."

He met Richard in LA back in 1966 and followed his career to
San Francisco when he performed at the Basin Street West. As an
employer for Columbia Records, Reverend Banks was keenly interested in Richard's career. Years later, in 1974, he signed Richard
to Warner Bros for his record *Is It Something I Said?* (1975). It introduced the world to "Mudbone," but Mudbone had been brewing
for a few years, since the "Wino and the Junkie" that I saw him do
in Mandrake's in Berkeley.

Bank's production of Richard's third album, *Is It Something I
Said?* was a turning point. It was the first album that had a concept, depicting Richard on the fire at an Inquisition! When Richard
showed it to me, I was just blown away. The cover was like a jacket
of a novel. It was Richard's second big hit.

Richard had a record contract at that time in 1969 with a David Drozen, president of Laff Records which produced his second record, *Craps: After Hours.* The contrast between David Drozen and David Banks was like night and day. While Reverend Banks was an intimate friend and a keen observer of Richard's work, Drozen was a con from the beginning. Richard had to use a couple brilliant lawyers (like Michael Ashburne and David Franklin) to pry Drozen out of his career. Years later, I talked to Drozen to interview him on Richard, but he was insulting and abrupt. When he learned that I was a friend of Richard's, he cut off our communication.

When I came into the room, Richard and Banks were arguing about a story that Richard was telling. When he was a young boy, about six or seven, he was coming across the railroad tracks, Richard recalled, when an older man called him over and made him have oral sex with him.

"If I wrote a book," Richard said, "I'd put it in the book."

"I won't put no shit like that in a book," Reverend Banks said.

"Why not? I want to be honest," Richard replied.

"I wouldn't put that in a book. And don't you put no shit about me in your book either."

"Let me ask you this," Richard asked, "If somebody caught you giving a woman head, what would you do?"

"If you caught me giving a woman head? You know what I would do? I'd get my pistol out and make you give her some head, too."

Richard was amused. "Why would you do that?"

"Because if you gave her head, the next time you tried to tell about me giving her head, you wouldn't be able to talk about me without tellin' on yo'self!"

Richard fell out laughing. He really liked Reverend Banks' answer. Richard was brutally honest. He expected others to be as brutally honest as he was. Often he would ask somebody's opinion about his comedy and he expected him or her to tell him the truth. If he wasn't funny, he didn't mind somebody telling him that. But if they tried to lie about what they thought, he wouldn't have anything more to say to them. This was one of the reason he liked Reverend Banks.

I remember too that he was brutally honest to the point of being scary. I told him I was going to take him to a party in Berkeley where he would have no problem scoring. I said something like, "You wouldn't even have given them your name." We went to the party and he wouldn't say his name to the girls. He sat in a corner waiting for a girl to come up to him. When he didn't get any action, he said to me, "You said I wouldn't even have to say my name!"

I meant that as an exaggeration, not realizing that he was holding me to it literally. That would mean that a girl would want to sleep with him so bad that she wouldn't even ask his name or he wouldn't have to say it. That was asking a bit much – even for the Berkeley girls.

When Reverend Banks and I would talk about Richard, he was always impressed how well Richard was able to translate the Black people's struggle to young white hippies. "The white hippies love him," he would say, "because he won't conform."

I agreed with him. Richard was a non-conformist to the letter. Richard's apartment was always neat. When he lived with Alan, Alan did everything for him. Alan worked at the station from six in the morning to two in the afternoon, while Richard slept. When he returned, he made Richard breakfast.

But now that Richard had his own crib, he kept it spic and span. His kitchen was always clean. He would stack his dishes neatly on the dish rack by the sink. He made his own breakfast, lunch, and dinner. When he left his little apartment, he was always so well dressed that judging from his appearance you would have thought he came out of a mansion up in Beverley Hills.

Reverend Banks had an office with Columbia Records in San Francisco, but he lived in Oakland.

One day I went by Richard's apartment on California Street and found him reading a copy of Alex Haley's *The Autobiography of Malcolm X* and listening to the radio.

He told me he was following the trial of Huey P. Newton. It wasn't long after that—August 5, 1970—that Huey was released from prison for shooting Oakland police officer Frey.

A few days later, Richard and I were listening to his radio in his room, when we heard the news that George Jackson's young brother Jonathan Jackson was killed during a shootout with the police at the Marin County courthouse. Ten days later—August 15, 1970—Huey Newton appeared at the funeral of Jonathan Jackson.

Through his friend Alan, Richard had begun doing a radio show on KPFA, the most political radio station in the Bay Area, if not the entire country.

Richard kept telling me he was going to have his own radio show, called "Opening Up." I didn't think much about it, but one morning, he told me to show up at the station. I was to be there at six in the morning. I had spent the night with friends in San Francisco. As I pushed the bell, I could hardly keep my eyes open.

The inside of he station looked like a revolution was going on right there. People ran back and forth. There were slogans and messages posted everywhere.

Inside, I found Richard sitting behind a desk with a microphone in front of him.

"Sit down. We have our first guest."

Another man was with him, and it turned out to be comedian Paul Mooney. After I had talked a bit about the pigs, he turned to the Black man who was with him in the studio.

"Now, I want you to meet Paul Mooney!"

This was the first time meeting Paul. Richard had told Paul about me and me about Paul, but this was our first meeting. Richard had a talent for bring people together, even if these people had little in common except that they both were friends of Richard's. I remember meeting Jim Brown and realizing I had nothing in common with him, except the fact that Richard liked him. But with Mooney, it was different. We got along right away and remained friends for the next four decades.

Richard was in command. It must have reminded him of the television shows he had made, where he was always some white guy's guest.

Now he was in the role of the white guy and I was the "guest."

"Well," he said, "Tell us about the literary world, Mr. Brown!"

"Take a seat!" he said. Richard took out some red records and put one of them on the turntable.

"Lenny Bruce!" He announced to us.

As he played Lenny Bruce's comedy for the first twenty minutes of the show, I got a belly full of what Bruce meant to him. There was a very good reason why Pryor got hot under the collar if you mentioned he was a "Black Lenny Bruce." Reporters who asked that were usually given a scowl, and a short answer. He so hated the comparison to Lenny Bruce that he once broke off an interview.

The reason he was so sensitive on that subject was that he had taken so much from Bruce. Not just the structure of his bits, but the very themes themselves. Before Richard did the junkie, he heard a similar one on recordings. Before he did the characters in a pool hall, he had heard Lenny do the Jewish underground hoodlums. The idea of using impersonations of other characters as extending, or deftly characterizing with an intonation, or a slight gesture, even the social commentary of a satiric bystander—all this he heard first from Lenny Bruce.

Then, on the other hand, why should he emulate Lenny Bruce, who was trying to imitate the black male ethos himself? As Albert Goldman, the Bruce biographer, said, Bruce based his act on imitation of the cool black masculine style. Back in 1970, I could see that Richard's admiration for Lenny Bruce was great. Yes, Richard respected and recognized Bruce's achievement. But Richard was in Berkeley to find himself, to find out who he was, not to find out how much he was of somebody else! "If I died today," he once said, "would they put in the paper, Richard Pryor, who imitated Lenny Bruce, died today?"

This was the real reason why he hated being called the Black Lenny Bruce. The one time that Richard really got pissed off with

Alan was when Alan asked him if he was the Black Lenny Bruce. Richard went off, Alan recalled to me.

After this Lenny Bruce introduction, which consisted of his playing twenty minutes of the comic, he finally got around to me.

"I want you to meet my dear friend Cecil Brown. He is a writ-er...He wrote a book called *The Life and Loves of Mr. Jiveass Nigger.*" He spoke to the radio community as if he knew them. At one point in the show, though, he had to ask the audience if they heard him. "Is there anybody out there listenin' to us? Let me know, by calling this number." He gave the number on the air. This was before call-in shows. It was so unusual that I made a note of it, because I was not certain that you could do what Richard was attempting. What he was attempting was to have the audience participate in the creation of a dialogue between him and the listening public.

Another innovation occurred in that early morning show. This has to do with the usage of the word "motherfucker." Due to the overuse of the word today, we have forgotten that there was a time when nobody used it in popular media.

In the course of my conversation with Richard and Paul, I forgot that I was on the air, and used the word 'motherfucker.' I said something like "Well, that motherfucker—"

Richard grimaced when he heard that obscenity. Then he pulled my arm. "Lissen, man, I got this little gig because this white boy, Alan, is trying to help me out. And here you come fuckin' it up."

"What do you mean?"

I was puzzled.

"You know you can't say motherfucker," he whispered, "Not on the air!"

"Oh man, I'm sorry."

No more than three weeks later Richard started using 'motherfucker' in his act down at Mandrake's. He never stopped using it to characterize his characters as natural and realistic.

Then the phone rang and Richard grabbed it quickly. "Yes?"

"Hey, man, I can hear you."

"Oh, who are you?"

"My name is Joe. I'm here lying in the bed…"

Suddenly we hear another voice with Joe in the bed. It sounds like a woman is giggling. Richard picks up on that quickly.

"Oh, you are not alone…?"

"Uh…no…I'm here with…my friend…"

When the "friend" laughed again, we could hear that it was a woman — and a white one at that.

"Say, brother…" Richard was laughing as he drew the brother out. It was funny, and it was just like when he had a live audience in front of him when he was performing.

The next thing we knew, he had drawn the brother out and was developing a skit around the fact that he called in and he happened to be in bed with his white girlfriend. Richard drew the implications out so that anybody within radio shot was laughing.

"Thank you, Richard."

Then he turned back to me.

"So what is happening in the literary world, Mr. Brown?"

I said a few things and then he asked, "Can you tell us something about the pigs?"

This was when I was in the 4H club as a boy and I had to judge pigs. In one of our countless conversations, I told Richard about this, and how one of the things you do in the club is to participate in contests. I was the winner of the pig-judging contest in our county. He would ask me, "How do you win a pig judging contest?" I would explain to him the different kinds of pigs. I would tell him about judging pigs by the way they stood on their hooves, and so forth on. You could tell how big a litter a shoat (a female pig) could have by the way she stood. He would show the most intense interest in my story, as if he didn't believe it, yet knew that it was true. He always loved that, and now he wanted to share his enthusiasm with his audience.

After the show, we went to get some breakfast. Paul told me fabulous stories about Richard's strange behavior with money—about how he walked off and left a Mercedes in the middle of the street in Santa Monica. "Why? Cecil, Richard is a nut! He doesn't want any material things like cars!"

I loved cars. I had paid 500 dollars for my old Jag, and while I was working with David Foster, I acquired an XKE from him. So it was hard for me to get my head around the concept of leaving a Mercedes in the middle of the street. But Richard was my cut buddy so stuff like that didn't faze me.

It was during this time that Richard became interested in the Black Panthers and the political world that the Black Panthers brought with them.

During the 1970-71, Richard became revolutionary, reading Black Panther books and listening to their speeches on his radio. It was during this time that he met Huey P. Newton.

In August 1971, Richard and I listened to the radio in his room and heard George Jackson's last interview. It wasn't more than a few days later that Jackson was killed in San Quentin prison in an alleged prison break out. We heard James Baldwin, and Jean Genet pay tributes to Jackson.

Then on September 13, 1971, prisoners at the Attica Correctional Facility in Buffalo, New York, responded to the George Jackson murder by revolting. The revolt lasted four days. The blacks held the white guards hostage. Governor Nelson Rockefeller ordered over 1,500 prison officials to attack the prison and a total of 43 people were killed, including 10 of the 38 hostages. Later autopsies showed that the hostages were killed, not by the prisoners, but by the police gunfire.

One of the convicts stated, "We do not want to rule; we want to live… but if any of you gentlemen own dogs, you're treating them better than you treat us." [4]

Using the radio program "Opening Up" as his means of communication, Richard read poems he had written against New York State, against "Attica."

CHAPTER SIXTEEN

SUPER NIGGER

LANEY COLLEGE AUDITORIUM

RICHARD PLAYED FOR a small, mostly white counterculture audience at Mandrake's in Berkeley, but when he performed at Laney College, in Oakland, it was to a large audience of black students. Not just Black students, but Black students schooled in the ideology of the Black Panther movement.

It was at this event that Richard perfected his routines about "the Junkie and Wino." While he had performed these bits back in Berkeley, here in Oakland the Black audience, which Richard entertained at Laney College, was revolutionaries. They were hipped to police brutality. They were aware of their history and the continuity of the oppressive system.

In skits like the "Junkie and the Wino" and "Wino Meets Dracula," they saw themselves. In addition to the "Junkie and the Wino," they also recognized themselves in the skit that Richard did on Superman called "Super Nigger." Fantasy was a Black way of criticizing the system. In American pop culture, the main man is Super Man, an embedded Nazi-figure that is so dear to the white man. The very idea of a token Negro with a cape is funny, and it makes Black people laugh. That's their demon, a powerful Black man.

The irony is that the Super Man character had been based on a 1890s black cartoon, "Steam Man", about a black man who can run faster than a train. After losing the black work force after slavery, the American imagination compensated by fantasying about a mechanical robot that was black. Over the years this black robot that had appeared in popular magazine was "whitenized" into the super man we know today.

"Ladies and Gentlemen, the crown prince of Comedy..."

The introductions were always lame and meant nothing except that he was about to go on and stand in front of the microphone.

Richard would come out. He would be wearing a change of shirts. Maybe he would have changed into some slacks with creases. He would have combed out his natural, but it would still be kind of funky. He didn't want to be different on stage than he was in real life to give the audience the sense that there was no real difference between Richard on stage and Richard off stage.

The junkie got the loudest applause.

"...Somewhere in Metropolis, they have Clark Washington. Faster than a speeding bullet! Faster than a bowl of chillins'!"

"It's a crow—It's a bird!—*it's Super...Nigger!"*

To put his skit into a minstrelsy context, Richard did a soft shoe dance. He was a janitor doing a soft shoe dance. Then, he was singing the spirituals. He acted out a scene from his imaginary scene in Super Man, or as it were, Super Nigger Television Show. He began the routine with Super Nigger singing a spiritual ("Nobody Knows the Trouble I See") as he worked at the warehouse.

As the worker in the warehouse, he pantomimed a scene in which he sees Lois Lane. He approached her.

"What's going on, Miss Lane?"

Lois Lane said, "There's fire in the warehouse!"

Richard addressed the audience. "As we know, Super Nigger can see through everything—except whitey! He puts on his cape!"

He went to his closet and tried to pick out a cape. He had so many capes! Damn, the brother had capes in every color and hue!

"Now, this one is a bad motherfucker!"

He puts on the cape and evaluated his effect on the public. "Shit, I'm clean!"

Super Nigger jumped out of the window.

"Look, it's Super Nigger."

He looked at Lois Lane. "Bitch don't call me nigger."

Lois Lane repeated the news: "There's fire in the warehouse! On 9th and Ward Street!"

"Ninth and Ward - That's where I got my *stash!*"

The audience went wild with that image of a Black man and his stash of marijuana, one of the main symbols of counterculture. *The stash!*

Super Nigger jumped up into the sky. After a brief time in the air flying across the buildings, he landed on the pavement on his feet on the corner of Ninth and Ward streets. He examined the building and discovered that his stash had been burned up.

"My shit burned up—y'all can't bust me. Nigger gonna pay me for my dope, four kilos."

Super Nigger went into a mild fit, he was so messed up in the head over being ripped off his precious stash!

This single skit was, in retrospect, a great achievement. It fell right into the absurdity category that Freud had written about. It left people howling in the aisles. It was so far out nobody knew quite what it is was.

During the last days of his Berkeley transformation, Richard came up with "Wino Meets Dracula," "The Wino and the Junkie," and "Super Nigger."

The first impression I had of this absurdity in his act was when he introduced the "Wino and The Junkie" (sometimes called "Street Corner Wino") one night on the stage in Berkeley. In these bits Richard showed the absurdity of Black life in the inner city.

The Junkie and Wino were absurd, but one of them, the junkie, thought he was *less* absurd and better off than the Wino. In fact, the audience found that they were both in the same situation.

What made the bit on the Wino and the Junkie so interesting were the distinctions between the Wino and the Junkie.

If you are white and an outsider to the Black world, you might not see much difference between a black wino and a black junkie. For you, they are about the same. But if you are from the Black world, there are a lot of differences between the two. You would know that Junkies don't like winos because of their bad breath and funky appearances. Junkies, on the other hand, seldom have bad breath because they don't have much use for alcohol. Junkies are usually cleaner because they don't live in the street. When they can afford their junk, they are usually well dressed.

Junkies are usually better educated than the Wino, which is why the Wino said, "See that boy? He was a genius, could remember the numbers without a pencil or paper." The Junkies were from the end of the segregation and the beginning of the time when integration took hold. This is why the Junkie said, "I put on my white voice." The Wino comes from a time when there was no such a thing as a "white voice," (at least not as a kind of hustle) because you couldn't get a job whether you had a "white voice" or not.

Even then the "white voice" had the effect of "freakin' the bitch out!" but he didn't want a job anyway because you have to do a lot of "shit" to get it.

The Wino was older. He may have been in the Korean War and has certainly been around the world several times. He has known Pancho Villa, and helped start the Merchant Marines. He was limited by his non-literate status, for he is "In-Literary." He spoke phonetically Black Speech that has not been locked down by the laws of spelling. He used sound poetics.

"I believe you have potential," he told the Junkie. "I know how to talk to the white man. I know how to speak Mexican. I said, 'What you say, Motherfucker?'"

His idea of speaking "Mexican" is ludicrous. But the Junkie's idea of the world they are living in was not much better. He would simply imitate the "white voice" like a parrot. Richard demonstrated with this skit that there is very little difference between these two social types.

That night in particular, Richard explored the Junkie further. The Wino is a kind of community leader, like ancient Socrates, who went around asking members of the community about themselves. And like the philosopher, he likes to "interview" the citizens. So he interrogates the Junkie about his life, specifically about why the police were looking for him.

The Junkie told him that he was sick, and then described the "Murphy game." The "Murphy game" is a common form of sexual exploitation well known in the street life of the 50s. In this version, the Junkie tricked a white man who was looking for black girls into pulling down his pants. After taking his money the Junkie runs off leaving the man holding his drawers. This is why the police were looking for the him, the Junkie tells the Wino.

The Wino was impressed by the Junkie's ability to maintain his dignity in an exploitive situation. Like somebody in a primary oral society, the Wino saw that the criminal was sympathetic because his burden is his own consciousness. If you kill a man in the oral world, your punishment is that you have to carry the body around on your back.

Richard used these bits to show the absurdity of Black life in White America. I saw this in Richard's comedy: the Junkie and the Wino were mirror images of each other.

The image of "Super Nigger" was a hilariously funny comment on Super Man. Richard employed the same kind of comic strategy when the Wino meets Dracula. It was one absurdity meeting another absurdity. "So the technique of the nonsense jokes," Freud wrote, "consists in the introduction of something foolish, nonsensical, whose underlying meaning is the illustration, the demonstration, of something else foolish and nonsensical."

The charm of the absurdity for Richard was the psychic release of energy, which the laughter brings. The longest and the loudest cry of laughter, the birth pains of insight, was when Richard impersonated the Junkie. When the Junkie told about freaking out the unemployment officer by putting on his "white voice," the audience's howl of recognition lasted longer than any other I had ever experienced. Richard would hang in a freeze like the Junkie in a trance, yodeling "WHAATSSSHAPPPPININNN!"

Now I understood what he meant by going for something extra. He had turned the comic bits into dramatic characters. He had become an oral actor, a one-man show who could speak from the point of view of that character he impersonated at the moment.

He was ready for Mudbone, which would be his crowning achievement.

CHAPTER SEVENTEEN

MUDBONE

THE VOICE OF the Wino and the Junkie was an echo for the major voice, Mudbone.

"Once I noticed him, inspiration took over," Richard once told me. The character just came over to him, and introduced himself. "Hello," Mudbone said, "I'm Mudbone..."

He talked about Mudbone as if he were somebody we knew. "As with other characters I did," he would say, "like the Wino or All Well, I suddenly knew everything about this old man who I called Mudbone. Every black town had someone like him, Mudbone is a trickster, a shaman from the Native Americans."

That first time he talked about Mudbone for two minutes. A month later he did half an hour of him alone.

Richard knew everything about him, and could express his whole worldview with a minimal of gestures and voices. "We all know somebody like him," Richard said. Mudbone was out of Zora Neale Hurston. The legend of Mudbone was one that African Americans shared with the Native Americans.

The African stories and the Native American stories crossed over from one group and back again. The wise old black man had its origin in African West Coast culture. It was taken to the West Indies and to the mainland America. Stories about the Old Wise Black man who survives on his wit go back to Uncle

Remus (a name given to him by a white journalist Joel Chandler Harris). In the Black version, he is John de Conqueror (a name given him by Zora Neale Hurston).

"You know, I was thinking about your act," I would say, "You know the best stories are the ones you tell in a persona, like a voice."

"Yeah," Richard said, "Yeah, like Mudbone?"

"Mudbone?"

On episode 21 of the Cosby Kids, October 20,1973, Fat Albert and his buddies learn about Native American culture when they encounter the Shaman named "Mudbone." Did Richard use that name because of the show? He certainly could have.

The Wino was a prototype, or model, for Mudbone. One of the qualities that indicated their connection was that they were both observers of their neighborhood. The Wino looked out for his neighbor ("This is a neighborhood, this ain't no residential"!). The Wino was a citizen of the city, but Mudbone was from down South.

The Wino was a city observer; Mudbone was an observer of storytellers, of men who are masters of the tall tale. One of these storytellers was Toodlum, who tells about the "Niggers With The Big Dicks."

"He could lie his ass off," Mudbone said, paying him the highest of compliments.

"You know everybody got an old man in their family like this guy we used to know, we call Mudbone."

I saw another connection. "Oh, yeah, he can be a kind of Nigger Jim in Huckleberry Finn!"

Richard sat there thinking about what I said.

A few years later, in 1976, on *Bicentennial Nigger,* he did a bit called "Mudbone Goes to Hollywood," in which he recalled details about D.W. Griffith. Mudbone brags that he came to Hollywood and met the famous white filmmaker and taught him how to do a close-up. He also met Mae West and shacked up with her for a while.

Although Mudbone would not be archived until 1975, in *Is It Something I Said?*, the seed that would grow into this archetype began in Richard's use of the absurdity in comedy. In *Is it Something I Said?*, he introduced Mudbone for about 17 minutes, then in 1975, he introduced Mudbone as the shoeshine man on his TV show; in 1976, he recorded "Mudbone Goes to Hollywood, and in 1983, in *Here and Now* (concert film), he did "Mudbone" (part one and part two). This was the last presentation of the Mudbone cycle.

In 1976, when I began working on the screenplay, *Which Way Is Up?* I wrote the character of Rufus being inspired by Mudbone. In the years 1974 to 1976, Richard brought Mudbone to perfection. All of our excitement derived solely from Richard's incredible work on the stage and the subsequent comedy records that widened his audience.

While still living in Berkeley, Richard had been making overtures to Hollywood. But now that he was living in Sausalito, he began to think seriously about going back to Hollywood.

In 1971, Richard met a young Pan Am airline stewardess Patricia, who lived in Berkeley and drove a Porsche. She was tall, witty, and funny. She fell deeply in love with Richard and became part of the gang.

After Richard began living with Patricia, Alan's role switched to being a road manager. Alan told me that one day, Patricia let him run an errand in her Porsche. When Richard discovered this, he flew into a rage. He got so mad that he threw a bottle of shampoo at him, punched him in the face, called him a faggot, and fired him. He hired him back, but he never apologized for calling him a faggot. Alan, being a devotee to Richard's genius, forgave him.

Not long after that, Patricia moved across the Bay, to the upscale town of Sausalito, where she rented an apartment. It was here that Richard became friends with Spencer, a street genius, who lived on a houseboat in the Sausalito harbor.

*Richard was still scruffy-looking when he
met Julian Bond (far right).*

Part of his plan included auditioning for new Black films. His opportunity came when he was called to audition for the role of Piano Man in he upcoming film, *Lady Sings the Blues*. Before he could get on the plane, which he missed five times, because he was afraid of flying, he got into fights with Patricia, who claimed that he broke her nose.

Auditioning for the part, he got it and performed his role of Piano Man brilliantly. After *Lady Sings the Blues* came out, Richard thought that he had a shot to become a star, or at least to get more movie work. He thought that he should have had the chance, he would say, but he was Black.

Richard and I would meet in Berkeley where he still performed. He told me he never read the script they gave him of Piano Man. "I just improvised it," he said. He had learned a lot from performing standup in Berkeley. He learned to create characters out of gestures and words. From bits like "The Wino and the Junkie," he had learned how to create memorable and admirable characters without writing them out or even writing them down.

This character was sketched out for him by knowing real junkies and winos. He knew Flip Wilson, who was a junkie throughout his life and career. Flip's nephew Rashon told me that Flip showed Richard how to play a junkie and Richard had used that little tutorial for Piano Man.

His performance in that role was his first fruits of working the room in Berkeley. When the film came out, the critics agreed that his portrayal of junkie musicians stood out. Even though Billy Dee Williams was the male star of the film, Richard was the unspoken hit in the film. Anybody who saw it had to be moved by his performance. James Baldwin observed that this performance as a new beginning in acting and wrote about it in his essay, *The Devil Finds Work.*

In 1973 I would meet Baldwin in Paris, and often talked to him about Richard and his incredible performance in *Lady Sings the Blues*. Like most viewers, Baldwin recognized Richard's genius from that small part in the movie. He wanted to meet Richard, and I promised him that when he returned to America I would introduce them.

CHAPTER EIGHTEEN

THE MACK

T HE NEXT SERIOUS part after "The Piano Man" in *Lady
Sings The Blues* that he was offered in a film was a small one
in the blaxploitation film, *The Mack* (1973).

Michael Campus, a young Jewish guy from Los Angeles, directed *The Mack*, starring Black actor Max Julian, who had made
several blaxploitation films. Richard didn't respect the exploitive
black films that were being produced by studios, but since he had
no other offers, he had no choice. He wanted to make films that
bad.

Back in the days before he came to Berkeley, Richard became
friends with Max Julian. Julian had written *Cleopatra Jones*, a blaxploitation film. Richard and Max Julian respected each other as
actors, so Max Julian brought Richard in to be in his next film, *The
Mack*, in which he was playing the starring role, Goldie, the pimp.
Richard played Slim, the sidekick to Max Julian's Goldie. He hated
the role and we would spend evenings hanging out and talking
about films.

Richard spent a year preparing the script with Julian and
Campus. But when they started the production in Oakland, Huey
P. Newton stepped in.

According to Elaine Brown, who, in 1974, had succeeded Huey
as the leader of the Black Panther Party, Huey demanded that

Campus put money in the Black Panther Party. "Huey's idea was this," she told me later, on May 15, 2008. "If you are going to come down here in the Black Community to exploit people, then you got to pay us. Huey looked at the film as any other kind of business adventure."

Huey P. Newton intimidated by the Black Panther Party and campus. He used other blacks like Elaine Brown and Bobby Seale to navigate the difficulties he was having with Huey. He said, "Huey cast the minor characters," meaning that he gave up some important decisions to the Black Panther leader.

Campus had hired Richard even though he was, as he puts it, a risk. "He had a bad reputation for being unreliable," he told me.

After preparing the film for more than a year, they were scheduled to finish it in Oakland. They had twenty-eight days to shoot it, and Richard was there for half of those days. He was usually late, and when he did arrive, he was stoned. He wouldn't know his lines. He had to be persuaded to do it. But then after many mishaps, he would get it together. And then before they knew it, he was incredible. He would come alive and do something during a shoot that had not been anticipated. He would surprise them. Michael Campus recited what came to be the usual reactions to Richard's performance. A few years later, Mel Brooks would describe Richard in almost the same words.

These directors wanted to work with Richard because his name was beginning to be a draw. But they didn't want to judge him on his own terms.

But when Pryor was on screen, Campus told me, his performance was electrifying. "We never knew what he was going to do next," Campus recalled, "so when he was on screen, he carried that quality. You couldn't stop watching him."

Only great actors like George C. Scott and Lawrence Oliver could do this, he observed. He put Richard in this elite category. "It would be like a burst of the sun."

There was one big problem. Richard couldn't sustain his performances. Yes, Richard's performances were like the bursting of sun, "and then…it would go out. You would have this incredible moment of light, and then it would be gone."

His acting style was like his moods—very mercurial. "We would be in the writing stage of the script, and Richard would be doing great, but he would go into the bathroom and come out in a completely different mood."

Campus attributes Richard's behavior on the set to a childhood that wrecked his life. "There is no question in my mind," he said, "that Richard never really felt inner confidence." Expressing the same observation as many of Richard's close friends from those days, he claimed that Richard's "demons put him in a rage, and his rage fueled his talent."

"It would have been great," he believed, "if Richard had gone into therapy, or got some help, at that early stage. That was his biggest problem. He would have lived a lot longer."

Campus doesn't believe that Richard's comic genius would have been destroyed if he had gotten psychiatric help early in his career. "There are people who say that kind of talent is always connected to tragedy. I don't believe that. He had so much talent, that had he gotten help, he might have taken a slightly different road but he would have been successful. He would have found some kind of peace that I don't think he ever found."

In 1998, Richard showed up for the 25th anniversary of the *The Mack*. By then he was victimized by MS and was not able to walk. "Richard came in his wheelchair," Campus remembered. "There was so much in his eyes about what had gone wrong and it was difficult for me to see him that way. I saw it was difficult for him, too, to be in such bad shape. When I knew him back in 1971, he was so vibrant, alive, giving it everything he had. It's a tragedy. It was a gift, but it was also a tragedy."

It was during this time that Huey P. Newton became a legend. For most young Black Americans, Huey P. Newton became a symbol of manhood. Richard was a legend in his own right and had conquered Berkeley and San Francisco, but Oakland belonged to Huey P. Newton and the Black Panther Party.

Michael Campus turned to Elaine Brown, one of the leaders of the Black Panther Party, to help him negotiate between his production company and the Black Panther Party.

Elaine Brown understood why Black people—especially Black men—gravitated towards Huey. She summarized it this way: "Everybody wanted to challenge Huey's manhood. "They [Richard and Huey] have "manhood issues." She remembered that Huey liked Richard a lot and Richard liked Huey. She said they not only admired each other, but they liked each other.

If other black men looked up to Huey, Huey looked up to George Jackson, who gave his life for Black people. A hero of the people, a poet, a leader, Jackson was for Huey the model that he most emulated.

Huey's attitude toward the film production represented the Black Panther Party's attitude. Both Huey and the party had the attitude that the film was exploitive of the black people living in Oakland.

"Huey had no problem telling the producers of *The Mack* to pay up," Elaine Brown told me, "If you are going to shoot a film here, [the Black Panther Party] can't allow you to exploit our people. We are feeding people here."

Huey saw the production of a film about a pimp as negative. He put it in the same category as the after-hours joints that line 7th Street and San Pablo Avenue in Oakland. Most of the after-hour joints and clubs had to pay Huey and the Black Panther Party a "tithe," as Huey liked to call it. To be even more accurate, he might have called it a shakedown.

"We opposed films like *The Mack* and *Super Fly*," Brown maintained. The Black Panther Party put so much pressure on the filmmakers that, "Ultimately, they had to change the ending of the film to redeem the pimping part, by having a big message out there."

Just as he did with the other outside business, Huey made them pay. "If you're going to come into the black community and collect money from black people, you have to pay us. Already we were getting money from those illegitimate capitalists like the pimps and hustlers, and the after hour clubs and joints. These were the illegal activities of the underground economy. They all make a contribution to the Black Panther Party."

Whether he was forced to do so or if he did it willingly, Pryor did give to the Black Panther Party. Brown claimed that Hollywood celebrities contributed to the Black Panther party, and not just the well known celebrities like Jane Fonda and Burt Schneider, but also Warren Beatty, Jon Voigt, and Donald Sutherland.

Meanwhile, Richard got to meet Huey P. Newton, whom he had only known through his reading and seeing him in the media. Richard met Huey at a party in Oakland.

Both Huey and Richard liked cocaine and a competition arose as to who was the baddest—who could stay up the longest. Elaine saw it as a badge of courage. "They were the only ones who could afford large amounts of cocaine," Elaine Brown suggested.

Huey had an unusual physical constitution when it came to imbibing drugs, according to Elaine, one of his most devoted admirers, now as well as then. "He had the ability to take incredible amounts of alcohol and cocaine in this respect. He was an incredible man."

In her assessment of the battle between Richard and Huey, Brown was well aware of Richard's street persona. Because of his comedy album *Craps After Hours*, which had come to saturate the nightlife of Oakland—as well as other black inner cities—Richard had become synonymous with the street culture.

This was one of the reasons, Elaine Brown believed, that Richard was attracted to Huey, the ultimate symbol of the Black Street Male, at least in Oakland, the home of the Black Panther Party. Like his competitive attitude towards Warren Beatty, his competition with Huey was inevitable.

If Richard thought that he could come into Oakland, make a pimp film, and on top of that, outlast Huey in a cocaine-snorting contest, then he didn't know what he was up against.

"There is no way that you can come into Oakland and take over," Brown told me. "Huey is going to go two or three days straight snorting and drinking. I know that Richard can do that, too. By that time, they would be crazy. But Huey was crazier! Was he crazy? Violent? Would Huey do things that were difficult to follow? Yes."

Being crazy, or being crazier — these are accurate expressions for how Richard and Huey competed with each other while snorting cocaine. For the average white person these terms would have to be explained. Richard had already garnered a reputation as being crazy, of saying or doing the most off-the-wall stuff and getting away with it. To be "crazy," you had to be honest, and truthful. You had to be courageous and willing to put your life on the line. You had to do the thing that most people would not do, the thing that the average person would not think of doing. When an Oakland policeman pulled a gun on him, Huey pulled his shotgun on the policeman. One night we were in the Basin Street West, and Richard was up there doing his comedy routine, and at the moment when the loudness had subsided, a young woman said, "That Nigger's crazy!" Richard heard the comment and made it the cover of his next album.

What Black people meant by the expression "that Nigger's crazy" is different from how white Americans understand the phrase. For Black people, it meant that in most instances, acting crazy was the right thing to do. Warren Beatty probably could not remember my name, but he never forgot Richard. Being crazy under the right circumstances isolates the crazy person and marks him with a uniqueness that makes him remembered.

This is why Elaine Brown, after many years, remembered the coke wars between Richard and Huey as crazy. "Richard liked to come up and hang out with Huey," she told me, "But Huey could snort anybody under the table."

With Richard and Huey, it was always a question of who was the craziest. The cocaine was just a means to that end. In Pryor's social context, cocaine is manna, a kind of sacred food. It was the food of the gods, as it were, useful to distinguish the "crazy niggers" from the ordinary Negroes or Black people.

Even though I snorted it with Richard, I never thought of it as anything but a symbol of separating the sacred behavior from the ordinary secular rituals of life. For Huey and Richard, it was a physical, objective correlative of an inner spirit. With cocaine, Richard and Huey could rise to the level where only the two of them would be alone. Who else would dare do what they did? Who else would want to?

Reverend Banks, who traveled with Richard when he was making *The Mack*, reported one of the craziest things that Richard did to Huey.

They were snorting cocaine. "Huey tried to strong arm Richard—and Richard slapped him," Reverend Banks said. Reverend Banks' story confirms my feeling that Richard was the king of craziness. "I was surprised, but then I realized that Huey was not such a bad motherfucker," Reverend Banks told me. "And I realized that Richard was crazy!" Without the cocaine, there would be no contest and without the contest there would be no report on who was the "craziest."

Even though Reverend Banks saw Richard pop Huey, Elaine Brown doesn't believe that Richard hit Huey.

"No, there would be no Richard slapping Huey," she laughed. "If Richard had slapped Huey, he would have been dead. If anything, it would be Huey slapping Richard, because Huey had [already] slapped Melvin Van Peebles. He slapped Melvin and when Melvin tells the story, he says the slap was like a kiss."

As Brown tells it, Huey went to meet Melvin in New York. Melvin was about forty minutes late, but when he showed up, he didn't mention that he was late, didn't apologize, and went on talking as if nothing was wrong. "Then Huey smacked him," Brown told me. But Melvin and Huey really liked each other. Like these men, Elaine Brown thought Huey was brilliant, a genius and a revolutionary.

When I told Melvin Van Peebles what Elaine Brown had said, he laughed at the idea that Huey slapped him. "No, no, no!" Melvin explained. "I don't remember that! We would do this thing of slapping hands. We would bump shoulders."

The matter rests mainly on the Black urban conception of "craziness." In early 1973, I did witness a crazy scene between Richard and Huey. After Richard had performed at the Circle Star Theater, Huey came by Richard's room at the Doubletree Hotel.

There were several people gathered in Richard's suite. He had a suite that had a staircase that connected the downstairs and an upper bedroom.

There was champagne and loud talk, attractive women, and boisterous men—a typical scene after Richard's concerts.

With most of the guests in the living room, Richard's bedroom was off limits. I was in the bedroom with Richard, Huey, and Huey's bodyguard.

Then Huey brought out a bag of cocaine and dumped it on an album cover and started snorting from it and passing it around. He was talking to Richard about Richard playing him in a movie about Huey's life. But as he pontificated to Richard, he forgot to pass the cocaine to the next person—to Richard.

Richard kept saying, "Pass the coke, nigger," But Huey kept yelling to him about how he wanted Richard to play him in a movie. After a while, Huey put his face about an inch from Richard's. This was how Huey liked to talk to Richard, his face up in Richard's.

"What's your problem, man?" Richard would say.

"Nigger, I ain't got a problem."

"Then, why the fuck you yelling?"

Richard said to cool Huey out. "Ain't nobody here but us!"

"I got somebody to look after me, too!"

Huey looked over to the bodyguard. Richard looked over at me. He made it look to Huey that I was Richard's bodyguard. I am a pretty big guy. Rashon was Richard's regular bodyguard, but he was downstairs on a mission. So I would have to stand in for him if something went down.

The room got very intense. Such intensity could go either way. It could get more intense, breaking out into a fight or scuffle. Or, it would break into a laugh, which would release the tension. With Black men, though, it was usually a combination of both.

With Black men, such situations are hard to explain, though not very rare, especially when drugs are involved. What is even more inexplicable is that Black men really enjoy these scenes. They bring out the most intense feelings and are fun to talk about later.

In short, some black men are crazy! As I look back on this scene, I realize how "out there" I was, too. I could have been killed, or shot, because both Richard and Huey were high and had guns near by. Richard probably didn't have a gun, but Huey and his bodyguard may not have known this.

Recounting this scene years later, Richard wrote, "The really scary people like Huey Newton didn't bother me. Huey and I met at a party in Oakland and then did cocaine in my hotel room. As we got high, he got angry because his woman was coming on to me and I didn't tell her to stop."

"The scene got very tense," he wrote in his autobiography. This was true. We were talking about jail, Richard reported. Huey was worried about going to prison. Richard asked him why he was afraid of going to jail.

"Cuz if I go," Huey told Richard, "everyone's going to want to fuck me," he said. "But if they put their dick in my mouth," he added, "I'm gonna bite it off."

"That would be the right move," Richard told him, "But right before you bite, you know, you're going to taste that dick in your mouth and wonder whether or not you liked it."

Huey's reaction was violent. Richard claimed that Huey hit him.

"Huey shot up from his seat and punched me. The blow caught me on the side of the head."

As I have already said, Reverend Banks claimed that Richard slapped Huey, but Richard says that it was Huey who hit him. I was in the room at the Doubletree hotel that evening with both of them. Richard and Huey didn't come to blows but they were close. Thinking back on it years later, Richard wrote, "It could've been messy. Both of us were high, we had guns, and we were out of our minds. Fortunately, I decided my best move was to watch as Huey grabbed his woman and marched out of my room. I knew that I could stir up more shit on stage than in a revolution."

Richard and Huey's egos were so strong that they had to go at each other, seeking some way to express their desire to be the best. Finally, Richard realized that his province was the stage and Huey realized that his area was politics. Huey recognized that Richard's contribution was setting up a "dialogue about racism in America through comedy;" though, ultimately, Richard was not a revolutionary but an entertainer.

At the end of the day, Elaine Brown said, Huey knew that Pryor, Max Julian, and Melvin Van Peebles were entertainers. They were not in the world to change anything for the masses. They were not there to change the dynamic.

"Richard didn't do anything revolutionary," Brown averred. "His contribution to the progress of the black race was limited to being an entertainer, which is what Huey reminded him of. Just like Melvin Van Peebles and Max Julian—these people forget that Huey was the leader of the Black Panther party."

Richard's fascination with Huey and the Black Panther Party ended when he finished his work with *The Mack*.

CHAPTER NINETEEN

"THE NEW PRYOR"

SINCE HE CAME to Berkeley, Richard had been going on the road with the new show. He would sit with me in the International Pancake House on University Avenue across from where he lived on 1988 California Street and show me the meager clippings he got. I would read the clippings as we ate. He always had the steak and eggs. In those days, he was about a hundred and fifty pounds and wore a leather, wide-brimmed hat.

"It was hard," he would say, "to come back with a new act to all those old clubs that knew the old Richard Pryor. 'Cause the same audience would come see me and get shocked—when I just decided that, 'Hey, man, this is the way I'm gonna be.' And the clubs started falling off. The first one was Mr. Kelly's in Chicago."

The late George Marienthal then owned the Chicago club. "George came to me and said, 'Now Richard, we don't want that shit on our stage!' I said, 'Mr. Marienthal, this is what I do now.' 'You know we don't want that shit now!' George repeated.

"I said, 'Well, look, man, I won't even come, rather than cause a lot of trouble, 'cause I like you and I don't want to go against that.'"

He complained to me that the one place he could still go was The Cellar Door in Washington, D.C. This club supported his new change from the very beginning. Hollie I. West, a Washington based writer, was one of the first critics to acknowledge that Pryor had changed his comedy style after moving to Berkeley.

"Richard Pryor altered his comedy style about a year ago to include bawdy street language and risqué routines," he noted. "His previous act was more like that of a proper college boy."

He quotes Richard's defense of this new bawdy mode: "I think what I'm doing now is more me. I could perform if I did what the squares want me to do. But so far everything has been nice. There have been positive as well as negative effects."

Some of the negative effects were that audiences might be turned off by the obscenity. Hollie conceded that some would be turned off by it, and goes on to explain that Pryor does not intend to shock his audience.

Although Richard was cracking up audiences at The Cellar Door, West explained, "his use of profanity may drive out the meek, but the way he deploys a sexual or bodily excrement term, is as natural as many people talk in private."[5]

Richard's practice of treating the audience as if they were in an all-night spritz sessions with the boys back in Berkeley was taking its toll and making itself known.

It was this intimate, insider's view of the profanity that convinced West that Pryor's language is not there to shock. "The [obscenity] terms fall into a definite context and are not intended to shock. Pryor is not like Lenny Bruce, who sometimes used coarse language for its own sake."

What West was driving at was that Pryor's language was part of a wider cultural practice by an African American community. Much of Pryor's comedy comes from the ghetto area of Peoria, Illinois, where he grew up.

Pryor grew up in a community of prostitutes and pimps. Therefore, West writes, his "routines about basketball, after-hours spots and boy-girl relations are spiced with colloquialisms and attitudes of American black youth."

Even the names of these characters reflect those of all African American urban communities. "Some of the characters he depicts

— Cool Breeze, Bubba, the Weasel or Jesse — evoke by themselves vivid images of what it is to grow up Black."[6]

The message was that humor connected millions of black people.

In fact, the Black humor — or Black worldview — was another thing that separated Pryor from Lenny Bruce. Both Bruce and Pryor are "irreverent" in their attacks on President Nixon, Pope Paul, the Protestant Church or the Apollo 11 Astronauts, but whereas Lenny is intellectual, Pryor is funny. Pryor always makes the audience belly laugh. Furthermore, West quotes Pryor's claim that he is even more influenced by Bill Cosby than he is by Lenny Bruce.

Richard loved the progress he was making. For every negative review he got, he relished the ones that were positive.

While on tour in the South, he was arrested for "disorderly conduct" in Virginia. He told a *Rolling Stone* magazine reporter that the reason he was arrested was racism. "A white man in North Carolina heard my act, heard me talk about Christ, called another white man in Virginia and said, 'Have that nigger arrested.'"[7]

The first real job Richard got in Hollywood was working with Mel Brooks on a script that became *Blazing Saddles.* Richard met with Mel Brooks' staff of writers. He would tell me about how jive they were.

One of the tasks Richard set for himself was to work bits of his comedy into the script. One of these such bits was having Count Basie's band playing in the desert. Richard had done this riff back in Berkeley and Oakland.

For all of his work on the script he was greatly disappointed. He told David Felton about how he couldn't get much respect for his work as a writer. Even though he had received an Emmy for a screenplay with Lily Tomlin, it was for his skit and comedy.

When he worked for Mel Brooks, he was so disappointed that Brooks didn't use his screenplay that anytime he discussed it with me, he became very sad and depressed.

Richard was not quiet about his writing experience with Mel Brooks. "My name appears on it," he told me, "but way, way down."

When David Felton brought up the *Blazing Saddles* movie and Richard's disappointment in not getting the lead in that film, he was impressed by Richard's response. "For several moments Richard was silent," he recorded, "his face silhouetted by the harsh, late afternoon sun screaming through the coffee shop window. Finally he leaned forward over the table, his forehead furrowed all crazy, and said haltingly, 'Frustration…is the worst thing, you know?' he lowered his head, studying the table, his mouth open and grasping for words. When he looked up, his eyes were filled with tears." [8]

The *Blazing Saddles* incident was his first big disappointment with Hollywood. Although he had won Emmys for his comedy albums, he was not able to cut into the film business—yet.

PART THREE:

WORKING THE BIG ROOM (HOLLYWOOD)

Find the good, and praise it.

—Alex Haley

CHAPTER TWENTY

THE COMEDY STORE

SOCIAL DRAMA NUMBER ONE

BY 1974, I had returned from a stay in Paris, France, where I met James Baldwin. Richard and I used to talk about Baldwin all the time in Berkeley.

I was sitting in a cafe in Paris, when another brother came up to me and said that Baldwin heard I was in Paris and would like to meet me.

The brother turned out to be Baldwin's secretary. He had read my novel and wanted to know what was happening in America. We made arrangements and I met the famous writer the next day for lunch.

I told Jimmy about Richard. He had seen his performance of Piano Man in *Lady Sings the Blues* and wrote about it in *The Devil Finds Work*.

I promised Jimmy that when he came to America again, I would introduce him to Richard.

I was back home in Berkeley, when Richard called me to come down to Los Angeles and work on some scripts with him.

I drove down to Hollywood and found his address in Laurel Canyon. We would sit in the backyard with drinks and go over the scripts he wanted me to work on.

"Man, Cecil, the stuff we talked about doing in Berkeley," he said, "We can now do!"

"Like what?"

"Like the Bert William's story!" Bert Williams was the black vaudeville performer, whose most famous comic song was "Nobody." I would end up calling my screenplay about him "Nobody."

"Yeah, I want to buy that story."

I was excited, but what I wanted him to buy was my novel, though he didn't mention that. Besides, it was still under option with David Foster.

"I have an idea of a man who gets out of prison and his punishment is to drive a group of kids across the country." This idea would eventually become *Bustin' Loose*.

We talked about how we were going to realize our dream of a real Black Hollywood. We would make our own films with black directors and writers.

"Not all white people are bad," he reminded me. "Just most of them."

"Yeah, like the ones we know."

"I know three that really want to help us. One is David Wolper. He is going to do a movie for television called Roots. The other one is Hannah Weinstein. She is getting a movie for me to do called *Grease Lighting*. The third one is Burt Sugarman. There is also Steve Krantz."

High on the list was the Bert Williams story. We never had to talk about money, because my agent took care of that. I had already sold options to *Jiveass Nigger* a couple times, was already in the Screenwriter's guild, and had an agent in Hollywood as well as Sterling Lord in New York.

Richard took me down to Sunset to the Comedy Store, the hottest comedy club in Hollywood. It was run by Mitzi Shore, who absolutely loved Richard.

I remember we were on the rooftop of the Comedy Store at a party Mitzi had thrown for Richard. As a prank, Richard told me she was into brothers and he told her that I was out to put the make on her. I watched her park her Jaguar in the parking lot and get out. When she came upstairs to the party, Richard introduced us. As I talked to Mitzi, I saw Richard over to the side cracking up. We laughed together when we realized that Richard had played a trick on us. Richard would come on Monday nights, when Mitzi encouraged comedians to try out new material. Richard treated the Comedy Store with the kind of experimental space as he had done at Mandrake's.

The Comedy Store was not the dinky little room that Mandrake's was back in Berkeley. For one thing, the Comedy Store was in Hollywood, the center of the industry that Richard wanted to crack. The folks who came in were not some hippies with their counterculture slant on the world, like the Berkeley people.

No, here were the sophisticates, the ones who had seen it all, and who were very hard to impress. Then, too, Richard had already been here, down on Santa Monica Boulevard at the Troubadour.

When we came up to the club, there would always be this white comic with a broad face and blonde hair. He would greet Richard, "Hi, King." Later when he got his TV comedy show, Richard hired him. His name was Robin Williams.

Paul Mooney and I would go with Richard or meet him at the Comedy Store. Paul drove his old blue Cadillac, and I would drive out in my red Fiat convertible.

The headliner, usually Robin Williams, would come out to the car to meet Richard as he got out. He would always say something like, The King is here! He would always open up with that line. Richard would smile at him and go on into the club.

Other comedians I got to know that headlined with Richard were Jimmy Walker, David Brenner, Marcia Warfield, Argus Hamilton, and John Witherspoon. Jimmy Walker became the star of "Good Times," Marcia Warfield made her mark in "Night Court," and John Witherspoon became famous in Ice Cube's *Friday.*

As Richard entered with his entourage, we would pass the guys waiting and genuflecting like he was a pope. Here would be the Puerto Rican comic Freddie Prinze and the Native American called Charlie Hill. They looked up to Richard more than any of them. Freddie Prinze was a rising star and eventually was a big star on "Chico and the Man."

It seemed that the minority comics liked Richard more than anybody, because they figured if he can make it, there might be a chance for them. But Richard would always say to them, "That pressure, man."

When "the pressure" came, Freddie Prinze shot himself with a .375 magnum. Charlie Hill (from the Oneida-Mohawk-Cree tribe) went back to the Cree reservation. Richard loved him. He was the funniest Native American comic any of us had ever seen (if not the only one). He would walk out on the stage of the comedy store, with his long straight hair, put up his hand, and say, "How!"

Standing in the wings, Richard would roll with laughter. Richard had him on his Richard Pryor Show, and there is a clip on YouTube of Richard introducing him to his first television audience. Not long after that exposure he disappeared from the scene. Today, he appears in a YouTube video, balding, overweight, still holding up his hand and saying, "How."

At the end of the show, we would all stand outside the comedy club with Richard milling around and shooting the shit. Nearly every night some celebrities would show up and jaw with Richard.

Some nights after the show, Richard would invite all the comics back to his place. There they would eat and snort as much as they liked. Richard liked to get a group of them in the kitchen and, with them all sitting around him, put on one of his comic clinics.

That year, 1974, Richard had his first major social drama. While he was adjusting to his new status of the prodigal son, he was in trouble with the law, the Internal Tax Revenue.

In a social drama—as opposed to on-stage drama or written drama (film)—he had very—little control. The social drama is largely instigated outside the theatrical world. He owed some

$68,504 in taxes to the Federal government from which he earned in 1967.[9]

In Richard's case, the breach was that he hadn't paid his taxes for all the time he had been hanging out in Berkeley. The judge was not sympathetic, as Richard reported to his audience on stage. In fact, the judge, hearing that he was in show business, said, "Fuck that nigger!"

He was sentenced to ten days in jail and given the prison number 2140-875. This was the second stage of the social drama, the crisis.

In the days before his defection to Berkeley, he might have become violent and depressed. But this was a new Richard. He took a different approach. As a member of the fledging new black comedy, he had an admirer in Flip Wilson. Flip Wilson just happened to have been the only Black man on television in those days.

While in the jail, Richard had met some pretty decent brothers. They had been really nice to him, and so he thought, why not return the favor with a gesture of appreciation. He decided to ask his friend Flip Wilson if he would come down to the jail and put on a show with him for the guys.

And guess what? Flip said yes, and so that June, Flip Wilson and Richard put on a comedy show for forty-five minutes for three hundred inmates. These were the days before the Internet and phone videos, so these can't be seen on YouTube, but you can imagine what an incredible scene that was! Here was Flip Wilson in his make-up as "Sheriff's deputy Geraldine Jones."

According to an eyewitness, she "twirled her purple panties on one finger," and "flung them at Prisoner 2140-875—and said, 'Put that on your cell wall!'"[10]

The prisoners laughed so hard that the roof of the place almost fell in. Then Richard took the microphone, "Thank you, brothers. We did this because we love you and respect you. When you get out, please stay out."

Richard found a way to take a bad situation and turn it into a good experience. Anthropologist of humor, Lawrence E. Mintz believes that the comedian as a social commentator can use his status to turn dishonesty, selfishness, disruptive and aggressive behavior, and licentiousness, into virtues.[11]

You might ask, How is that negative behavior becomes positive? It's a good question because the answer involves enunciating Professor Mintz's theory of comedy, a key to understanding Richard's comic development into a cultural hero.

In order to understand the role of standup comedy, Professor Mintz recognizes the significance of the comedian's traditional license for deviate behavior and expression. The reason Richard needed the license for deviate behavior is to be "exempted" from "normal behavior." Whatever Richard did that was not normal, like directing traffic in the middle of Broadway, was exempted. All you had to say was, "It's Richard Pryor." If it was Richard Pryor, then his behavior was excused. Comics depend on that exemption.

"Traditionally," Professor Mintz writes, "the comedian is defective in some way, but his natural weaknesses generate pity, and more imprint, exemption from the expectation of normal behavior."[12]

The comic becomes a negative exemplar. We laugh at him. His conduct is ridiculed and rejected, and our laughter shows us how much more sane we are than he is.

Yet, there is this identification we make with the negative exemplar. "To the extent that we may identify with his expression or behavior, we secretly recognize it as a reflection of natural tendencies in human activity if not socially approved ones, and he becomes our comic spokesman."

This is what Richard did. He literately took the mic and spoke as a representative of the prisoners. Back in Berkeley he read Malcolm X. He identified with George Jackson and he met the icon of the Black Power Movement, Huey P. Newton. He had also snorted coke with the founder of the Black Panther Party.

Thanks to these experiences, Richard created a cultural performance that gave him his voice and transformed him into a modern-day shaman. In this sense, writes Professor Mintz, "The comic spokesman serves as a shaman leading us in a celebration of a community of shared culture, of homogenous understanding and expectation."

It is the comedian as a mediator, which is what the shaman is, between the public audiences and "immense exaggerations of all we fear and reject in our own self-definitions." The comic, according to Mintz, is a kind of contemporary anthropologist.

Take Joan Rivers, for an example. "Joan River's comic persona is established as essentially negative," Professor Mintz writes.

"We laugh at her characterizations of herself as a failed or flawed woman, because she is unattractive, lacks the proper female attributes, is rejected by parents and friends, and inept in domestic skills such as cooking and housekeeping."[13]

These are all negative qualities. Yet for her audience of women, who reject male demands that women fulfill their romantic and domestic fantasies, her negatives qualities become positive ones. Like Phyllis Diller, "these female comics are voicing changing attitudes about gender roles that have begun to take hold in American society as a result of the most recent wave of feminist agitation."

The same process began with Richard. The negative qualities of being arrested for tax evasion were transformed through a live performance into a positive experience. An audience of black men in prison witnessed it. Just as the feminist movement helped make the negative qualities of Joan Rivers into positive ones, so the black experience helped Richard.

I once asked Richard if he thought that Rivers was funny and I was expecting him to agree with me that she wasn't. Instead he said, "No, you ain't gonna get me to lie. She's funny."

That afternoon in the Los Angeles County men's jail, not only did he identify with the prisoners, but also he spoke *for* them.

"I wanted to do a show," he said in an interview at the time. "The cats facing murder raps kept telling me to be cool. I wanted to do something to show my appreciation. Laugher makes them feel good. The vibes will last a long, long time."

In taking his comedy out of the nightclub and in to a county jail, Richard had come up with a new use of the comedy space.

He was moving the stand-up routine out of its traditional context and helped to relax the conflict created by the tax evasion event.

By going between the Real Life (RL) events and the on-stage (OS) events, he was able to create a fissure that would eliminate the drag on either.

Important to understanding Richard's interplay is the notion of laughter behavior, or audience behavior. According to Professor Mintz, both Richard and Red Foxx, his most important influence, developed a persona of a sexual libertine.

In doing fieldwork in audience response, Professor Mintz went to the Redd Foxx Club to observe the comedian at work and the audience's response. In fact, he witnessed a presentation by Redd Foxx himself. He reported that virtually all of Foxx's routine "dealt with the topic of oral sex. Foxx presented himself a successful practitioner of these taboo arts."

The audience revealed two different types of laughing behavior, Professor Mintz recorded. The older audience looked at each other nervously but "the younger audience leaned forward to Foxx, often applauded, raised their hands or fists as though cheering a political speaker with whom they were in agreement, occasionally yelling, 'yeah,' or 'right on,' or just yelping with delight." [14]

Like Redd Foxx, Richard mastered the poetics of participation, relying more and more on techniques of making the audience a part of his performance ritual.

Over the next twenty years, he would rely on his Shamanistic strategy, not only to solve personal problems, but to resuscitate his art as well.

His "Jail Comedy" reverses the usual performance occasion — where free people go to a place to hear jokes. The jokes are told in the prison for the benefit of the prisoners.

Richard had developed an on-stage routine about "Ben the Blacksmith." In that jail skit, the white warden invites a group of actors to put on a show for the benefit of the prisoners.

This bit was one of Richard's funniest, most artful routines, replete with brilliant impersonations, as I described earlier, but now that he was in the Los Angeles County Jail, he flipped the OS

(Onstage) to the RL (Real Life) — from his OS (Onstage) creations to the RL (Real Life) ritual.

This spin-off was to boomerang into the movie, *Stir Crazy*, where he and Gene Wilder play two city boys, imprisoned and forced to perform to the inmates in order to survive.

Between the comic sketches "Black Ben Blacksmith," the "Jail Comedy," and *Stir Crazy* there was an interplay that had been missing in cultural performances until Richard began to flip it in 1974. This would appear again and again; this kind of social drama that became his pattern of living and of creating comic art.

When *Car Wash* came out in the fall of 1976, Michael Schultz, who had been working with me on *Which Way Is Up?* introduced me to Joel Schumacher. He was a gay Jewish guy who had only written one script (The Wiz) before he wrote *Car Wash*. Schumacher was living proof that a white guy had a better chance writing Black movies than a Black person.

Schumacher was from New York where he studied design at the Parsons School of Design and became a window dresser. When he talked about his life as a window dresser, he would always throw his head back and laugh.

He had written the screenplay for *The Wiz* a few years prior, but it was a financial and commercial failure. This, however, did not stop him from a successful career.

Car Wash was not a great film, but it did show that there was no harm in having a lot of leading black actors in a comedy. One critic said, "When you leave the theater, you feel good."

Richard knew him, of course and pointed out to me that the film gave many black actors work in Hollywood.

I felt encouraged because *Car Wash* didn't set the standard too high. If a Jewish guy could write a film about Blacks, why couldn't I?

Michael told me that if Joel Schumacher could do it, so could I. I was to learn quickly that in Hollywood everybody was connected to each other. For example, Joel Schumacher was destined to be a big time Hollywood producer and director that had already been initiated into the industry that produced Black culture. *The*

Wiz was an all-black Broadway musical that became a vehicle for Hollywood. It was directed by Sidney Lumet, produced by Rob Cohen, and written by Joel Schumacher. The all-black crew included Diana Ross, Lena Horne, Michael Jackson, and Richard Pryor, who played "Oz".

Richard didn't care much for *Carwash* nor did he care much for the minor role Daddy Rich, which he played as a caricature; but this role was a step up from the blaxploitation films. Richard's attitude was that it was like picking cotton: you did it because you had to eat. He knew that there was going to be a time when we would move off the sharecropping land. After sharecropping, we would own our own land.

During this time, around 1976, when *Car Wash* came out, Richard was still the talk of the town because of his stage act. All of the action was centered on his stand-up performances, mainly on Sunset at the Comedy Store. It was on the stage that he began his creative distortion of his social life.

He began to collect a group of black friends around him, ranging from the Pointer Sisters to Alex Haley, who was virtually unknown then. In his stage act, he started bringing people backstage to meet and greet.

The Pointer Sisters were in *Car Wash*, and they showed up at one of Richard's parties. I met them again after being their teacher at Merritt College a few years back. We all drank and laughed about our days at Merritt College, where I taught them *Othello*.

When Richard was in the dressing room at Universal, he walked passed a dressing room and saw a black hairdresser. His name was Robert Stevenson.

"How does this suit look?" Richard asked him. Richard was wearing the white suit that he wears for the role of Daddy Rich. He warned him, "Don't lie!"

Robert told him it looked great. Richard asked, "Are you working for anybody else?"

"No," Robert said.

"Then come work for me."

That was the way Richard hired him and he worked for Richard for the next thirteen years. This is also a good example of how Richard recruited his personal staff. He never went through agencies for people to work for him. After meeting somebody we wanted to work with, he would go by his instincts and hire them - and it usually worked out.

Around this time, I started going with Richard and other members of his entourage, including Paul Mooney and David Banks to the Comedy Store on Sunset Boulevard.

I soon discovered that a concert with Richard was divided into two basic forms. There was the OS (Onstage) performance that drew crowds that were becoming whiter and whiter and richer and richer.

Then, there was the second part: the invited guests who came into the little dressing room after the show where Richard took the energy from his OS performance and interplayed it with the guests. He wanted to meet people, but he wanted to meet them on his own terms. People who came back stage became part of his "community," or as the anthropologist Victor Turner would call it, "communitas." Through his OS performance he had screened them out as members of his group that represented his way of thinking.

Alan Farlan told me that this was how he met Richard. He went to thank him for a wonderful show, and Richard asked him, "Where do you live?" He said, "Berkeley."

Richard said, "When are you going back?" Alan said, "Now." Richard said, "Can I come with you?" Alan said, "Sure."

Richard was blowing up around the end of the seventies. In addition to the films, he was growing into a symbol, not only of the counterculture, but the rich and the very hip people, especially the rich folks of Hollywood.

No better example of this widening phenomena is the fact that he had become a role model, as it were, for the New Age crowd.

At that time, Werner Erhardt represented this group of way-out social types. He was a guy who suddenly found that life could be lived differently from the counterculture. Focusing on the Easlen

Institute as a Garden of Eden, Erhardt and his group preached a life of wealth and happiness.

All that was necessary was that you found a person whose life you could imitate. Erhardt tried Buckminster Fuller. Nothing there. Then, he tried the German philosopher Heidegger. Nothing there. Then, he turned to Richard Pryor.

It was generally known among the in-crowd that Erhardt was telling everybody that if they wanted to get their stuff together they should imitate Richard Pryor.

One night while he was performing at the Circle Star in San Carlos, California, I was scouring the audience with Paul Mooney looking for interesting people to bring backstage to meet Richard.

I spotted Werner Erhardt in the line waiting to come back stage. I went back into the dressing room and told Richard. Richard told me to bring him backstage into the dressing room.

Before I left, Richard said that he was going to climb up on some boxes that were stacked near the door. On top of the boxes, he was going to perch. I was to sit in front of the door and when Werner came into the door, I would give Richard a signal. "I'm going to jump on his ass!" The idea was to freak him out. If he was so hip to what Richard was up to, let him figure out why Richard jumped down on his ass!

I did not know at the time that Richard had already met Werner Erhardt. Joel Schumacher, who wrote the Oz role in *The Wiz* for Richard and the Daddy Rich role for him in *Car Wash*, was a big fan of Erhardt's. He had opened a seminar with Schumacher called "The Forum," which famous Hollywood heavies attended. *The Wiz*, according to The Grove Book of Hollywood, "was influenced by Werner Erhardt's teachings. Actress Diana Ross and writer Joel Schumacher were "very enamored of Werner Erhardt."[15]

I went to the line and told Erhardt that Mr. Pryor wanted to see him right away. He had two beautiful women with him. I went in ahead of him and took my place in front of the door. Rashon or Mooney opened the door.

Erhardt started to the door, got to the entrance and stopped. He just stood there smiling and refusing to enter. He stood there so long that it freaked me and Richard out. It was as if he was trying to "out-nigger" us. Finally, Richard got down off the boxes and Erhardt strolled in and shook Richard's hand.

Richard was blown away, as if Erhardt was tricking him. Later, we talked about it and couldn't figure out how he knew what we had planned.

Richard gave him the old shock treatment. Glancing over at the women, he said, "Hey, are we going to screw tonight?"

The women laughed and Werner laughed. One of the women laughed too long and gave Richard the license to assume she was interested. The guru Erhardt was a model for the upscale rich hippies, but Richard was the person he modeled himself on. He had been born John Paul Rosenberg and became a California-based salesman and training manager of encyclopedias.

Then he had a revelation and stared the Erhardt Seminars Training course in 1971. By 1977, over 100,000 people had completed his course. After the success, his Est philosophy was parodied in many films like *Semi-Tough*, starring Bert Reynolds. Still it was strange that Erhardt had modeled himself on Richard, who rejected Erhardt's putting him into this role.

After the shows, Richard's dressing room would be like a police raid on a whorehouse. The dressing room would be crowded with women flashing their wares, men flexing their muscles, and Paul Mooney and Rashon and I would be seeing that everything went alright.

One night Miles Davis came backstage with Cecily Tyson, his date. Miles leaned into the dressing room and said, "I didn't come to see you!" He said to everybody, "I came to see Richie!"

"Sit here!" Richard said to Cecily and motioned to an empty chair. Miles took his handkerchief out and dusted the chair. Then, as we all watched, instead of Cecily sitting down in the chair, he sat down on it and then, placed the handkerchief on his lap, where Cecily finally sat down. Richard's eyes were glistening with laughter. Long after the event, we would talk about the gestures that Miles so masterfully made that evening. Richard would redo the scene, and reenact it with great amusement and pleasure.

Richard's dressing room was the inversion of his onstage performance. While he was on stage, he entertained the audience. But when they came backstage, they entertained him. Many people (especially show business stars) wanted to come backstage and greet him in his dressing room. It would be something to talk about. It was also a side of Richard that the general public never saw, but if you were luckier enough to be in one of those events, you were not likely to ever forget it.

CHAPTER TWENTY ONE

FRANKLIN

FINALLY, RICHARD HAD become a big success in Hollywood, not for stand-up but for his role in films. He decided not to go for the big bucks, as he would say, but for the creative possibilities of his comedy.

When critics wanted him to slow down, he wanted to go ahead. "My manager at the time didn't understand," he told a reporter. "He knew the futility of asking me to tone down the shit I did on stage. But he pleaded with me to think sensibly. He wanted those monies."

By 1975, Richard was finally getting recognition for his comedy. James McPherson, a *New York Times* journalist, claimed that his new comic style was noteworthy. "Pryor's vision comes from the peculiar experience of black people in America." This insight was what Richard had been working for since the Berkeley days.

It was at this time that he was introduced to David Franklin, the lawyer from Atlanta, Georgia; the only powerful black manager in America. Richard introduced me to him in a hotel on Sunset, next to the Comedy Store.

Franklin was a short, pudgy, light-skinned black man with a stutter. He had very blue eyes and a twinkling glint in his smile. He was very likable, and Richard was proud of their relationship.

During the Berkeley days, his manager was Don Pruitt. Pruitt was away somewhere presumably looking for money to produce Richard's films. "Fuck all that," Richard would always say, no matter what the subject was, regarding film making and black people, "it's all gonna change when Don gets back." Don never did get back, and as far as I know, he is still out there somewhere getting the money together for Richard's films.

The next manager was a white guy named Don Debasio, who had a limited view of Richard's talents. Richard fired him shortly after he came back to Hollywood. Then came David Franklin. The story Richard and I heard was that the singer Roberta Flack told David Franklin, "You've got to save Richard Pryor!"

When David took on the job, he discovered that Richard was being ripped off royally. Even though his third album was a runaway best seller and the recipient of an Emmy, he had made only $100,000 in 1974. Using his lawyers, like Michael Ashburne from Berkeley, Franklin broke the contract with David Drozer and had the master redistributed through a new producer, Warner Bros. Franklin set out to make Richard a "cross over star," a black actor who appealed to white people too. He started booking him in venues like New York's City Center and Pittsburgh's Heinz Hall, where white people went.

Some of the deals that Franklin made were incredible, like getting Richard $300,000 dollars for each episode of the Richard Pryor show-and two million dollars for not appearing in any other television competition! Richard didn't want to do television anyway, and yet Franklin got him 2 million dollars to do nothing (or, to do "nothing" that he wanted to do.)

He trusted David Franklin and saw him as a savior of his career and life. He was also grateful. One day in May, when Franklin drove out to Richard's house, he was surprised by a gift from Richard: a $52,000 black Rolls Royce.

Richard said, "I felt as if I'd found the guy who could help me become the hero I envisioned." But he recognized and glorified the difference between him and Franklin: "We couldn't have been more dissimilar. David was straight, upright and uptight. I was a mess, short-fused, paranoid, unpredictable."

But these differences didn't matter to Richard, because they had the same goal. "However, we have a common interest: respect. Both of us wanted it. For ourselves and for our people. We were going to break down the barriers. As teammates, he'd block, I'd move toward the goal line."

Franklin fit right into the cut, and became a regular part of the operation. We had many good times together.

CHAPTER TWENTY TWO

THE SUNSET MARQUIS

AFTER KNOWING RICHARD since 1969 in Berkeley, things were finally paying off. As I kicked back at the Sunset Marquis, I remembered those days in Berkeley. If Richard had escaped Berkeley to the big time, so had I. Richard and I had talked a lot about this back in Berkeley.

I remembered how we used to drive around in my car and fantasize about what kind of films we would one day make when we made it in Hollywood. We wrote black liberation poetry, read *Being There* as a vision of the future of American politics and sympathized with prison activist George Jackson. We talked often of black stereotypes and of the betrayal of blacks by white marketers of black culture.

Here was the chance, at last, to do some of the things we had long talked of. Producer Steve Krantz called next, and I flew down to Hollywood on the first day of 1976 and met with him at Joe Allen's on Third Street. At lunch Krantz and I talked about how deplorably blacks are treated in Hollywood. In those days I was full of dreams about how blacks could improve Hollywood—and about how great a writer I was. I met Michael Schultz who was scheduled to direct "Which Way Is Up?" He and I sat down to a vegetarian meal in the Old World Restaurant on Santa Monica Boulevard.

By the time I got back to Berkeley, I got a call from him. He said they wanted to invite me back down to work on the script.

When I came back to Hollywood in 1976, I was asked to write the screenplay for Richard Pryor's first starring role, the film was to become Which *Way Is Up?* I met with Michael and the producer Steve Krantz. Steve Krantz was one of those people Richard had mentioned as being serious about helping black people in the film business.

I want to first get something straight about Richard Pryor himself. In LA, in Hollywood, at that time, the entire image of Pryor as an insane, dope-addicted, violent blow-top is the creation of the media, just as blackface minstrel caricatures were a creation of whites during Reconstruction to deal with the white public's fear of black progress.

David Felton, of *Rolling Stone* magazine for example, called him a "fuck-up" and wove a fabric out of this material, which Pryor had to wear, but the thing was so tight it kept choking the brother. This stereotype did its job of attributing all of his success to the support of his white audience and all of his negative qualities to his coming from a black environment.

Unfortunately, Richard had this same mindset of his work. Seated in the Brown Derby with him, I listened to him explain to a reporter how careful he was about showing up on time when he was working on his "Piano Man" role in *Lady Sing the Blues*.

"Sometimes in my life I have to fuck up every now and then just to keep it together," he told the reporter Gregg Kilday. "I was glad Berry Gordy, the producer, gave me that chance." He sucked on a cigarette. "I made it a point to show up to prove that it was not true what they were saying."

The one critic who got Richard right was not white, but black, and he didn't live on the West Coast, but the East.

He was Mr. Hollie I. West, and he was an extraordinary journalist. Back in the early sixties, he had tried to get into journalism after graduating from Ohio University where he had been a journalism major in 1959.

After West graduated in 1959, he enlisted in the Army and worked as a public information specialist for three years. When he finished, he moved to California and began the search for a reporting job. He applied to the *San Francisco Chronicle* whose editor told him, "Hollie, we want a Negro reporter, but we want one with five years daily experience."

He tried the *Oakland Tribune,* but they only offered him a copy boy position. He turned it down and decided to try his hand at the civil service. After taking the exams, a friend encouraged him to stick with journalism. He went back to the *Tribune* and took the copy boy position.

In 1974, he saw something else. He saw that Richard's art was to blur the line between on-stage comedy and the "dreary and blemished routine of daily life." Surely he adds a few things here and there, but West sees that Richard "tailored the situations to fit his view point." The audience gets the real thing: "lives lived by people, mostly in black neighborhoods." Richard's comic style is to take the ordinary situation and dramatize them, showing the hypocrisy, contradictions, and foibles of people. "Pryor's point of view is almost always black," he wrote. [17]

He got exited about Richard's accomplishments, including the fact that his latest recording album *That Nigger's Crazy* sold over the million mark, and his other albums sold well.

In his interview with Richard, West reported that Richard got a lot of autograph seekers from Hillbillies.

"What has changed since you became a public figure?" West asked him.

"Being popular, man. It's a lot more people than there used to be when I worked at the Cellar Door in Germantown, but I could also tell a [nigger] to kiss my [ass] when they come on to me funny."

West appreciated Richard's humor "and his everyday talk." He liked him because he is emotionally direct, honest and profane.

As a leader and spokesman for black people, Richard said, "I hope I do something good. I have to do it. It's not that I just help my family get a house or something like that. But I hope I do something to help people. I hope I don't misuse this chance."

"How would you help people?" West asked him.

"With money. Or make it possible for others to make money, to get a job."

As for his art, West judged Pryor's success by his "masterful use of facial expression."

At the Kennedy Center performances, he portrayed a man whose female friend was leaving him. The grimaces were genuine but also funny. "Many times he has several characters talking in the same skit," West observed, "and they may be of different races or ethnic groups."

This was Richard's use of faces to recall the memory of another event that happened in Real Life (RL). For Richard meaning doesn't take place until he has reenacted the RL event in a performance On-stage (OS). As West indicates, the facial expression is a theatrical style. It is also the way that Richard adds meaning and passion to what has happened to him in RL. It becomes a tool of communication through feelings.

West connected this style to the Yiddish tradition of humor, the way of telling jokes that flourished in early 20th century urban Jewish culture on the borscht circuit or in community groups. And out of this approach have emerged in recent years Jewish and Non-Jewish comedians - Bill Cosby, Mort Sahl, and Lenny Bruce.

To this tradition, Richard brought "a sensitive understanding of black working class life."

"I guess I experienced all of it," Richard told him.

"Sometimes some people are in the audience and the wino (one of his characters) might be doing something. I used to do a thing where the wino pissed in a bottle. I got that idea when a nigger in the audience said 'Now (piss) in it.' Then I started using it. People just tell you shit like that. So you use that. That works a lot. My experience is in there. My awareness is their (blacks) experience, too."[18]

Here Richard is talking about the difference and the interplay between his Real Life (RL) experience and his On-stage (OS) experience. The person in the audience who suggests that the wino piss in the bottle is in RL. When the wino pisses in the bottle on stage that is in the OS reality where art expresses itself through symbols and symbolic gestures.

As West reveals in his insightful probes, Richard is aware of the oral tradition in the streets as a source for his art and satiric genius.

"I started comedy in school with plays," he recalls, *"I got a feel for the stage, you know. Not just what I did in the streets, but in the streets it's like standing on the corner. Like in the white community, they have all those outlets.*

They stay at the school afterward or go to somebody's house and have a little theater group. But ours is on the corner. That's where we niggers rehearse. If you want to a public speaker, you rehearse your speech on the corner. You tell your stories. You talk [shit]. Singers start there. Groups do their thing. Players run their game. It's like that. That was my stage.[xix]

This is the inversion of the theater culture. The street is his theater. Another factor that had come into Richard's career now was not just stand-up, but the films as well. To his credit, West pointed out, he had played a musician in *Lady Sings the Blues*, a detective in *Uptown Saturday Night*, and a pimp in *The Mack*.

He had recently come under fire from the "sisters" because a photograph with him and a white woman had been seen.

"That was my lady," Richard told Hollie, referring to the picture of him with a white woman.

"How did the racism affect you?"

"It hurts."

"Why?

"Black women's lack of acceptance. I don't think nobody can deal with that."

"Are you doing what you want to do?"

"Yes, and will continue to do what I want to do. I ain't never minded nobody in my life that I know of and I ain't going to mind nobody now. That ain't none of nobody's business whatever I do. I ain't telling none of them how to live. Ain't none of them [bitches] got nothing to do with it"

Richard said he wanted to make a film about the life of Muhammad Ali. "You know what he went through. Lose all that because of his stance against the Vietnam War and come back. His life is a movie script—a movie script whitey don't like and we Blacks can't get the money to produce."

West said Pryor impressed him as somebody who is "speaking out in his own way about social conditions. Comedy is his framework, but he's dealing with serious issues, and he says he wants to continue."

"I don't want to lose my humanity, man. And I won't want to be exploited. But I also want to help people," Pryor said.

The jive lingo that he spoke did not originate with him but comes from a community of black working people. It is the language of maids and butlers, of preachers and sinners (none of whom had real churches or really sinned), of handymen, gamblers and porters. It is the lingo of the smart-ass, citified, badass, black-is-beautiful, I-ain't-taking-no-shit-from-nobody northern black, and it is the opposite of the Uncle Tom "yes'm" of the South. It is through this language that Pryor found his voice and asked strange questions.

I started to work on the script. I was put up in a three-room apartment in the hotel Sunset Marquis. It was there I met several screenwriters. I met Bill Thompson, who was a friend of novelist Thomas McQueen, and I met John Kaye who was writing *Where the Buffalo Roam*, starring Bill Murray. Peter Fonda and his buddy Jimmy Buffet were regulars around that time.

One day, soon after I finished the first draft of the script, I went to see a documentary of the farm workers' strike so that I could give *Which Way Is Up?*, which dealt with farm labor, as much authenticity as possible. I sat in the screening room alone and witnessed the horrible injustice dealt to the Mexican farm migrants. It reminded me of the kind of thing I experienced as a boy on a farm in North Carolina. The agri-growers in the film kept saying Mexicans were lazy to justify their exploitation. When I emerged from the screening room I went to talk to Krantz about my reactions.

"O.K.," he said when I'd finished, "O.K., go write it out! Write out everything that's in you."

"What do you mean?" I asked. I couldn't believe my ears.

"That's right," he said, assuring me that my impression was correct. "Write how this movie relates to you! You are a black man! Write it from a black man's point of view!"

I was delighted. I left his office and went straight to the hotel and started to work.

Judith, Krantz's wife, wanted to have lunch with me. I met her at the Hamburger's Mary on Sunset Boulevard. She told me she was thinking of being a writer, and wanted to know how I went about writing a novel. I told her what I knew, and what I could tell her during an hour lunch. It may have done her some good, for about a year later, she had written a novel called *Princess Daisy*, which became a best-seller.

Meanwhile, Leroy Jones, the hero of my script, was somewhat similar to Chaplin's hero in *Modern Times*. In that film, the total discontinuity of occurrences is the source of humor. The world is ruled by casualty and not causality. As I sat down in the hotel I read the notes on *Modern Times* from my notebook:

"The eating machine that beats him up is supposed to help make the production more efficient and profitable. It tries to get more out of the worker, but instead of getting more it harms the worker in a ridiculous way, not by killing him, which would have been an easy way out, but by worrying him to distraction. The machine ends up beating him in the face; the monotony of the machine runs him so batty that anything that faintly resembles a bolt appears to him to be in need of screwing down."

I scratched my head, wondering how I could get such a scene in my movie. I remembered the documentary film. There was one scene in it in which a machine that picked oranges was demonstrated. What if our hero was asked to demonstrate that machine to his fellow workers? They look at him, knowing that he is showing them a machine that will put them out of work. They don't like it, but he has been promoted over them. As he is demonstrating the machine, what if it goes haywire and picks him up by the seat of his pants and throws him into the field? His friends would laugh, and the point about the machine destroying honest human labor would be made. I figured if Charlie Chaplin could do it, we could too.

Many years later, John Williams, the great American novelist, wrote a book with his son Dennis on Richard Pryor (*If I Stop, I'll Die*). He said that *Which Way is Up?* was Richard's best film. The authors recognized my Chaplin's influence when they commented, "Some of the most hilarious lies and expressions on record are in his film. Chaplin would recognize it"

I wrote the scene and brought it to Steve Krantz. Krantz answered the door at his house in Beverly Hills, praised me for the additional scene and told me he would "clean it up" for me.

The next Monday morning we met in his office to discuss the material I'd done. He said he had to cut most of it, but as a compensation he had come up with a few funny jokes of his own. He then had me read the jokes he had put in the script.

Kid: If I eat Wheaties, Uncle Leroy, will I grow up big and strong?

Leroy: Yeah and a baseball player — and white!

To say the least, I didn't think this was very funny.

Another joke he included was:

Thelma: Leroy, don't you get involved with none of this union mess, you hear? . Scabbing was good enough for your grandpa.

(She motions to a picture on the wall; Leroy looks at the picture on the wall.)

Leroy: Mama, that isn't grandpa. That picture was on the wall when we moved in.

The implication was that blacks don't have a heritage; that they are so uprooted that they don't remember their parents. In short, what Krantz had done was to write coon humor into the script.

Two blackface white comedians, Lew Dockstader and Press Eldridge, first invented coon humor during the 1890s. It was a derogatory humor, which viewed the black man as an inferior animal. A black vaudevillian comedian Ernest Hogan sang the most famous coon song, "Every Coon Looks Alike To Me!" Other comedians carried it onto radio and television. This was the type of humor that in 1978, my producer was writing into our movie. I could not believe it.

As I sat in Krantz's office, other things clicked into place in my memory. I remembered once hearing James Baldwin say: "A black writer cannot write black stereotypes the way a white writer can." Baldwin went on, "He cannot think of himself that way. A black man cannot see himself as a stereotype. He does not exist the way whites see him. That's why it's hard for black writers to write the things whites want to see."

I told Krantz I didn't see the humor in some of his jokes. "O.K.," he said, "We can cut them out," and he drew a blue line through the jokes. When we finished going over the script he promised to have it retyped; he would send me a copy back in Berkeley.

A few months later, when filming started, I flew down to Houston with Paul Mooney to assist Richard. We traveled from Detroit to Houston, Texas, and then to New York. From behind the stage, I helped Richard with his entourage.

It was during this period, that he called me one day to come to his place, he had a surprise for me. When I arrived, he was sitting in the room with two Black men. The room was dark oak and lined with books.

One was tall, and light skinned, the other one was brown-skinned and shorter. The shorter man was Alex—Alex Haley, as he would become known to the rest of the world upon the publication of his novel, *Roots*.

As it turned out, David Wolper, who was to be the producer of *Roots* was a good friend of Richard's and would be his producer as well.

"Alex can trace his ancestors back to Africa," Richard said exuberantly, when we had all settled down with a drink. Richard also wanted me to meet Alex's assistant, the scholar Alex brought with him who was very impressive with his knowledge of oral traditions and who spoke and understood several African languages. When this scholar finished talking, Richard looked over at me. Then, he would ask me to respond to what they had said. Richard was on the vanguard of exploring black life in history and culture.

The scholar described a journey he and Alex took to Africa, where with the help of the oral historians and bards known as Griots, they were able to race his family tree back to a specific village. In this conversation, I heard the term Griot for the first time.

Naturally, Richard and I were blown away by their story.

We were as excited that evening to hear Mr. Haley talk about how he discovered his ancestors, as the readers of *Roots* would be a year later. Richard was always ahead of the general public because he had a personal curiosity and interest in anything that reflected the progress of black people.

CHAPTER TWENTY THREE

ROSALIND CASH

URING THIS TIME, Richard and Paul and I hit the party
scene in Hollywood. One night Richard and I and Paul
Mooney went to a party. There were many actresses, and
we were looking for some girls.

We saw Rosalind Cash. She was then one of the leading black
actresses in Hollywood, and had been trained in New York, where
she was a well-known stage actress. I think we all saw her at the
same time. She had just been in the *Omega Man* (based on Richard
Mathewson's novel, *I, Legend)* with Charleton Hester. She had
avoided the blaxpoitation films . In addition to being one of the
most talented black actresses in Hollywood, she was very beautiful. I was about to discover a very wonderful person.

But when Rosalind was introduced to me, she laughed and
said, "Ah, the writer!"

What nobody realized, certainly not Richard, was that Rosalind
and I had met before. We had met before in New York through the
playwright Lonnie Elder.

In 1969, Roger Straus threw a publishing party for my first novel. When Roger Straus in LuChow (a famous German Restaurant)
lionized me for the publication of *The Life and Loves of Mr. Jiveass
Nigger*. Jon Voight, David Foster, and Robert Altman were all in attendance. Lonnie Elder, the playwright, took me under his wings.

Lonnie was there to introduce me to the theater society. He had written the Emmy award winning play, *Dark Ceremonies In Old Men*.

Lonnie Elder was at the top of his game as an up and coming playwright with the potential to be the next Lorraine Hansbury. I went to see his play and moved by his art. I got to meet him and, as with Richard, we hit it off.

One evening, he took me to see the Negro Ensemble performance that Rosalind Cash starred in. I sat admiring her and falling in love with her on stage. I had no idea that I would be sitting next to her at a table drinking together an hour later.

I had never been that close to a woman like her. Though I am a very talkative person, I fell silence when she was near because I was not used to those feelings.

Lonnie was so proud of me that he introduced me to her as an equal. Since I couldn't express myself, I drank. By the end of the evening somebody said, "Let's go to Harlem," I was barely able to make it to the car.

We drove up to Harlem and half way to our destination, I threw up. I had to roll the window down and eventually had to be dropped off to my hotel.

My only relief was that I would never have to face Rosalind Cash again.

Now, a few years later, we were looking at each other.

"Oh, the writer!" she laughed.

I knew what she was thinking. How I had been drunk!

I had made such a fool of myself, and she enjoyed laughing at me! I smiled and told her it was so nice to see her again.

"Hey, I'm taking everybody up to my house," Richard said. He looked at me and then at Rosalind. "You want to come?"

In those days, if Richard Pryor said he was taking everybody back to his house, people ran to get their cars. The one party you wanted to make it to in Hollywood during the mid seventies was Richard Pryor's.

Rosalind looked at me.

"What do you want to do?" she asked me.

Richard looked at me, as if to say, "Oh, shit!"

We laughed together and we took to liking each other from that very moment. If we didn't become lovers that evening, then it was the next one.

When Richard called me the next day, he said, "Hey, man, how was it?"

I had Rosalind's head on my shoulder. We were in my bed.

"Man, I can't talk now..."

On the night of the recording of the *Bicentennial Nigger*, which took place in the Comedy Store, I took Rosalind. The place was packed with celebrities. Everybody was there to see Richard: Minnie Ripperton, Smokey Robinson, and Mick Jagger.

I went backstage and found Richard in his closet of a dressing room. He was smoking a cigarette and sipping on an orange juice and vodka.

He asked me if I had seen the house. I told him I had. He said he was nervous because he might not be funny. He didn't want to not be funny in front of so many Black people.

I gave him encouragement and went back to my seat with Rosalind.

Richard came on and the Big Room was quiet with tension. Richard was stiff. He talked about snorting cocaine, about the preacher who told the crippled people to find another church to come to.

"I like to say to the cripple peoples that come here—can't you find another church to go to? Goddamn, you come in knockin' shit down and breakin up furniture and shit. And you deaf and dumb motherfucker, we don't need you here!"

He still wasn't loose. This went on for a few more minutes until somebody yelled out, "Richie, get crazy, man!"

Richard seemed shocked. Then, he stepped up to the edge of the stage, peered out at the heckler and said, "What you talkin' 'bout, *nigger?*" This retort brought the house down. "You wanna fight, nigger!" When he hurled this epithet the audience went crazy and this loosened him up.

Then he went into one of his most memorable routines. He had everybody roaring with laughter.

We were seated in the special guest section of the main stage. That night Mick Jagger was in the audience. When he got up to go to the john, Richard spotted him. "Hey, Mick, save some for the rest of us!"

Capping on Mick like that made him think of something else that white folks had done recently. it made him think of the science fiction movie *Logan's Run*.

"I went to see *Logan's Run*. And there ain't no niggers in it!" he screamed at the audience in a hysterical voice.

There were no black people in the film, which was about who would survive America. "White folks ain't plannin' for us to be here."

As the audience applauded that insight, he said, "That's why we must make our own films!" Big applause. "But we shouldn't make anymore pimp films. White people already know enough about pimping. We Black people are the biggest whores they got!"

The audience broke up. Then looking over at me and Rosalind and Minnie Ripperton, Natalie Cole who were sitting a special section that Richard had arranged.

"I would like to introduce you to some of my friends," he started.

"This is Rosalind Cash!"

The audience applauded her.

He continued. "She's just finished doing the story of Angela Davis. But she's a Shakespearean actor. She ain't no poot butt. !" Don't you just love it when niggers who can do anything. I saw her in *King Lear*. Shakespeare may have been the greatest, but the motherfucker wrote funny."

He mimicked a few lines from comic version of a Shakespearean passage. "She's a great person. Miss Rosalind Cash!" The audience clapped long and sincerely. When they were finished, Richard added a quip: "Fine woman! I been asking her for some pussy for seven years. Bitch, won't give me no parts of her pussy. 'Please, Roz, just let me smell it.'"

Then he turned to me.

"I want to also introduce a brother, who is a novelist. A hell of a writer and a good friend. This is my friend, Cecil Brown. Nigger wrote a novel called *The Life and Loves of Mr. Jiveass Nigger!*"

They applauded me and I acknowledged their appreciation.

"And he is with Rosalind Cash!" Richard went on. "Nigger gets plenty props from me. I asked Cecil how it was. Did you smell it? All the nigger does is just grin, 'hehehe!'"

What he really felt about me and Rosalind being together in RL certainly influenced him enough to want to reenact it on-stage.

They thought that was the funniest thing in the world. But I knew that this was the shock treatment.

Then he turned to Natalie Cole, who was seated next to us.

"I know you are thinking, I don't know her. Well, there she is—Natalie Cole!"

The audience and the lights flashed on Natalie, who simply, glowed in the attention.

When they had quieted down, he said, "And now! Minnie Ripperton! She has the most incredible voice." After they had their fill of Minnie, Richard ended with a punch line that made everybody chuckle. "Minnie has such a high, beautiful voice, don't she? What if you were making it with her and she let out one of those high notes! Hearing that high note makes your dick hard right away! 'Is it good to you, baby?' Hahahahiiiieee! That note'll fuck you up!"

Then, he got around to addressing the Bicentennial Nigger motif.

In a bitter take he talked about the *Bicentennial Nigger* who gives up being a king in Africa to be a slave in America, have his life expectancy shorted from two hundred to fifty-two years, see his family sold by the slave master, and can now look forward to the next hundred years of the same treatment.

That night we all had a great time. I didn't know at the time that the jokes were being recorded. It wasn't until a few weeks later, when I went down to see him on the movie set of his first film, *Greased Lightning*, that he told me that his joke about me and Rosalind would be on wax forever.

As it turned out, *Bicentennial Nigger* garnished Richard a third Grammy and made him over a million dollars.

On the cut, "Black Hollywood" Richard tells a joke about Cecil Brown. When I hear that joke, a tribute more to a person I was then - I smile with nostalgia and longing for not only a time that has passed, but a time when we were all at the top of our form, a time when Richard was American's comic genius.

This was another example of On-Stage (OS) drama to comment on Real Life (RL). By putting it into the context of an On-Stage (OS) routine, he dealt with any sense of rejection. By acting out his desire to "sniff her pussy" maybe his dispensed with the desire in RL.

Later that night, back at his Northridge place, Richard was anxious because in a few days he was flying to Georgia to star in his first movie. The film was called *Greased Lightning* and I was invited to go with him. I was going because I was working on Richard's next film, *Which Way Is Up?*

"Tomorrow, I'm getting a personal trainer," Richard said.

"A friend of mine said Pryor was looking for a trainer," Rashon told me a few years later. "I went to the Hotel Sunset Tower and went up to the room. He was sitting on the sofa, had a beard on, and was all fucked up."

He looked up at Rashon as he entered the room.

Richard said, "What you gonna show me, Motherfucker?"

Richard worked out with Rashon for about eight or nine movements of 15 sets a piece. Rashon told me he just wanted to give Richard an idea of what to expect from his workouts. After they finished, Richard said, Go downstairs and somebody will let you know."

Rashon went back downstairs and waited in the lobby.

"I'm sitting in the lobby," Rashon said, "when the ambulance pulled up. Fifteen minutes later, they are bringing Richard down on a stretcher."

When Rashon saw Richard coming out on a stretcher, he was naturally a bit concerned.

"I said to myself, 'Was it something did that caused this? I might have fucked up the gig.'"

David Reverend Banks, who worked for Richard as a manager and producer, came behind the stretcher and said, "You got the job." His pay started that day.

They were taking him out on a stretcher, yet I had the job!

For the first three years, Rashon told me that he and Richard never spoke. Rashon would pick up all of his instructions from the office.

The first six weeks it was weird. But the checks were always on time.

One day, Richard and Rashon went to get the box office. The box office is the tally up of the money. Rashon was only twenty-two, and from that moment on, he realized that Richard trusted him. Richard trusted him with the money.

He knew that Richard trusted him then and that he could relax. Rashon accompanied Richard to Georgia to shoot *Greased Lightning*" in which Richard would play his first leading role.

Chapter Twenty Four

Greased Lightning

I T WAS THE fall of 1976. I was on my way to meet Richard on the set of his first real big film, *Greased Lightning*, which was scheduled to be shot in Atlanta, Georgia.

As the plane prepared to land, I looked outside the window and saw green Georgia pines. The white man next to me asked me if I had somebody to pick me up. He said he was a rich business-man, and would like to be nice to any black person. He was very nice, but I refused his offer. I told him that somebody was going to pick me up.

When I got to the airport lobby, I was surprised to find that there was a limousine there to pick me up and take me to the set. When I got in the limo, I saw that there was another person already inside.

"Hello." It was a woman's voice. "I'm Hannah Weinstein."

It didn't take me but a split second to realize that she was the producer of the picture. Richard had told me about her. "Cecil," he would say, "Man, listen there are some white folks out there who really want to help us. We just got to find them!" She was one of those people! Richard had finally met one of those white liberals you hear so much about.

When you know that you are riding in a car with somebody who could change your life, you are going to give it your best shot.

I told her I was a friend of Richard's. "That is great" she said, "He is such a genius." I told her I majored in English at Columbia University and the University of Chicago. That really impressed her. Born in New York City, she knew the weight of those degrees and opened up to me.

"Journalism is the best way to get into the business," she said. She had been working for the *Herald Tribune*. She was living in Paris in the 1950s, when she made her first television film about the French Resistance and sold it to an American television company.

She came back to America after making over four hundred films for TV. She recently started the Third World Cinema with James Earl Jones, Brock Peters and Ossie Davis.

"Have you seen *Claudine*?"

"Yes, I liked it." *Claudine* starred James Earl Jones as a garbage collector who marries Diana Sands. She had produced it.

"I loved it." That was no exaggeration either. During this time, it was the only film that had a realistic relationship between a black man and his wife in a working class situation.

"It was a cross-over picture," Mrs. Weinstein said, glancing out the window at the hills rolling by, and then she turned back to me.

"I'm hoping that *Greased Lightning* does as well."

"Oh, it will!"

"There are things that blacks suffer through that whites relate to, too, like *Grapes of Wrath,* but people have forgotten that," she said.

"It will be a great film," I assured her.

She started telling me that Melvin Van Peebles was a great director, but maybe he wasn't right for this picture. I had no reason to think that Melvin wasn't going to stay on as director.

She had three daughters, she said, and all of them were in the film business. It was hard for women in the film industry on the executive level, she bemoaned. Both her daughters, Paula and Lisa, were producers at Warner Brothers and Columbia, respectively. They were both, as it turned out, down on the *Greased Lightning* set.

Arriving at his rented house (away from the crew and other cast members including Cleavon Little, Beau Bridges, and Pam

Grier) I was greeted by Rashon Kahan. He had been hired a few weeks ago to be Richard's Man Friday. He would be with Richard for the next decade or so. He nodded for me to go inside.

Richard was sitting at a desk with two shiny pistols. No sooner than we had hugged each other and said hello, the door swung opened and Pam Grier came in, she went directly over to Richard and gave him a long kiss.

"Damn!"

Richard looked from her to me.

"This is my friend, Cecil."

"Hi, Cecil!"

She turned to the door. "See you later." When she had closed the door, I said," Man, you talkin' about me, huh, with Rosalind? What about Pam?"

He grinned. "She fine, ain't she?" he asked and I had to agree.

"And Richard what about that joke you told on me. You didn't record that, did you?"

"Oh, yeah!"

"Man, you didn't put that on a the record, did you?"

"Yea, nigger," he laughed, "It's on the record forever!" We laughed about it. "It's called *Bicentennial Nigger*—and it's going be there forever and ever!"

He showed me a copy of the *Bicentennial Nigger*. I was embarrassed that everybody would know about Rosalind and me.

"So how's the picture going?"

"We had to fire Melvin!"

"Why?"

I knew how much Richard admired Melvin. Back in the Berkeley days, we would sit up and talk about *Sweet Sweetback's Baadasssss Song* all the time.

"Yeah - he's just not for this picture."

Melvin was the man who invented the independent film in America with *The Story of a Three-Day Pass*, which was produced and shot in Europe.

"Maybe, he was too independent," Richard observed as he drew on his cigarette.

Melvin was the one who set it off for everybody! They wanted control; if they could control Melvin, to break him, then they would have won.

Richard said, "Maybe that independent don't work."

Hannah Weinstein wanted to fire Melvin and hire Michael Schultz. Richard could have stopped it but Richard and Melvin didn't get along.

To make everybody feel better, Richard threw a party that evening, where Richie Havens performed.

I was sitting right next to Richard as Richie Havens sang, "Here Comes the Sun." Richard cried. The song moved him so much. "Man," he said, to Richie, "That was so beautiful!"

In the film, Richie Havens played Hutch, a pit mechanic. Standing next to Havens was Wendell Scott himself. As the man upon whom the story was constructed, it was a great honor for him to be present.

He was the one the film was based on, the first black racecar driver. Richard was attracted to his story, because Scott fought against racism in the racecar events. He even had to fight against the Ku Klux Klan. To build his character with plausibility, Richard spent a lot of time with Scott.

"We have a very good relationship," Scott told me, after I got to know him. "But back in them days, I was more militant than he is in the movie."

He said Richard didn't cuss around him. This was because Richard had such respect for the suffering of black people like him under segregation. After all, Richard grew up in a segregated city. It was interesting to watch Richard work with a model of a real person, not something drawn on paper. Scott was from the most segregated history of the South - a history Richard respected because he felt a part of it.

Cleavon Little came over and Richard introduced us. He and Richard had made up over the squabble they had about Blazing Saddles.

Richard was one of the writers on *Blazing Saddles*. When he was telling Cleavon and some other people that he was going to play the lead, Cleavon said, "Excuse me, but I just signed up to play the lead." To show him that he had no animosities any longer, Richard got Cleavon hired on to act with him.

After I left Richard, I went back to the hotel and found a group of people hanging out. They were boom operators, directors, sound people, hairdressers and make-up artists.

Melvin was there standing in the middle of the group, smoking a cigar.

Then he saw me. "What's happening, partner." He said he was headed back to New York.

"I don't have any hard feelings," he said to the group. "All I'm concerned with is that my people stay."

The group cheered.

I met Robert Stevenson, and his wife Rosalind Stevenson. Robert had joined Richard's personal team when they both worked on *Car Wash*. Now Robert worked for him on his wardrobe and hair.

His wife Rosalind was a script consultant. Back in Hollywood, she worked for Norman Lear—who was a producer of the *Good Times* comedy series. (Rosalind would later help me get a gig writing an episode "The Evens Dilemma" for *Good Times*.)

A few days later, with Melvin out of the way, Michael Schultz took over. The film hummed right along. After a while, the whole set opened up. Richard was so loose and free. After shooting a scene, he would rush back to a crap game we would be having with some local brothers on side of the road.

One day, while the racetrack scene was being set up, I sat with him in the bleachers.

I was picking my nose. Richard said, "Pick me a winner!"

We laughed.

"Can you believe that we are actually shooting a black movie?" he asked.

"You mean, when we were back in Berkeley, we would talk about this shit and now it's happening?"

"Life is a fucking dream!"

"Well if you think this is something," I promised him, "wait until you read *Which Way Is Up*?"

He laughed. "You got some shit for me?"

"I got some shit for you, brother."

"I can't wait to read it."

I went back to Hollywood and shacked up with my typewriter in the Sunset Marquis. These were the good times. We were on a roll. We were on our way to changing Hollywood.

CHAPTER TWENTY FIVE

BLACK HOLLYWOOD

A FTER COMPLETING *GREASED* *Lightning,* Richard returned to Hollywood a rich and famous man. During the summer of 1977, he had a great time.

David Franklin made multiple deals with Warner Brothers, Universal, Columbia, and Paramount. As Richard wrote in *Pryor Convictions,* "After *Greased Lightning,* the pieces fell together. Everyone in town wanted to be in business with me."

Franklin negotiated multimillion-dollar deals. His dealings allowed Richard to buy a Spanish *hacienda* for $500,000.

It was located on three and a half acres in Northridge. The address was 17267 Parthenia, and it was about forty minutes drive outside of Los Angeles. In Greek mythology, Parthenia means birth. It is the Greek word for virgin. Parthenia is the Goddess Athena's own personal epithet.

I remember when Richard invited me up to see it. We walked around the fields, which had a lot of trees on them.

"This is mine," he said, waving over the fields of citrus trees.

We entered the gate and walked down the long driveway. To the left was the stucco mansion and to the right where the dog kennels of Alaskan Malamutes. Straight ahead were the guest cottage and the apartment for the live-in Mexican housekeeper, next, basketball court, and then the boxing gym. To the left of the gym were the swimming pool and the tennis court.

All the time he was in Georgia working on the *Greased Lightning* movie, the spot was getting groomed up for the "big time partying" that was going to happen when he got back.

We entered the house. In the center of the living room, he had this big fish bowl. The goldfish, he told me, were shipped in from somewhere in Japan. You passed the goldfish, and you were in the middle of the most amazing thing: an aviary-atrium filled with exotic birds. On one side of it was the master bedroom and other the other side was the dinning room.

As he talked about his plans to finish up the decoration, I was reminded of him sleeping on Alan's sofa back in Berkeley.

His story was really like the rags to riches legend. He knew that I would appreciate it, because I had seen him sleeping on Alan's sofa, and his fans had not. I had been with him when he moved into his little one bedroom apartment in Berkeley, and the Hollywood people had not.

It was around this time that Richard began to throw parties - usually disguised as a "wrap party."

We all went out to Parthenia in Northridge for the "wrap party." In reality, it was celebrating Richard's rise, to show everybody that he had finally made it.

I came into the gate with Rosalind. When we arrived, there was Roshan directing the cars. The parking lot was full.

I could hear the loud voices of a celebration just as we walked into the backyard.

Just as you came around the main house, your eyes could feast on any number of activities. Any one of these activities would blow your mind. There were three such eye-poppers.

To the right were the swimming pool and the party that was surrounding it. Turn to your left, and you had the skating rink - and the party that was surrounding it. Straight ahead was the tennis court, where Richard and Pamela Grier were having a match.

"Man, this is like Caesar's Palace!"

"Did you get a gift?"

Roz Stevenson showed me a bracelet that Richard had given her.

"He is the most generous of all the movie stars," Robert said. "He gave away more gifts than any of the other black stars like Eddie Murphy or Flip Wilson."

They were speaking truth. As Richard's reputation exploded, so did his generosity to other blacks.

He was known among the black technicians and movie staff to be the most generous of the new black stars.

"He just wanted to give the people who don't like to swim or play tennis something to do."

"What do you think of Richard?" Rosalind asked.

"Richard is his own worst enemy," Rosalind Stevenson said."He has a big heart but his worst enemy is himself."

He was suspicious. When it came to giving Robert his per diem, he gave it to the white boy and not to Robert. "It kind of hurt my feelings," Robert said. "He knew that black people always wanted something from him when you try to get with him and be his personal friend, but if you push for that, he don't want people that close to him. Especially if you work with him."

Just as we arrived at the Tennis Court, Richard and Grier were playing tennis. Richard and Pam were not great tennis players. Richard was better than she was. She kept hitting balls that went flying off the court. A reporter wrote, "After Pam Grier beat him for a second time at tennis, he wouldn't speak to her for a day." He had it all wrong.

It wasn't that Richard was a great player—he wasn't, but Pam was awful.

When her ball went off the court again, she yelled, "Richard, I need to give you a few lessons!"

"You gonna beat my ass and give me instructions too? No way!"

"The Richard Pryor Tournament prize goes to—"

"How much is the prize money?"

"Ten thousand dollars!"

When it came to drugs, he would bring in piles of coke so nobody would be without.

"Hey, Rosalind! And Cecil!"

We greeted him. "Do you like gambling?" he asked. He had a handful of one hundred dollars bills. "Here is something to gamble with."

He gave us a stack of crisp hundred dollar bills.

We went to the swimming pool. When Rosalind went to change into a bathing suit, Richard came up to Robert and me.

"What do you think of Pam?"

"She's beautiful," I said.

"Robert, what do you think?"

"She's great!

"I want you to take her a flower for me." He took a flower from a vase that was near by. "Give this to her, and tell her I sent it."

Robert laughed. "Now?"

"Now!"

We watched Robert take the flower over to Pam. She turned and smiled at Richard when Robert gave it to her.

"Robert," he said to him when he got back. "You are happily married."

"Right."

"How you do that?" We all laughed. "How you stay with one woman? I can't do that."

"You are just lonely."

There was a commotion as everybody turned. It was All Well, the pimp that Richard had made famous in one of his routines. Everybody turned to look. Here All Well came driving up in a purple Cadillac with a packed seat of good-looking women.

Driving the Cadillac up to the party, he called out to Richard.

Richard was busted. He just looked at him and grinned. He had blown All Well up so well that now All Well responded to the fantasy that Richard had created.

One of the biggest parties that he threw was for Ike Sutton, the photographer for *Jet* magazine.[20] I remember seeing Ken Norton,

Michel Jackson, Marvin Gaye, Sheila Frazier, and Lonette McKee, both of whom would later work with us in *Which Way Is Up?*

When Richard was down and out in Berkeley, one of the favorite songs was Marvin Gaye's "'What's Going on." At that party, he had a chance to talk and entertain Gaye whom he regarded as one of the greatest singers of all times. It was quite something for Richard to meet one of his idols who had been his inspiration to aspire for a better life.

CHAPTER TWENTY SIX

THE RICHARD PRYOR SHOW

THAT EVENING, ON Tuesday, September 23, 1977, we sat in Richard's living room and watched the premier of the *Richard Pryor Show* on NBC.

Richard used the upstairs office as a room for the writers he hired to work on the television show. NBC had signed him to do ten one-hour shows. David Franklin had worked out the details, like the fact that the shows would be aired on Thursdays from nine to ten. Richard wanted this time slot because he wanted to aim his comedy to a grown up audience. He didn't want the family viewing hour from eight to nine. He didn't want the censors biting on his material.

When Richard came back from a vacation, he found out that NBC had rescheduled the shows. Now, the network had changed the airing to eight to nine. Not only was this going to reach a more unhip audience, this slot was putting him in competition with "Happy Days" and "Laverne and Shirley," the most popular shows on television.

The problem was how to translate Richard's oral performances into a mass media without the censorship of television.

After the Comedy Club closed, Richard often invited the comics back to his place. He hired Most of the comics that he knew from the Comedy Store, to work in the Richard Pryor Comedy Show.

There were people from the show sprawled out on the slick hardwood floors. In the middle of it, Richard got up and walked downstairs and went outside.

"You know," he said, as I came up to him, "I hate this shit. You feel like you are trapped. I can't do this. It ain't art!"

"So what are going to do?"

"I know one thing, I'm quitting this shit!"

He seemed almost about to cry.

"I can't do it!"

He went back inside and addressed the group of writers and comedians.

"I'm sorry, Paul," he said to Paul Mooney, "I can't do this, I bit off more than I can chew. They give you so much money, you can't refuse."

"But you've got the chance to do something different on television," said Marsha Warfield. Marsha was a young comedienne from the Comedy Store who took a special supportive role to Richard. She was one of the writers hired to write the *Richard Pryor Show*.

She loved working with Richard. But Richard simply did not want to do the show.

"You want to see me with my brains blown out?" he told Marsha.

"I'm gonna have to be ruthless here because of what it does to my life. I'm not stable enough. I don't want to drink and I don't want to snort and I can't do it no other way."

Richard felt constrained by the television. When he consented to do the Richard Pryor Comedy Show, I had never seen him in as much pain.

"I hate this," he said as I came into the dressing room where he greeted me.

"What's the problem?"

"I don't have a live audience," he said. "I always look beyond the camera."

Richard was so uncomfortable that he got Franklin to re-negotiate the contract with NBC. He would do five shows. Part of the deal was that they would give him an extra two million dollars if he didn't go to any other network.

When the last show was finished, Richard got all the actors together. On the day that the last show was taped, Richard called all of the writers and their friends together. There was also a studio audience that joined in with the others. They had no idea that what Richard was going to perform would not be seen by any public until twenty years later.

Richard enters through the audience to the stage. The audience is mixed, mostly blacks. The camera focuses on two attractive black women in their twenties.

"I wanted to walk through the audience," he begins. "I'm going to do a little stand-up on TV but this is not being edited. So this is going to be offensive to a lot of you. Because I'm going to say fuck, suck, and shit and doodoo." He laughed with the audience, and then said:

"No, this is my last show. The people are saying that my show was cancelled. Motherfuckers didn't cancel me!"

Big applause.

"We were never cancelled," he told the audience, "I was not canceled; we were only supposed to do four shows—and get the fuck out of here! No, seriously they will make you kill a nigger. The shit they be tellin' a nigger to do. 'You can't do that!' 'Say what the fuck you mean?'

"NBC got a motherfucker from the Gay Liberation and then called me up. This is the Faggot Expert. [Voice of a hillbilly:] 'Will this be offensive?' The motherfucker said, 'Yes, I think that is offensive.' Who the nigger you call up?"

The contradiction was that NBC would censor him if a gay person objected to what he said, but the same censorship was not exercised if he used a racial epithet.

"The white boy muttered," he said. He imitated his stuttering. "Uh. Uh. Uh...well, we never gave a shit about colored people anyway," he finally admitted.

Finishing up that bit, Richard said, "I want to do Mudbone—"

A stagehand brings out a big chair for him to sit on.

In Mudbone's voice, he says, "Chairs too comfortable! I ain't use to sitting in shit like this!

"That's what I need—" he said to the stagehand, who was bringing him a stool. "That's what I need, a stool..."

He was now in Mudbone's persona and voice. The set up is ingenious and effective. The narrator (who is never named) slipped easily into the Mudbone character of an old, illiterate, black man, who is himself very old. But he was young back then, when he met an old man named Mudbone. "He sits down by the pool hall. And he dipped snuff and spit in an old Maxwell coffee can and talked shit! That was his job! I never seen him do no work."

He took the stool. "I'm going to start all over now."

"Mudbone had a old Maxwell coffee can. He told interesting stories. He freaked me out."

In the middle of his monologue, a stagehand, a young black man, came over to Richard to tell him to "do a clean start."

"Clean start? This is as clean I'm gone get!"

Then the young black man cautioned him that we were on television.

"Television? Mudbone don't give a fuck about television!"

The audience laughed harder, because they sided with Richard against the NBC television censor. This was pure shamanism.

"Mudbone was born in Mississippi. I knowed him well.

"I came up to Hollywood by mistake," Mudbone says, before that he worked on a plantation. "You young folks don't know nothing about plantations. Mr. Johns was a good old white man but he had son named Junior. He was cock-eyed. He was hard to work for. He would say, 'Hey, nigger, pick that up!' And fo', five niggers bend down!"

I had seen Richard do "Mudbone" many times before. But now he used it to get back at NBC and its producers.

The plantation was merely the frame for a story about revenge. Junior ordered a mail bride, and Mudbone must drive his horse Ginger to the railroad station to pick her up. She turned out to be a fat, stuck up, violent woman. She hit him in the face several times (*"bitch slap me upside my head!"*) and he planned his revenge by cutting the bottom out of the outhouse, causing her to fall in.

That afternoon Richard brought the house down with that routine. He organized his standup the way the oral performer did in oral cultures - by arranging the episodes in a different order and creating a different mood and outcome.

I had heard all of these bits separately, over many years. I had heard about "Toodlum," especially that time the New Orleans girl put a spell on him and he had to go to Miss Rudolph to get it taken off. In that bit, Toodlum is left in the zoo with tiny feet.

Tonight, however, Toodlum has a different function. He is talking indirectly about the TV censors to the censors.

He introduces some other black narrators, two brothers that like to tell stories themselves. He calls them the "Niggers with the big dicks."

"They put their dicks out over the Golden Gate Bridge," he said. "One says, 'The water is cold!' The other one rejoined, 'And deep, too!'"

The end was his triumph over the television censors who had blocked him from his real audience. This skit was never released for television, but Richard used the comedy skit to get his anger off his chest.

In the fall, *Which Way Is Up?* was finished and ready to come out in November, and I anxiously awaited the days. Richard and I met at the Comedy Store and he apologized for what I had to go through. I had no idea that the producer Steve Krantz was so corrupted that he would bring another writer in the project after the studio had accepted my script.

Since *Jaws* had been a big hit for Universal Studios, the Universal producers thought it would be a good idea to bring in one of the writers to look over my script. David Franklin had suggested to me that I shouldn't get screen credit since I had not written a screenplay before.

I went to the Writer's Guild and had an arbitration. The Writer's Guild decided that I had written the script and my name would be in the credits. Even though I had to fight to keep my name on the script, I was excited because my name would in the credits.

I was so hurt that Richard had to sit with me at the Comedy Store and tell me about his treatment by Mel Brooks on *Blazing Saddles*. When he had worked as a writer on *Blazing Saddles*, Richard was given credit, he said, "a long ways down on the credit lists."

As a black writer in Hollywood, Richard had a hard time, too. He had written a few episodes for Sanford and Son before he broke with the shows producer Aaron Reuben in a disagreement.

"They say at Sanford & Son they wanted black people writing the scripts," he told Gregg Kilday, LA Times, "but they change the scripts to the way they thought black people was." He told the reporters the same thing as he had told me. "They used me," he said, "and that's not fair." It was a thorn in his heart, he said. That thorn in his heart stayed there a long time, too. So now that night, he wanted to console my having to fight for my script. Hollywood did not like black writers. That was what we had to fight, he said.

CHAPTER TWENTY SEVEN

THE HOLLYWOOD BOWL

SOCIAL DRAMA NUMBER TWO

AROUND THAT TIME, Lily Tomlin, with whom he had done a television special together, asked him to perform at a gay benefit at the Hollywood Bowl. The benefit, called "A Star-Spangled Night for Rights," had been organized by local gay leaders to raise money to fight Anita Bryant's anti-homosexual crusade. Among the celebrities backstage were Bette Midler, Paul Newman, and Robert Blake. This invitation came a few days after he closed his Richard Pryor Show.

This incident was the most complete example of what I mean by Social Drama. According to Victor Turner in *From Ritual to Theater*, the Social Drama has four distinct divisions: 1) the breach, 2) the crisis, 3) the redress, and the 4) reintegration.[21]

The setting was a benefit event for the Human Rights event at the Hollywood Bowl. The performers were Bette Midler, Tom Waits, David Steinberg, War (the rock group), The Lockers, The Los Angeles Ballet Company, and, among the headliners, Richard Pryor.

The audience was mostly gay and was, according to *The Los Angeles Times'* Lee Grant, "pretty much taken with itself."[22] Richard got out of the Limousine with me, Rashon, and a few other guest. We went backstage, where one of the first people we met was Michael Schultz, who had just finished directing *Which Way Is Up?*

We all greeted him. Richard started looking around and saw the black dance group called The Lockers. The Lockers threw sticks with fire on it among each other. The fire marshal came up to them. "You can't do that," he told them. He told him that they couldn't use the fire torch.

One of them said, "Well, sir, we have been doing this for some time everywhere we perform." They were polite. The highlight of their show was twirling torches, but the marshal said that he didn't care where they had been doing it, they couldn't do it here. He said it in such condensing way that Richard got offended.

Observing this interaction between the fire marshal and the black dancers, Richard looked over at me and Rashon. "They were messin' with these black dancers," Richard complained. He added, "That's what I'm going to talk about."

The show had started at 8:15 with the Hollywood Festival orchestra playing "The Star Spangled Banner" to a standing ovation. Then the MC introduced Christopher Lee who read a song while the orchestra played. Next, came Lily Tomlin, who told jokes about gays in the fifties, "Back then nobody was gay, only shy."

Then came The Lockers. They were called the "last word in disco dancing" in the program, because disco was on its way out. But they could have been called the "first" word in hip-hop, because their innovative dance was one of the first signs of the hip-hop phenomenon that was poised to sweep the country.

After doing two dance numbers to the music of *Star Wars* and the "Flight of the Bumblebee," they went off stage, signaling the intermission. Just as the first half had been introduced with a black American dance troupe, The Lockers, the second half was presented by a white ballet dance troupe.

Backstage, Pryor had seen how the two dance groups were treated differently. He noticed how the white concert coordinator treated the white dance troupe with respect, but treated The Locker's hip-hop innovation, with disdain.

"When the white dance act went onstage," Richard said to me and the others standing near him, "Every damn body and his brother went to fix the lights. But when the Lockers came on," he said, "They didn't do shit for the Lockers." When it was time for him to go on, he said, "Watch this!"

Richard came out on the stage like a lion and stalked the stage like he was on a prowl. He looked at the audience and saw a sea of white faces. The audiences of white people were charged up, too.

Richard shouted back at his hecklers. "There's only four niggers out there...niggers!"

This was a direct reference to the famous lines that Lenny Bruce had used back in the 1962 in a routine Richard knew well, called "How to Relax Your Colored Friends at Parties."

It was based on a real incident, which Richard also knew well. The incident is about how Dick Gregory and Grover Sales, a well-known hippy writer and critic, walked into the Hungry i cafe on Broadway in San Francisco and saw Bruce in the middle of his performance. Sales reported that Dick Gregory, one of the leading black comics at the time, had never seen Lenny Bruce perform. Spotting Dick Gregory, Lenny peered at the audience for an unnerving interval, and said, 'Are there any niggers here tonight?'

Grove described Dick Gregory's reaction: He "stiffened like a retriever." In 1962, nobody had ever heard that word on stage, not in a white nightclub.

Lenny certainly shocked the white audience that night with that forbidden word. But here at the Hollywood Bowl, Richard used the word "faggot" in the same way that Bruce had used nigger, as a way to shock the audience into realizing a crucial shortcoming.

Scanning the white faces, Richard went on, "I don't see no niggers..."

He started in by noticing that he was the only performer who had admitted to having "fucked a faggot."

The audience clamped up when he said the word "faggot."

He didn't like the gay experience, he said. "I'm the only person at this thing," he went on, "who's admitted to having a homosexual experience... fucking a faggot."

The audience groaned. "Get him out of here!"

The audience's reaction to him increased to a loud protest. But Richard went on. "Black people can't deal with the word homosexual. There may be a faggot in the family but there ain't no homosexuals."

Richard kept pushing them. In the theory of comedian as shaman, what he was doing was trying to bring the audience's demons out. By "insulting, goading, looking for reaction," as *Los Angeles Times* reporter Lee Grant put it; he was trying to get them to show their fears. Once their fears are out there in some symbolic way, he can exorcise them.

"Anita's getting over," Richard roared back, "How can fags be racists? I thought since this was a night for human rights there be some human being here."

There were more catcalls and swelling boos.

He told them they should give the money raised "to the people on welfare."

There was a deadening silence.

"Where were you when the niggers were burning down shit; you were on Hollywood Boulevard fucking and didn't give a damn. You are not concerned with human rights, you're just concerned with fun."

Pryor continued to insult the audience for their hypocritical stance of being for human rights but being more concerned with their hedonistic, self-centered lifestyles. What he attacked them for was their repressed bigotry towards blacks. "Fags are prejudiced," he joked, "The Locker dancers came backstage dripping with sweat but all you could say is 'Oh, that was nice.' But when the ballet dancers came out dancing to that funny music you said, 'Wow, those are some bad mothers.'"

The audience booed him.

"I just wanted to test your soul," he shouted back to their hisses. "I wanted to test you, to see where you were coming from.

They're not paying me to do this. Where were you faggots when niggers burned down Watts."

Some cried out for Bette Midler, hoping apparently that Richard would cool down. Then, he turned his backside to the audience, and tugged his pants and said, "All of you can kiss my rich, happy, black ass." Then he stalked abruptly off the stage. The audience was loud and raucous in its dismissal of him, but above the loud noise, one lone voice said, *"Tell it like it is, Brother, Richard!"*[23]

Having said that, Richard bent over towards the outraged and jaw-tight audience, turned and pranced off the stage. The show's director came out to apologized for this scathing attack.

Then onto the stage came Bette Midler, "Is there anybody out there tonight who wants to kiss his rich *white* ass?"

But her comic remark couldn't calm down the angry audience.

Lily Tomlin came on and said, "That's what you get when you invite Richard Pryor."

But the cat was out of the bag. This confrontation with the audience drew immediate critics in the gay community in Hollywood.

Michael Schultz told reporters Fred Robbins and Dave Reagan that Richard had been reacting to "blatant racism."

"The show's representative was definitely giving the black group different treatment and talking offensively to them," he recalled. "Anybody else would have tried to rationalize it. Pryor came out and told them how upset he was and exactly what was on his mind."

I had seen Richard become outraged about racism behind the stage and on movie sets before. I saw him get angry at the way whites acted towards blacks that were not recognizable super stars. Richard resented the way whites would kiss up to him because he was famous, but ignore another black person standing right behind him. He did the same thing with the cast of Neil Simone's The California Suite. On that set, Richard defended one of the black actresses who complained that the director was rude and dismissive.

Lee Grant, who covered Richard for *The Los Angeles Times*, defended Richard's right to say what he pleased, arguing, "If you hire Richard Pryor, you get Richard Pryor, someone who challenges, who tells the truth."[24]

Sometime that day, Richard's lawyer David Franklin called me to say that the film might be held up, because Richard had insulted some Hollywood producers at the incident. We had finished *Which Way Is Up?* and were all waiting for the upcoming opening, on November 9, 1977.

Irate gay supporters responded to the article by marching with picket signs outside Lee's newspaper office. The *LA Times* published about eighteen letters from the readers, nearly all of them calling Richard an antigay bigot.

"Regarding Lee Grant's review of the show," Jeanne Karaffa from Beverly Hills, wrote, "Pryor was abusive, filthy and racist." Rick Clark from Orange County said he was "bigoted." "In this country of free speech," wrote Martin Matson from Pasadena, "presumably anyone has the right to express his hostility toward minority groups. But for Pryor to accept an invitation to perform at a benefit for gay rights and then to use that benefit as a forum for expressing his hostility towards gays is the ultimate double-cross."

One or two of the responses defended his right to say what he wanted to say. "Richard Pryor is one of the few people in this town who has not compromised his ideals and his humor to achieve success," wrote Patrick Quinn from Manhattan Beach. "He has grown as an artist and a human being without succumbing to censors or a negative reception."[25]

When Lee Grant's phone rang, it was Richard.

"You've been taking some heat," he told Grant and thanked him for defending him.

He felt the pressure from the studio executives and worried that the publicity might hurt his career. Record companies said they would stop distributing his albums. A gay group took out a full-page ad denouncing him and promising to boycott his movies and concerts.

I drove out to Northridge to see Richard and to find out what was happening with *Which Way Is Up?* After being buzzed in at the gate, I parked near Richard's Rolls Royce before going up to his den and office. Facing West and looking beyond the guesthouse, I could see the tennis court and bathhouses; to my right were the boxing gym, the dog kennels, and garages. To my left was the main house. I knocked on the back door of the main house and the Chicano maid opened it, greeted me politely and said Richard was out by the swimming pool.

I found him sitting by the pool with a cigarette and a drink. He looked depressed. He motioned to me to sit down, and as I did, he sucked deeply on the cigarette.

"I guess I fucked up, huh?" he said.

"No matter what happened," I said, "You still got this." I waved to the house and the swimming pool.

"All of this," he gestured to the house and swimming pool, "is the price I've had to pay to do my work. I keep this bullshit going so they'll leave me the fuck alone!"

He asked me if I had seen what had happened. "When I got there," Richard said, "I didn't know what kind of benefit it was."

"Right!"

"All I knew was that Lily Tomlin asked me to do a benefit. But as I walked around I could see that it was mostly white boys with each other."He looked at me. "Damn, if I don't apologize," he said, giving me another look, "I won't have a career."

"When they interviewed me in the gay press, I said I wasn't scared. But I was scared. I was scared about what I'd done but I was so happy because I knew I'd done the right thing; I'd said what was in my heart."

"Somebody asked me, 'Do you fear your career is over?' and I don't know what I said, but what I thought was this: 'If my career is over because I said what was in my heart, then I didn't have a career to start with. So fuck it.'"

"That's right," I said.

I reminded him how it had been in Berkeley. Back in Berkeley, he had slept on Alan's sofa. Had he forgotten how he had finally got his own apartment, and had lived on his own? From that, he had conquered Hollywood. He had done that by being true to himself.

I had another idea: ancient history. "Remember Aesop!"

"Aesop?"

Black Aesop, the ancient slave who invented the fable, was the first black writer in the ancient world. Delphi was a city in ancient Greece that was famous for its "piety, learning, and wisdom."

When Aesop came to the city of Delphi, he was disappointed that the city had not lived up to its reputation: it had become a cit of intolerance, arrogance and corruption, and in an unguarded moment, he spoke his true opinion.

Somebody told the city authorities of Delphi what Aesop had said. These officials knew that when the word got out about the city, visitors (their principle source of income) would stop coming. Therefore, they used a trumped up charge that Aesop had stolen a sacred vase and condemned him to death: his fate was to be thrown over a precipice. Like Richard, Aesop had held the mirror up to the ancient Greek society, the city of Delphi.

As Richard shook the ice in the glass, his face full of pain, he gazed off beyond the estate, towards the distant mountains, as if he were looking at the abyss that Aesop went hurling over.

He gave me another look as if he had made up his mind. "This morning, I asked Lee Grant to write a piece about me apologizing for what I said. I need to be myself, true to myself," he said. "I'm not going to apologize." He got up abruptly and went across the swimming pool into the house to ask the reporter not to publish his apology. Lee Grant got the article pulled and it was never published. [26]

Though everybody had predicted that his career would suffer, that was not what happened. When the film *Which Way Is Up?* came out a few weeks later, it made a big box office success. It cost about two million to make and it grossed nearly ten million dollars. In those days, a low investment was seen as a risk because the film was black. When the return was over five times the invest-ment, the studio was happy.

The producer, Steve Krantz, with whom I had many fights, explained away the lucrative investment and the Hollywood Bowl event by claiming that there were two societies—the Hollywood society and the rest of the country. He said, "The people in the rest of the country don't give a damn about [Richard's] attitude towards gays."

The Hollywood Bowl event was a significant turning point in Richard's life - a turning point that defined who he had been and who he was going to be. Richard had inadvertently turned the mirror up to the society and the society did not like what it saw.

One member of the audience said in a letter that appeared glowingly in the *LA Times,* "We made him," meaning that the white society had picked him and given him his success.

White society (least of all white gay society in Hollywood) did not make Richard Pryor. This is what those of us who were close to him, his friends, knew. He held the mirror up to a society, which could not bear to look at itself, could not afford to look at its own foibles. That society would attempt to smash him, and leave him shattered like so many millions pieces of glass.

That afternoon, down by the swimming pool, I experienced Richard at one of the most significant turning points in his life.

He saw the fall beneath him, Aesop's fateful pit. Yet, he decided to stay with his conviction. He didn't invent society, he simply reflected it. If they couldn't handle it, that was society's problem. "I'm testing you," he told them. Some of them didn't get it then and still don't. Some did, though, thank God.

Lee Grant's phone rang, and it was Richard.

"He wanted to apologize for his performance at the benefit, pressured apparently by studio honchos worried his burgeoning film career would be threatened. So I wrote that story."

The next day, according to Lee, Richard called again, changing his mind. "I need to be myself, he said, 'true to myself,' and promised that he'd owe me if I could get the article pulled. I managed that and developed a relationship with him that lasted until his death."

This was the point. Richard had shown them their demons, but some didn't want to accept the truth. He did reach the members of the audience, as a *negative exemplar* who had became their spokesman. Some of the audience did look inward. They had heard the laughter of the community and had replaced their lack of social concerns with a renewed vigor to become part of a larger community.

If you do not believe that Richard is to speaking the truth, one black homosexual wrote, just try going into a gay club as "black, fat, ugly, or a woman alone."

One critic marveled at what Richard had accomplished. "You can call it talent, or even genius," he wrote, "but Richard managed to insult 17,000 people (gay and straight, young and old, rich and poor) all at the same time..." Richard's social drama had a powerful ending, for it used satire to bring a communal laughter that help heal the rift caused by the inevitable breach in society's fabric.

CHAPTER TWENTY EIGHT

THIS IS THE WAY UP!

INSTEAD OF HURTING Richard's career, *Which Way Is Up?* came out and made him a superstar. Lee Grant, the *Los Angeles Times* reporter assigned to cover Richard, turned his attention to the extravagant parties that Richard threw to celebrate the success of the triumphant of this movie.

In an article for the *LA Times,* he wrote about how Richard thanked his crew for working on *Which Way Is Up?* by paying for two full pages in the trade papers to tell the crew that he appreciated them. "The space listed 117 names," Lee wrote, "everyone from the stand-in to the cast. He threw an elaborate wrap party Sunday evening at a disco in Westwood." He reported how Richard had hired Marsha Reed, a still photographer, to take over 2,500 photos during the shooting schedule.

"I'm going to save these photos for the rest of my life," Richard said. "This film is the most special thing I've ever done." [27]

The redress of the social drama, in this case, was that Richard had made a great movie. He was becoming so popular that when he was coming out of the Playboy club, there were so many people waiting at the door for his autographs that he had to leave through the kitchen.

Once he was in the kitchen, however, there were ten black people who wanted autographs, too. Since these were the black cooks and dishwashers, he complied.

Which Way Is Up? was the hit movie for blacks all over the nation and won the praise of important film reviewers. Vincent Canby gave it enthusiastic praise for Richard's ability to play three characters.

The whole episode was Richard's mastery of life, of his koans. Like a hero out of Alejandro Jodorowsky, he had rebounded as though he was a magician, a modern day guru, or even (according to Reverend Banks) like Jesus.

Richard was in a good mood, too. He flew to Chicago for the opening of *Which Way Is Up?* When he flew back to Peoria, his hometown, the *Chicago Tribune* interviewed him. "I love being a superstar," he told Maggie Daly, *Chicago Tribune* columnist. "I love the publicity. It gets me up. The day may come when I go out into the street and hope somebody will just say hello."

Pryor told Ms. Daly, "I'm going to write for the next couple months. I'm going to write a movie all by myself for Universal or Warner Brothers."

With the success of *Which Way Is Up?* Richard began a behavior pattern that was to characterize the rest of his life. As I have said, I call these social dramas. These incidents would be distraction to his career. Just when his career would take off, some incident would occur that would block the momentum. Whenever there was an event that gave him great satisfaction, he would follow it with a disaster.

He expressed his excitement about being independent. "I'm glad I make a lot of money and there's nobody but me to decide what to do with my life. I'm going to keep going. That's what everybody wants."

Six days, later, however, the social drama took a turn. After all his great press, telling everybody how fantastic his future was, he has a heart attack! The headlines of the *Chicago Tribune* for that November 10 was "Comic Pryor in Peoria Coronary Unit."

He checked into the Methodist Medical Center in Peoria. The officials said he was in the coronary care unit. The paper noted that he had been in three movies, he was a local boy, and "The Richard Pryor Show" did not survive this television season.

I was flying back to Oakland on PSA. One of my seatmates asked if I had heard that Richard Pryor had died of a heart attack. I became alarmed, and asked if it were true. It wasn't until the plane landed that I was able to call back to LA and ask Reverend Banks (who was practically his personal manager) if Richard was dead or alive.

Rolling Stone magazine wrote a mock column about the "Death of Richard Pryor," called "An Attack of the Heart," it went on:

Peoria Ill (UPI) "Black Comic Richard Pryor, whose violent temper and obscenity-laced spoofs of black society kept him at loggerheads with television censors and the law, died here today after being admitted to Methodist Medical Center for what doctors termed "exhaustion and poor color."

David Felton, the *Rolling Stone* writer who had profiled him in 1974, where he termed Richard's stand-up act, "Theater of the Routine," wrote this spoof of Pryor's death. Now, he does a white boy shuffle on Richard's new style.[28]

The spoof was in bad taste, or even more to the point, pointless.

As with all social dramas, there is end of the cycle and things return to the normal. Anthropologist Victor Turner coined the term social drama, while he was doing fieldwork in a small African village. The social drama has four phases: breach, crisis, redress, and reintegration.

Richard's heart attack was such a social drama. The final phase occurred after the heart attack at the Methodist Medical Center in Peoria.

When Richard got back to California, he was excited and anxious to get on with the next project. He was ready for the next breach in the social fabric.

One day, in his pad, I read Gene Siskel's review of *Which Way Is Up?* in the *Chicago Tribune* to Richard. "This will be remembered as the year Richard Pryor became the leading black box office film star.

Richard loved our success. I read on: "Young black audiences respond to Pryor like no other performer working today. He's an impudent Bill Cosby."

Excitedly Richard slapped his thighs. He loved it that that he had outpaced Cosby. Siskel pushed this idea further when he suggested that Richard's presence was typically of a street-smart guy who is for himself and always gets his way either by "charming or fooling the hell out of you." He applauded Richard as a "superb silent comedian. There are plenty of scenes where he doesn't need to speak. His expressive body immediately registers fear, love, and exhaustion."

This review really impressed both of us. We had tried so show the non-verbal art in black film culture, and here was a critic actually recognizing it. Gene Siskel was definitely on our side. *"Which Way Is Up?* is made for Pryor fans," he concluded his great review, "For those who think he's an uppity, women-hating comedian, forget the picture."[29]

It was not long before Richard was back at the Comedy Store on Sunset. Every couple nights, he comes to the store to work out some new material. At the end of his show, he would hold court outside the Comedy Store club on Sunset Boulevard. Comics who were at other clubs that were closing would show up.

This was one of the best times I had hanging with Richard. He would always be funny and relaxed, shooting the breeze, as we say. People would be coming up to him and talking shit and he would be loud talking, too. Cutting people up and handing out insults and swipes and praises like a chef dishing delicacies.

One night Thelma Huston the disco diva showed up with her entourage. She had this hit, "Don't Leave Me This Way!" Richard and I were checking her and her crew out. She was traveling with some good-looking partners. Richard nudged me. She invited us all to her place, which was across Sunset Boulevard, just down the block.

"Come on, man, let's go get some of that."

I got the address and walked with Richard across the street. We got past the doorman and went upstairs to the seventh floor.

When we walked in, Richard said, "Wow!" There was a view of Los Angeles beneath us. The whole pad was laid out in a lavender color, with mirrors and sleek furniture. The next thing I knew we were all snorting cocaine and listening to Thelma's new release.

After a few snorts, Richard got up and said he had to get home.

Soon everybody was gone and as I picked up my hat, Thelma asked me to stay. It was then that I realized she had her designs on me and not Richard. And just like what happened with Rosalind Cash, I was sideswiped into love.

We stayed in bed for the next few days. She sent her maid to get my things and I never saw my little old apartment again, except in my imagination.

I went out to see Richard a few days later. He took one look at me and said, "Nigger, what happened to you?"

He was looking at my new digs and the Gerri Curl I had. I had been transformed by one of Hollywood's singing divas!

During this time, Richard began to have more parties out at Northridge. It was normal for me to find myself out at his house at three in the morning in the kitchen being entertained by Sammy Davis, Jr. and his wife.

In the meantime, Richard was hanging out with Paul Mooney and me one afternoon at the Daisy on Rodeo Drive when he spotted this sister with a flashing smile and very large buxom. Richard sent Paul over to her table to invite her over.

Her name was Deboragh McGuire, and it wasn't long before she and Richard were dating. Not long after that, they got married.

While Richard was going through his changes with Deboragh, I was going through mine with Thelma.

My sole reason for being in Los Angeles was to write a novel about my experience of being in Hollywood. I was doing okay, as I saw it. I had friends, I was hanging with crazy people, I could make a living, and I had a great girl, Thelma. One problem: Thelma's jealousy. That threw my plans off. I would tell Richard about how jealous Thelma was and he would tell me how to handle it.

We were in Richard's office, which was also his playpen and writing studio. I was telling Richard the following story:

I was down at the swimming pool (at the Sunset Towers on Sunset Boulevard) where Thelma and I lived. I was lounging there talking to a friend, sipping a martini, when an attractive woman came up.

This young actress had just graduated from UC Berkeley's drama school. She wanted somebody to talk to. And since I was from Berkeley, we agreed to talk further.

I told her that I would meet her at this French restaurant on Melrose Avenue. We would meet at 8:30. No sooner than we sat down and ordered a bottle of wine, I looked over the dining room and saw Thelma sitting at another table staring at me. She got up and walked over to my table and before I could open my mouth, she strolled out.

How did she know I was here? As I put the key into our apartment I noticed that there was a garbage pail next to the door. I went over and discovered that some of the clothes she had bought me were cut into small pieces and thrown in. I opened the door and walked in. Thelma was sitting there with a drink, laughing. *"I broke your mother fucking face!"*

In those days of that particular time in Black Hollywood the expression "I broke your face" was new. But the way Thelma used it was that she wanted to actually break my face! I was still picking up the pieces when she gave me the cold shoulder and I knew then that our relationship was going to be very, very difficult.

I told Richard about the scene and he cracked up.

He looked at me in disbelief. "Don't you know what's going on?"

I was clueless. "No?"

"The gays!"

"The gays?"

"That's right. Thelma is famous right? She knows all the gays in Hollywood. They dig her!"

This was true. Where we went in public, gay men would come up to her and perform rituals of appreciation.

"You see, what you don't realize man is a famous singer like Thelma is protected by all the gay people in the whole fucking town, man, and if you make a date with any woman within earshot of any of these motherfuckers, man, they going to run back and tell her."

"How?"

"Think back, man! Where were you when you made the date to meet her in the French restaurant."

"I was at the pool..."

"Who was at the pool with you?"

I thought about it. "No, it was just me—and...

"...And who?"

"Rudy! What's his name..."

"He's gay, right?"

"He works with Thelma. He's gay. He's a friend of Thelma's!"

"That's right! He went straight to Thelma and told her where your ass was going to be and with whom!"

The next time I would watch to see how many of these guys around Thelma were gay. Richard was right. I couldn't do anything without Thelma's spies finding out about it. Not only was Thelma jealous but also she had one of the best spy systems in Hollywood. I concentrated on writing my novel. She was so jealous that I had to rent rooms to work on the book alone. When I hired a secretary, Thelma found out about it and met the girl in the elevator.

When the secretary came to me she was crying and told me that she couldn't work with me any longer. In the elevator, Thelma didn't say a word. She just stared at the secretary and, in the clichés of that times, *broke her face.*

CHAPTER TWENTY NINE

BLUE COLLAR

SOCIAL DRAMA NUMBER THREE

I N 1978, I started my novel *Days Without Weather,* and Richard went to shoot *Blue Collar* on location in Kalamazoo, Michigan. Richard had reached his peak as a stand-up comedian around this time. In 1978, he got that chance to be in a drama film in which he was not being funny. That opportunity came with the movie *Blue Collar.* He had agreed to make the movie, but Paul Schrader, the director, still wouldn't give his girlfriend the money. At this point in his career, Paul Schrader was the celebrated scriptwriter for *The Taxi Driver,* starring Robert De Niro.

Although *Blue Collar* was one of the first socially conscious films, and it was based on a great idea, it had a rocky beginning.

Blue Collar was his first serious acting role that was not pure comedy, and Richard had a hard time working with Paul Schrader, the director. Richard didn't get along with Yaphet Kotto or Harvey Keitel.

He and Rashon would come back and tell me stories of their adventures on the set Richard would say how it depressed him to make the film, and that he hated Harvey Keitel, Yaphet Kotto, and Paul Schrader today because of that movie.

When Richard came back, he would tell me about his ordeal with Paul Schrader. Schrader said he had problems working with Richard. "Not a day went by without a fight," he claimed. "Right after I said, 'Cut!' a fight would start. Richard hit Yaphet with a chair on camera, so I knew things were bad,"[30]

The problem, which centered around the movie had to do with Richard's conviction, since the Berkeley days, not to do a film that demeaned black people. Richard's character in the film, Zeke Brown, was a difficult role for Richard to play. The story featured three men, one white (Harvey Keitel) and two blacks, Yaphet Kotto and Richard.

Set in an automobile plant in Detroit, the story is about how these three autoworkers are mistreated by their management and union brass. They decide to rob their employer by breaking into a safe. The safe has very little money, but they find a ledger that reveals how the Union has been cheating them. They decide to blackmail the Union, but finally decide they have to turn the ledger in to the union boss. Each of them suffers a different fate. Smokey James (Kotto's character) is murdered. Richard's character Zeke snitches on the other men. Richard was so uncomfortable with that role.

"Man, I can't see it," he would tell me. "I can't see playing a Tom like that."

His disagreement with the director Schrader was about how to redeem his character and not make him a sell out. He thought that the other two characters were being used to keep him from giving dignity to Zeke. The other two actors thought that Schrader was favoring Richard's character.

Schrader was playing all three of them against each other. He had the notion that if he could keep the actors at each other throats he would be able to fan some of the raw fire into the characters in the script. It was a notion he had picked up from the Actor's Studio. Later, when I interviewed him, he explained to me that he wanted to "keep them under pressure to stimulate the characters' emotions in the story."

As it turned out, Richard pulled a gun at Schrader and told him there was no way he was going to do more than three takes for a scene. This incident, according to Richard Pryor biographer, Jeff Rovin, may have caused Schrader a "nervous breakdown."

I would ask Richard how the movie was going.

"It was okay," he would say, "I had to pull my gun out."

"Oh, yeah?"

"It was in a script conference."

"What happened?"

"They wanted to put something in the script."

"Some shit?"

"Yep!"

The best way to explain and understand the animosity between Richard and members of the shooting crew is through the paradigm of the social drama and the four phases: breach, crisis, redress, and reintegration. The social drama paradigm shows how Richard used disruptive behavior to force the outcome of the film, which turned out to be what he saw as his best work.

According to Richard and Roshan, the breach in the community started when one of the actors, the late George Memmoli, said something to Richard that Richard thought was offensive. The offense (whatever it was) breached the social fabric of the film shooting crew community.

Richard reacted by grabbing the actor, who plays a minor character called Jenkins. He had been in *Mean Streets* and was a personal friend of Martin Scorsese. When Rashon saw Richard scuffling with George Memmoli, he thought it was a scene from the script.

Then, he saw Richard pick up an apple box.

At that point, he rushed over to separate them. In trying to get them apart, Rashon ended up hitting George across the head, too. They didn't know he had a plate in his head, and the actor ended up going to the hospital!

Richard accused Rashon ("You fucked him up!") and Rashon accused Richard ("You fucked him up first, by hitting him with the box!")

"Pryor took offense at something Memmoli said and slugged the actor," Jeff Rovin, a Pryor biographer, wrote, "when Richard grabbed a chair and hit him over the head. Memmoli ended up with a fractured skull, Pryor with a one-million-dollar lawsuit."

This phase of the social drama, "the crisis," was a perfect example of the second phase of the four-part social drama. This is the phase that divides the community, (in this case, the film community) and stopped the movie production.

What astonished everybody was that Richard would come out of his "fit" and act as if nothing disruptive had taken place. After such a disruption, hours later..." Richard would "be the sweetest man alive." Folks from the primary oral culture do not hold grudges.

Another problem with Schrader for Richard was the script itself. Richard may have known about the controversy surrounding how the idea of the film originated. It was said that Schrader and his brother (who is listed as screenwriters in the credits) had stolen the script from a black writer. Given the racism that Richard had experienced with the producers about his own scripts, this didn't sit well with him.

"The idea of *Blue Collar* did not originate with Schrader," Andrew Sarris, the famous *Village Voice* film critic, wrote in an article titled, "The Shameless Cinema of Paul Schrader."

The idea came from a black writer named Sydney A. Glass who attended a Writers Guild seminar in which Schrader spoke.

In his interview, Schrader told Sarris that he "invited Glass over to his house. He asked him, "What do you really want to write about?" Glass said he wanted to write about his father who worked in Detroit auto plants and committed suicide the day before he was scheduled to retire. Schrader thought said this was something to write about but that it shouldn't just be about a black guy. It had to be two blacks and white.

Schrader said he began to sketch out a bit of plot then sent Sidney A. Glass away. When Glass had left, Schrader said, "I thought, 'Why should Sidney Glass write it?' Finally deciding that I should write that."

The man with no shame had a brother named Leonard. He was three years older than Schrader, has never sold a script on his own, and like his brother, is reputed to be very smart. Schrader was able to get financing to shoot *Blue Collar* based on the participation of Keitel and especially Pryor.

The item made it into the trades, which was where Glass discovered it. Sydney Glass got a lawyer, apparently had a very good lawyer. He also had the backing of the black caucus of the screen Writer's Guild of America.

Schrader was busted. Sidney went on to write an episode for the television adaptation of *Roots*. Sidney's picture appeared in Jet magazine on May 11, 1978.

I was a member of the Black Caucus in the Writer's Guild. Sydney Glass came to thank me for mentioning the Schrader rip-off in my article "Blues for Blacks," published in 1981 in the *Mother Jones* magazine edited by former neighbor Adam Hochshild.

One of the difficulties with Richard and Hollywood was the difference between an oral culture and a literate one. One of the sub-forms of Hollywood anthropology of filmmaking is the script conference.

It is in the script conference that Richard became most irritated with Hollywood, which was usually represented by a white Jewish director or writer director as was the case with Paul Schrader, Michael Campus (*The Mack*), Herbert Ross (*California Suite*), and Andy Breckman. They were always the same.

The situation was Real Life. On one side of the table would be the director, usually a highly educated individual, who had read all the books on film-making and gone to a film school and who is wondering how an illiterate black man who was raised in a whorehouse could possible know as much about the script as he did? Yet it was this illiterate black man who was the hottest property in Hollywood, and was the reason for you getting work as a director.

Richard's black directors were Sidney Poitier (*Stir Crazy*), Michael Schultz (*Car Wash, Greased Lightning, Which Way is Up?, Bustin' Loose*) and Oz Scott (fired from *Bustin Loose*.) The only social drama with Oz Scott was that Richard stood up to the studio to hire him.

There were no social dramas associated with any of these films directed by black directors. It is only when the rest of his forty films which were directed by white directors where you find the social dramas. Why was that?

This was especially true if the director had written the script, as in Schrader's case. Never mind that Schrader stole the script from his student Sidney Glass, who would later win a lawsuit against him.

The script conference would invariably end with Richard pitching a "fit," or in at least two cases, pulling out his gun.

White screenwriter Andy Brechman is a case study. He describes such a conference. "The whole cast sat around a big conference table," he said.

"At some point in the script, there was a scene where one of the characters—a senile old lady—takes a crap in the backyard. Shamelessly in broad daylight. Like a dog...but Mr. Pryor felt that this scene didn't work. I respectfully disagreed. We went back and forth."[31]

What an awful scene. I could see why Richard didn't want it in. Why would anybody, except somebody with no taste for black culture, want a scene like this in a movie?

The director turned to Richard and said, "Richard, is this something you feel strongly about?" And this is what Pryor did, Brechman remembered, "He reached into is jacket and pulled out a gun! A real gun. A derringer—with short barrels. I'd never seen one before but I could tell it was definitely real. I was so scared I almost blacked out." Wow, talking about a fool !

Never once did Brechman consider that the scene was so offensive that Richard didn't want to discuss it. Apparently, the only way he could get his point across was to pull out a gun.

I got to know Paul Schrader when he came to Berkeley to make the Patty Hearst film. Tom Luddy, the film producer, told Schrader I knew some of the people in the Symbioses Liberation Army (SLA.)

Schrader had based the script on Patty Hearst's book, *Everything Secret*. In it, she wrote that the members of the SLA gang had sexually abused her.

Schrader had cast the actress Natasha Richardson as Patty Hearst. He told her that my friends and I had been in Berkeley during the time of Patty's kidnapping. Poet David Henderson and I went over to San Francisco to meet Schrader and his cast. When I arrived on set, Natasha came rushing up to me and threw her arms around me, thinking I was Cinque.

During those days in Berkeley, nobody knew what the SLA was really up to. In fact, for a while, no one knew just how large the group was. Were there only a hundred of them, or more than five hundred thousand? Richard and I had sat around in his apartment, wondering about how large they were. It was a revelation when the public realized that the group consisted of less than a dozen people.

So I agreed to help them, and got a walk-on in the film. I asked for $1,000, but was told that there was no money in the budget. As a counter-offer, Schrader offered me an interview and to buy me dinner at Chez Panisse. I figured I could sell an article based on his name (I couldn't) but the idea of dining at Chez Panisse I liked.

But all Schrader wanted to talk about was Richard's genius and his bad behavior.

"Every day," he told me, "there was trouble with Richard." One day Richard hit Yaphet with a chair on camera. Another day he cursed out Harvey Keitel. Schrader broke down and started crying, and Richard consoled him: "You pussy...are you gonna be a man or not on this movie?" Then he told me the script conference scene in detail, about how Richard pulled out a magnum and put it on the table.

The script conference motif illustrates how these directors wanted to work with Richard because he was a hot item, but they resented him at the same time.

For actors like Billy Dee Williams and Yaphet Kotto it was the same. They were trained actors who had gone the traditional way for success in Hollywood. Yet, here was somebody who was raised in a whorehouse and who had been kicked out of grade school after smacking his teacher, who was the real star.

Richard would tell me wonderful stories about working with Billy Dee and Yaphet Kotto. When an interviewer asked him how was it working with Keitel and Kotto, he was not dishonest when he said, "Keitel taught me about acting." Richard didn't see taking a chair to somebody's head as such a horrible thing, especially if you are learning great stuff about acting from them.

"We'd do a scene over and over." Richard explained, extolling his acting friend Harvey Keitel. "He'd say: 'Be that guy, till we've finished with the movie.'"

Harvey's bitterness lingered longer than Richard's. When I lived in Berlin in the 1980s, I would attend the Berlinalle Film Festival, where I once ran into Harvey Keitel. I told him that I was a friend of Richard who often spoke of him. "Yeah? What did he say? How's that white honkie?"

If we are able to look at the script conference as another part of the social drama that was the source of activity for Richard, we can better understand his art. The personal animosities grew out of the stupid, over literate prejudice that white directors like Schrader and others had of Richard. In the final phase of the social drama, all the dependent parts are put together, and the parties that didn't agree have to compromise.

After all the fights he had with Schrader, Kotto and Keitel, Richard was proud of the film and his work in it. He said, "I carry no negative shit about that movie." He said this in retrospect.

"I knew while we were doing it that we were doing something very good. The energy was right, and the actors are superb in terms of their art. There was a lot of pressure, and it was he hardest work I've ever done, but it came out well."

Richard's bodyguard Rashon Kahan played a vital role in saving the film. "Kahan had been hired to serve in the rather unusual capacity of both spiritual and athletic adviser," one journalist wrote, "and several times a week would he jog with Pryor to keep his body fit. They discussed faith and philosophy to get Richard's spirit in shape. He was constantly on the set; when Pryor would get upset, he'd take him aside and try to soothe him."[32]

Rashon not only saved the film by helping Richard, he also helped Paul Schrader. Schrader came down with a terrible stomachache. Rashon told me how he had made him some juices, and gave him some exercises and nursed him back to health.

Richard felt that the social drama was, in a way, necessary for his art. It was the canvas that he painted on. The problem was it was difficult to explain this to smart, overly educated guys like Schrader, Keitel, and company. Even though the film was a financial flop, making a dismal four million dollars, it was still a film Richard felt proud of.

CHAPTER THIRTY

HOW TO SHOOT A CAR

SOCIAL DRAMA NUMBER FOUR

THE DAY AFTER the New Year 1978, my phone rang. Thelma and I were still in bed but getting up for breakfast. We had been out at Richard's place for a New Year's Eve party. After midnight, we headed back to Hollywood and had a drink with Billy Preston.

It was Richard. "Hey, man, I'm sorry about last night," he muttered.

"We left around one o'clock."

"I acted a fool man."

"I wasn't there."

"Oh, man, thank you!" He said he was so happy I wasn't there to see him act a fool.

He wanted me to come out to the house, because All Well was coming out and he wanted me to be a witness to something.

I had read the LA Times headline: "Richard Pryor comedian, Freed on Bail on a Charge of Assault."

The article went on to say, "A warrant had been issued for the entertainer earlier in the day because of a shooting incident at his home, but he could not be found. No one was injured in the incident. Lewis Bobbit, an investigator, had said that the authorities would give Mr. Pryor until tomorrow to surrender before pursuing him."

The article went on to say, "A complaint against Mr. Pryor was filed yesterday by two women friends of the comedian's wife, Deboragh."

According to the *New York Times* : "Witnesses said the three women were ejected from the house by force, chased around the yard in a car by Pryor and shot at when they escaped into the street. Earlier, witnesses said Pryor had rammed the victims' with his Mercedes Benz five or six times.

Later that day, I went out to the house and found Richard in his office alone. Richard and Rashon were talking about what had happened that night. Richard was in a light mood. He and Deboragh and her two friends, Edna Solomon and Beverly Clayborn, had been sitting around in the morning when they got into a playful argument with Richard.

"I told them to leave," Richard told me. "Shit I wanted to go to sleep. And they kept ignoring me."

After telling them to leave they argued for about two hours. Finally, Richard ran them out of the house. His wife sided with her friends. Richard said, "I'll give you bull-dykin' bitches five seconds to get out of my house!"

Chasing them out of his front door, he got into his Mercedes and ran the women onto the lawn and rammed their Buick when they tried to drive away. They ran down the driveway and into the street.

"I rammed their Buick a few more times," Richard said.

Then he went inside and got his .357 Magnum. When they saw that he had his gun, the women scaled the eight-foot fence that walled in Richard's paradise. We all laughed at the description that Rashon and Richard gave of these half-drunk women leaping over that fence.

"I went outside and shot my Mercedes," he said. "I knew that Deboragh was going to take it and pick them bitches up in it."

After shooting the car in the tires, windshield, the mainframe, and then taking out the engine, he went inside.

"Fuck em," he said.

I was excited to hear Richard tell it. "What happened then?"

"The police came and arrested my black ass. I had to put up five thousand dollars bond and have a pretrial hearing in February. In the meanwhile, Beverly says she is going to press charges."

We were beginning to discuss what happened when the buzz on the entrance rang, and the person on the intercom was All Well.

Richard buzzed him in.

"Now what happens," Richard said. "This nigger is going to try to jack me up."

He said he had been drinking vodka. "These ugly bitches started fucking with Deb. I told them all to get the fuck out of my house."

Before he could go into details, All Well came in. After a few words of hello, All Well went into the pitch about the women wanting to sue Richard.

"They say you shot at them."

"So what are they saying? That I had a gun?"

"Well, you shot at them!"

"So how much they want?"

"Twenty five thousand dollars!"

Richard looked at me and winked.

"See, I told you that! This nigger is trying to extort me!"

"I ain't tryin' to do shit. I'm trying to prevent them going to the police and saying you shot at them."

"How much you getting to tell me this?"

"I ain't getting shit!"

"Man, I ain't going to let you extort me."

Richard dragged on his Marlboro. Then, he had an idea.

"I tell you what. You get them on the phone and let me ask them."

All Well telephoned one of the women. She came on the phone and Richard spoke to her.

But as Richard and Roshan related the story of what happened it appeared that it was All Well who ran Beverly out of the house and down the road to the gate. She and Edna Solomon jumped over the fence when the gate didn't open because they heard Richard firing the magnum.

"Did you tell All Well that I was to give you twenty five thousand dollars?"

"No," she said on the phone.

"See, Nigger, I ain't going to give you shit!" He slammed the phone down.

"If you weren't here, Cecil, that nigger might have jacked me up!"

Finally, in a huff, All Well left.

Richard asked me to go down to the courthouse in Sherman Oaks where the case was filed to see if they had put in the police report that he had a gun. What I could gather was that they had not said that Richard had a gun.

Michael Ashburne suggested the Richard turn himself in.

This was a social drama in full bloom. Star groupies like All Well, Beverly Clayborn and Edna Solomon played their parts in a script that nobody had written.

What was the redress? Wearing a neck brace, Beverly Clayborn appeared in Los Angeles Superior Court and sued Richard for 17 million dollars.

"If that bitch gets 17 million dollars from me, I'll marry her," Richard laughed when he heard that news.

Michael Ashburne got Richard to enter a no-contest plea. The assault charges were dropped. There was no evidence that Richard had threatened them with a gun. Richard was put on probation and ordered to do 480 hours of community service for a good civic cause. He was allowed to fulfill them by giving free concerts in order to pay his debt to society. By December of 1979, he had given five free concerts.

Even though the redress had solved the crisis, there were still the lingering emotional scars left because, when it was all said and done, Richard really did love Deboragh. He would tell me about her, and say things like, "She would say to me, 'Fuck you! I'm going to Paris.' And then she would go to Paris! Man, she was so beautiful. I love her for being so real." He told me, "I love my wife. I don't know how things go so out of hand."

After the incident, Deboragh McGuire Pryor moved out of his house and found an apartment in the Marina. She enrolled into the Junior College and accepted a settlement of $2,480 every month.

Around this time I was finishing up my novel, *Days Without Weather* (1983) and I gave it to Richard to read. It was a story about a young comedian, Jonah Drinkwater, and I had hoped that Richard would recognize himself in it. When I asked him for a quote he wrote the most touching response.

"There is nothing corrupt about his pride," he wrote. "I have never met a writer who loves his work as much as Cecil Brown. The humor, the warmth and even the smells are beautiful. The gentleness with which he handles the memory of his characters is great. I have had many 'Days Without Weather' too."

Despite his congratulating me on finishing my novel, the incident with Deboragh had put Richard into such a funk that he decided to put it into his On-Stage routine.

He went out to Debbie's House in the Marina. He was talking to her about reconciling. The two of them had had a bad turn, they agreed. As he was talking to her, though, he had a revelation, a kind of koan experience. In this experience, he was suddenly back in his house without remembering how he got there.

CHAPTER THIRTY ONE

LIMINALITY

A ROUND 1978, RICHARD went on tour with Patti Labelle as an opening act. This was not long after the car shooting social drama had calmed down. In March of that year, Richard and Jennifer had taken off for Nairobi, Kenya. He came back from Africa ready to go on tour.

With this tour that took him to twenty-two cities, he would have a chance to "clean it all up" by making a show out of the whole thing. His way to "reintegrate" the disparate elements was to throw them into the creative pot, go on stage and see what happened.

The first stop of the tour was up north in San Carlos at the Circle Star. He was family with this place, because he performed there back in the early seventies. That night, Patti Labelle opened for him. Paul Mooney, Roshan, and I were in attendance.

I came by Richard's suite around one o'clock in the afternoon in San Carlos as we sat in a room after brunch. I found him watching a football game with two women. As he was introducing me to the two women, I turned my tape-recorder on and sat it on the table. I was going to ask Richard some questions for an interview I had envisioned publishing in *Playboy* magazine. I had made out a list of questions I was going to ask Richard. I had intended to interview him for Playboy.

As I had turned the tape on, I forgot to ask Richard the questions, and later I forgot to turn the tape off. Today I have the tape, and it tells me more about Richard than I had anticipated in those days.

"Man, sit down." He introduced the beautiful chocolate colored sister next to him as Juliet, and her girl friend as Nidra.

"Juliet said something last night," he said. "You said that next to David Brenner, I was the funniest comedian you had ever heard."

Juliet laughed and tried to explain why she put David Brenner over Richard. Richard had opened for David Brenner back in the East at the Cellar Door.

"It was honest, what you said. I like that."

"She did this dance for me, man. It was incredible," Richard was saying. We met at an orgy," he said, "at Don Cornelius's house."

"I did that dance just for you," Juliet said.

"And then we went home together," Richard continued. "I liked her so much that we didn't even make love."

"That's right," Juliet confirmed for us.

"Matter of fact, we didn't make love last night!"

"Yes! That's right!"

"I don't think I could make love to you now." Richard said.

"Why not?" she asked.

"Because we know each other too well now."

A pause and we laughed.

"Then, she brought me this beautiful gift." He passed the "gift" over to me.

As we snorted and laughed and sipped drinks, the football game growled in the background.

After an occasional shouting for a player, Richard turned back to reminiscing with us about what was on his mind. What was on his mind was Deboragh. The whole incident of shooting the car, and being arrested, and then breaking up with Deboragh still weighed on his mind and soul. Even though the event had receded from the public median, he was still hung up about what had happened.

"I asked Deboragh a question," he said, and described how he had tried to reconcile with her. He went down to her apartment in Santa Monica and met with her. "I had one question that I was afraid to ask. It'd been on my mind for months."

"The only way these two women friends of hers could sue me is if they had Deboragh as a backup."

Then I said: "Oh, I see. She was a witness. She couldn't testify against her husband?"

"All she had to say was, 'I'm not going to go against my husband.'"

"What did she say?"

"She said, 'Richard, I'm not going to prejudice myself!'"

Then, hearing this, something happened to Richard. Suddenly, something picked him up and put him in his car and drove him home.

"I don't know how it happened," he said to the two women, and me "My car just drove me home. I was going in and out of consciousness."

He ended up at his house, convinced that he would never be with Deboragh again. This decision was made because he saw that Deboragh didn't really have his back. She didn't seem to understand how deeply she had disappointed him.

"Deboragh made me more mad 'cause she found out that I was really the man that she feared I was," he said, now accessing it all.

"She broke your heart," I suggested.

"No, I broke hers too. She saw too late that I was not afraid to tell the truth, even on myself." Told like a true shaman!

"I needed a woman who could stand up to the man I was," he said. As he had done in other relationships, Richard used the experience with Deboragh to measure his own failure. He wanted to grow and he wanted someone to challenge him so he could get better, more insightful about his life and art.

An important key to Richard's growth as an artist was this period of ruminating orally over a past event, and draining it of its significance.

Forbidden topics like his own demons he was prepared to talk about in private would be a kind of rehash for what he would talk about in public, as he did that night. This was the period of "rehearsal process," to use the term from the anthropologist Victor Turner.

Richard liked talking about his father—a subject that would appear that night in his routine. He was rehearsing with us.

"My father was good in the gym."

I had often talked to him about his father, starting as early as the Berkeley days, when we would sit in my apartment and talk about our upbringings. This time it was a bit different.

Like his father, he was good in the gym, too. He described a fight he had with a white guy whose parents were in the audience. He hit the guy and knocked him out in 22 seconds.

Then he segued into talking about his father's funeral. I had heard this before but this time he mentioned that his father was buried in the schoolhouse. His mother had his father's funeral in the gymnasium of the high school.

"It was a blessing for me," he said. "It helped me see how ludicrous life could be. I considered that my gift is looking at life from the point of view of how it was to see my father in that gymnasium."

"Was this the moment you would be a comedian?" I asked him.

"Yeah, I think so. I saw that would be my gift. The absurdity of it all."

For a moment, he was silent. I could see he was thinking about his father.

I was reminded of how the shamen worked. They would take a journey to find the lost souls of their patients. On his trip to find the lost soul of the sick person, the guardian spirit would encounter animals. Each person has an animal soul. This is the underlying meaning of Richard's skits with animals.

The conversations with me in private were part of a rehearsal process. Now, he would reenact his view of his father, for everybody to see. He was performing the ritual of a shaman looking for his soul.

At the funeral, Richard started telling jokes about death and laughter. Richard had made many jokes about death, most notable the "ultimate test" being death. In many African tribes, notably the Dogon, joking is permitted at funerals. Death is "cleansed by the joking," as Mary Douglass reported. [33]

So this was how Richard used the On-Stage drama to cleanse the social dramas in his life. The role of the jokester at the funeral could call attention to the deceased individual personally.

In Real Life, Richard paid attention to signs from the spiritual world. He told us that afternoon about how he carelessly connected words that came out of his mouth with the death of his mother.

"It was New Year's Eve," he recalled to us, "and we went to a movie. Then, we went to a restaurant. We came on the restaurant and I said, 'Long live the King, the Queen is dead!' When I got home I got a telegram that my mother had died."

He said that when his father died, they did an autopsy and found that he had 47 heart attacks. Then one time, he had a heart attack and they thought he was joking. He died on New Year's Day in 1967.

After the session ended with the girls, Richard took Rashon, Paul, and me to dinner before the show.

That afternoon, in Shoreline Circle Star Theater, with Patti LaBelle warming up the packed coliseum, he walked onto the stage, and talked about his father. When Richard went on stage that night, I stood on the sidelines and flipped on my tape.

The audience was rearing to go. The mood was intense with joy.

"Ladies and Gentlemen, Richard Pryor—"

He came on stage and looked at the audience with a long stare. He looked at a member of the audience at the Shoreline Circle Star Theater, which is on a dais that turns around.

As he had done that afternoon in the hotel suite, he started talking about his father. "My father was going to woods, you know. Rabbits would be fucking!"

"They could do anything but hunt. They run in eleven different directions. Going into the woods and rabbits would be fucking."

He imitates Rabbit. "Rabbit, can you hear me?"

Richard was like the shaman on his journey to find lost souls. Like the comic spokesman, who takes you out on a journey, his community, on a fantasy to bring out their demons.

"Out here you don't know why this has happened to you! 'Cause in the woods, your shit is quiet. And you don't know why it's happening to you. I want to shit. Or jack off. Fuck nature. Or shit on it." He pretended to sit on a log. "In the woods, your feet make that noise. And everything makes that noise."

He imitated walking the woods.

"You can't see it! The deers!" He imitated a deer turning his neck around. The audience even cheered that! They were so ready to face up to their shortcomings.

Then he took them on another journey. This time it was the horrible world of being beaten up as a child.

"My grandmother would whip my ass and make me say, 'Yessuh!'

"Whip me with a douche bag!"

He imitated her beating him. She would scream at him, "Don't you run!"

By putting his demons from his abusive childhood on display, he won their sympathy. Many of the audience could relate to what he was saying, even though they were not black.

"My father had such an attitude that he was afraid to hit me because he thought he would kill me."

The audience empathized with him.

"He had a temper like mine," he told them as he strolled across the big stage, "Yeah, he gave me his temper, but he didn't give me his other shit, his gentlemen part. I was going to have a fight with him."

He described a scene in which he confronted his father because he wanted to go out. "A girl done offer me some pussy tonight."

"Then, he hit me in my chest! Whoa! Then he grabbed me by my neck. And took a bottle and beat me! 'Black greasy mother-fucker. I'll kill you!'

"I said, 'Dad!'

"'No, you're a man!'"

A big applause swept the arena.

His father's brutality enlightened him, he said. "That shit helps me."

This was a replay of a horrid experience, a childhood trauma. Yet through his reenactment, Richard recreates it into something manageable. These beatings helped him reintegrate the fragmented life of his childhood. If the anthropologist Mary Douglass is right—that "a joke unleashes the energy of the subconscious"—then this was an excellent example of that.

He added: "I know how to deal with people!"

That's right.

The dais was turning. "People taking pictures and ain't got no film in the camera.

He caught the eye of a young girl. "She looks like she is used to sitting on faces!"

The audience burst into giggles.

"Y'all acting like you never did it. Ain't nothing like somebody sitting on your face! Yes I love it. That would get me off coke."

A heckler shouted something. Wheeling about, Richard went," Hey, man, you fucking up. I'm going to invite you to my next New Years Eve party!"

The audience focused immediately on the subject of the New Year's Eve incident. The bit about shooting the car had been so ingrained in the popular mind that by the time it came for him to do the routine on stage (like now), all he had to do was ask one question.

"Would you like to come to my New Year Eve's Party"?

He could also do it in an even more clever way.

"Have you ever killed a car?"

The audience cheered him and anticipated the retelling of the incident.

"Ever killed a car? I killed a Mercedes. I shot it so many times, it got good to me. My dick got hard!"

After the audience had quieted down a bit, somebody asked, "Why did you do it Richard?"

"What would you do if you were in love?"

This explanation had the advantage of concealing the real reason. As he told the judge, "What would you do if two bitches were trying to fuck your wife—and they were both ugly?"

To the audience that night, he told them that his wife was going to leave him, and he was in love with her.

"You may leave," he joked publicly, "but you will be walking."

He took out his magnum.

"I had a magnum...and the vodka, said, 'Go on! Shoot something else!' Then the police came. So I went in the house! They have magnum, too. And they don't kill cars! They kill *Nig-ARS*!"

That was the epithet he used to end the show. The contents of this show would later be filmed as *Richard Pryor: Live in Concert* in 1979. Much of it began as a reflection on his life that he bounced off a couple girls and me one afternoon in a hotel room.

I found a recollection on the Internet site that sums up what most people felt after seeing and experiencing Richard's live performance at the Circle Star Theater that night.

"I went to see Richard Pryor in concert at the Circle Star Theater in San Carlos, California," this anonymous person recalled.

"I was 18. He was rude, profane and sexist. But there was also this undercurrent of vulnerability and melancholy running beneath the comedy that exposed an uncanny understanding of human foible...I looked around me in that theater that night, in which I and my little friend Kathy were among a fair minority of whites, and I realized that they were all laughing uproariously together at this shocking dirty, racially charged stuff. As someone who grew up in a racist household...It was an enormous, overwhelming relief...He was right up front, saying it all clearly without restraint.... And it didn't matter. Nobody, not one person in that

*audience was angry. In fact not one person in that audience was anything but doubled over in paroxysms of hysterical laughter. He had our number, all of us, the whole flawed species."*34

This person expressed the sentiments of thousands who attended Circle Star Theater that night. As Richard's fame grew thousands were joined by millions who found in Richard's satire a universal laughter that united them and gave them relief from their own oppressive guilt.

Chapter Thirty Two

Albert Goldman

ONE DAY, NOT long after moving in with Thelma, I was walking down Hollywood Boulevard and ran into my old professor Albert Goldman.

"You know," he said, "I didn't recognize you behind that bush."

That bush he referred to was my mustache. It also referred to my manhood. When I was in his class at Columbia University, I was a mere boy, but now, as a writer in Hollywood living with a legend, I was a man.

I took my old professor to meet Thelma. When we walked into her apartment, he grunted. When he met Thelma, who was aware of his status as a writer, he grunted even louder.

We sat at the table over looking Los Angeles, sipped champagne, and rattled on about life in Hollywood. Professor Goldman was researching his book on Elvis. He had already written the book about Lenny Bruce, *Ladies and Gentleman, Lenny Bruce.*

Born in a small town in Dormant, Pennsylvania and raised in Mount Lebanon, Pennsylvania, he had been a small town boy like me. Like me, too, he had earned a master's degree in English from the University of Chicago in 1950 when I was a boy of ten. He had completed his Ph.D at Columbia University in 1961 on Thomas de Quincey, when I was entering college.

As an undergraduate at Columbia University, I had heard about him, as had all the hipsters who wanted to take a class from a professor who was a known wit. He did not disappoint. His classes were packed with the best students and each one ended with the students leaping to their feet and applauding him.

Professor Goldman had a solid reputation as a brilliant lecturer, and taken I had two classes with him at Columbia. One class was satire of the Roman satirists, Horace and Juvenal. I got a B+ on my paper on Juvenal, the great Roman satirist. For my senior paper, I needed a seminar, and I managed to get into his class on the Romantics. We had to read Thomas DeQuincey's, *The Confessions of an English Opium-Eater.*

I was pretty impressed to run into him in Hollywood. It was a time in my life that I still wanted to impress my teachers.

I wanted the professor to know that I admired his work, and that my success was due, in part, to his teaching. Was there anything I could do for him, to return the favor?

"Well there is one thing—"

"What is it?"

"You hear about free base—?"

"Would you like to try it?"

"Yes."

So I decided to turn my old professor on. It was such a small request. I was impressed that he made the connections between Dequincy's opium habits and his brilliant writing. Was there a connection between freebase and comedy? I was willing to find out.

We made the connection, which was not hard for me.

We had to go out and cop some coke on the street. I remember waiting at a gas station with Albert.

We cooked it up in Thelma's kitchen and smoked it. As we puffed, we would pause and discuss the effects.

"Reminds me of Thomas Mann's *Mario and the Magician.*"

The novella was about Cipolla, a hypnotist, who had a fascistic control over his audience. This was like a pop star like Elvis having power over his audience. Albert had just received a big advance to write a book on Elvis. The advance was a million dollars. He gave me a jacket cover of the book, even before it was finished.

I really got a kick out of shooting the breeze with my old Columbia University professor. He made me aware of something that I had not quite put into perspective.

Having been psychoanalyzed for over 12 years, he was familiar with Freud's theory of comedy. Remembering this, I looked at the book again to try understand what Richard was doing. In order to put Pryor's humor into a universal context—a context that might be a substitute for the missing political, historical, and racial one—in order to give them a handle, I read Sigmund Freud's *The Joke and its Relation to the Unconscious.* Freud divided jokes into two categories—the innocuous, or innocent, jokes and the tendentious jokes.

My professor told me his theory about show business. He said that the Hungarian Geza Roheim got it right; that comedians like Lenny Bruce were the shamans of our society. Like the shaman, he puts the audience into the area like the shamans use to do the tribe. By coaxing the audience with jokes he gets them to reveal their unconscious thoughts and repressed desires.

Once they are out there in the open, he blasts them with insults and jokes that are so terrible that it evaporates them. This operation gives the audience relief and they experience a catharsis—they are purged of their repressed evil. They are better equipped to go outside and fight the real demon in American society: reality.

From this moment on, I had a glimpse into the connection between Richard's art and the popular culture. As it turned out, he was the first professor to ever teach a course at Columbia University in popular culture.

It was so easy for me to see what Richard was driving at because I had spent countless hours watching him develop his craft. It wasn't only the craft that I watched develop, it was the ritual surrounding the everyday reality of the comedian that I had observed, too.

"Since you have Pryor's ear," he said to me, "You might tell him about Charlie Parker."

Then he laid some insight on me.

"Charlie Parker," he said, "according to my friend Ross Russell, Parkers biographer, Charlie Parker killed a man."

"A lot of people kill people," I said.

"No," he insisted, "This is different. It was covered up."

Goldman had dedicated his book on Lenny Bruce to his friend, Ross Russell, who had written the book on Parker called *Bird Lives!*

When I got back to Richard, I said that we should do the Charlie Parker story. He agreed and a contract was drawn up. I started to sketch out a film script on the life of Charlie Parker. Sometime in later years, Richard sold the idea to Clint Eastwood. The reason why the Parker story was important to me was that it was an idea that I gave to Richard who acted on it immediately.

CHAPTER THIRTY THREE

CALIFORNIA SUITE

SOCIAL DRAMA NUMBER FIVE

N 1978, RICHARD Pryor was assigned to play in Neil Simon's *California Suite*. He threw a party for the cast even before the movie started. Sheila Frazier, who played Bettina Panama in the movie, and who was a great admirer of his, was the hostess. She later became the president of Richard's film production he called Black Rain.

As the guests mingled downstairs, Richard and I were upstairs looking at the party below.

"Cecil," he said, drawing my attention to the big name actors and producers below.

"Yeah, man, can you believe this?"

He pointed out the various ones below. "That's Neil Simon over there."

I looked at the little be-speckled man with white hair. I knew who he was and his accomplishments.

"That's Ray Stark..."

I didn't know who Ray Stark was. Ray Stark, as it turned out, was the producer of *The World Suzy Wong*, *The Night of the Iguana*, The *Sunshine Boys*, and *The Goodbye Girl*, last year's big hit. He had produced films with John Huston and Sydney Pollack. He had produced 11 scripts from his friend Mr. Neil Simon.

That man next to him, he said, was the director of his new picture, Mr. Herbert Ross. Mr. Ross had directed *The Sunshine Boys*, too.

Mr. Ross, Mr. Stark, and Mr. Simon—these were the guys Richard was working with now. They had already made a dozen or so films together. Now they had some new blood, Richard Pryor.

We turned from the window.

"What about the Charlie Parker story?"

He smiled. "Warner Brothers is interested."

Since *Which Way Is Up?*, he had not talked much about the direction he wanted to go. I knew how much he loved the film, so it would be a matter of time before we did another film like that. In the meanwhile, the Charlie Parker story was my next goal.

Neil Simon had made it up the stairs and was in the room.

"Richard, you are a genius! You are the most brilliant comic in American today!"

Glasses went up in the air in an array of toasts.

His wife Marsha Mason surrounded him. Soon the room was full of the cast. Among them was Bill Cosby.

Seeing him surrounded by the big brass in Hollywood made Richard happy. When he was happy, he had a way of looking at you and winking.

That Monday, the movie began shooting on the lot. I was in Richard's dressing room in one of the trailers.

Robert Stevenson was making Richard up. He looked over and saw me paging through his *California Suite* script.

"What do you think of the script?"

He had given me the script to read. Neil Simon had adopted the screenplay from his play of the same title. The file is about guests staying in a suite in a luxury hotel.

It is about four couples who have experiences of four different attitudes towards marriage. It opened in June 1976 and is one of his least successful works both commercially and artistically, critics say. The story is told in four different unrelated stories. There's the couple dealing with infidelity (Walter Matthau and Elaine May); there's the couple dealing with divorce (Jane Fonda and Alan Alda); these's couple dealing with gay lifestyles (Maggie Smith and Michael Caine); and there's the black couple (Richard Pryor and his wife and Bill Cosby and his wife).

The problem with the black couple is that they are doctors. Bill Cosby had no problem playing a doctor, but Richard did. Nobody believed that he was a doctor. Neil Simon couldn't write the kind of dialogue that Richard could use.

"I think perhaps Richard was miscast," I heard Mr. Simon say one day on the set. Richard's solution was to spoof being an upper class doctor. This became embarrassing to watch because it was too phony.

The script was already dead, but adding Pryor didn't help any more. A big effort was made to make Pryor into a white Jewish character. This film marked the end of Richard's insight that writing scripts was the way blacks could conquer Hollywood. But David Franklin's influence was to get as much money as he possible could. That excluded any black writers working for Richard - even Richard himself. The only way he could make the most money was to yield the screen writing to writers like Neil Simon.

Ray Stark was one of the biggest producers in Hollywood. He went after Richard Pryor big time. After he produced the dude *California Suite*, he went on to get Richard in an even bigger dud, *The Toy*.

It was not long after the shooting began on the Columbia lot that some tension developed between the black actors and the director Herbert Ross.

One actress complained to Richard that director was not respectful, and that he was not as open to them as he was to the white actors.

Richard had gone to talk to the Director Herbert Ross, and told him that black actors were important too, even though they were not stars. What Richard had to learn, apparently, was that he was out of line to speak to him like that, so Herbert went to the producer Ray Stark.

Somebody knocked on the door of the bus and said, "He's coming!"

Richard and I were sitting in his trailer playing dominoes.

We could see Ray Stark as he came walking rapidly to our trailer. Smoke was blowing out of his ears.

By now from talking to Richard, I knew who Ray Stark was. Like a lot of these Hollywood producers, he had been part of an old boys club. He had worked as a agent representing Marilyn Monroe, Lana Turner, Richard Burton and Ronald Reagan. A major stockholder in Columbia Pictures had trained him, where he had produced over 17 movies.

He had clout that could break anybody in Hollywood. But could he break Richard?

As the stout Stark strolled across the lot, we could see him out of the window.

"Watch how I play this!" Richard told me. How he played it is an example of the Perfect Fool at work. The Perfect Fool is one who can use a nonsense action to expose the nonsense in the object of its attack.

"Richard!" Ray Stark begins, as soon as he opened the trailer door. As he raised up to our level, Richard looked at him and said, "Ray, are you out of your mind!"

Before Ray could say anything further, Richard pointed at the man's shirt.

Ray looked down at his shirt, expecting to see something. But that drew my attention to a wad of green money sticking out of his shirt pocket.

"Ray, you got to learn! You can't go around black people with money sticking out your shirt like that! This nigger, here," he said, pointing at me, "might be from the ghetto. He'll hit you across the head and take that money!"

Ray Stark looked down, and saw the money and looked over at me. "Yah, Richard, very funny!"

The laughter brought the temperature down, and before he knew it Ray Stark and Richard were discussing race. Richard had a chance to explain to him his side of the argument. Richard often used humor to undercut nasty situations.

This was another example of how Richard used comedy (On-Stage) poetics to influence the Real Life (RL) situation. After Ray Stark—one of the most powerful and the richest white men in Hollywood—had been calmed down, Richard began to tell him about how the director Herbert Ross was not being nice to the black actresses. Ray Stark promised Richard that he would look into it.

Since *California Suite* made over 30 million dollars for Columbia Pictures, the studios were more after Richard now than ever.

Ray Stark and his company tried to get another picture with Neil Simon writing another film for him. After Simon and Stark went down to the Comedy Store and saw Richard's act, they were full of ideas about screenplays.

Even though these old white guys were discovering the "black" Richard Pryor, it was too late for them. They had no idea of how to access Richard's humor. Since Richard has a bit in one of his routines about a "macho man," Simon came up with a script called Macho Man. It would star Richard and Simon's wife Marsha Mason.

They even came up with the ludicrous notion of redoing the *Odd Couple* with Richard and Bill Cosby, but nothing worked. Richard was aware of the problem, too. In order to get millions from Simon and Ray, he had to endure their untalented scripts and dumb ideas for films.

Chapter Thirty Four

Richard Pryor: Live in Concert

Social Drama Number Six

A COUPLE TIMES A week, Paul Mooney and I met with Richard to work on a new script. Paul Mooney and I had an office on the Warner Brother's Lot. We would arrive around eleven. I would drive my red convertible Fiat. Paul would always have flowers sent to the women who worked in the office.

I would take the notes we made with Richard and make copies while Paul would be on the phone arranging parties and ordering clothes.

In the days before, Richard depended on Paul for his fashion sense. Whatever the new look was, Paul would get it. Then Richard would get it. I'd follow suit.

One day during the script writing session, we talked about making a film about Richard's childhood. Richard wanted to do a film about his life. We had developed the idea that Richard would have an Alter Ego, somebody who was a reflection of his real self.

Richard said, "Let's work on the idea that just before he dies, his life flashes before him." Both Mooney and I nodded. We had heard this plot idea before. Richard had a bit of an obsession with the idea of one's life flashing before you just before some horrible incident.

One of the first stories he showed me back in Berkeley was called, "Uncle Sam Wants You Dead, Nigger," (published in *The Realist*), and contained that motif. In it, Johnny (character and the narrator) is shot in Vietnam. The film script opens just before Johnny dies. The rest of the script is about his life as it flashes before him, as a boy growing up in his grandmother's bordello.

On this particular day, as Paul and I were getting read for the script conference, Richard came in with a very pretty woman in her late twenties, and introduced us to her as Jennifer.

She was an actress and had been in *Sunshine Boys*. What we didn't know was that she had been working at Richard's estate as a painter, an assistant to the decorator who worked on Richard's house. He suggested that we think of a part she could play in his autobiographical film. I must have looked puzzled at that suggestion, because Richard gave me a sharp look.

Later, Paul said to me, "Don't say anything about Jennifer. He's in love with her and wants her around him all the time. Even in the movie."

From this point, I began noticing how much control Jennifer exerted over Richard's creative life.

A few days later, Richard invited me and Thelma out to dinner with Jennifer. Thelma and Jennifer got along. Thelma was a real diva and lived that life of a diva. Jennifer was not a diva. She had been in some movies but she rarely had a speaking part. Her strength was that she knew a lot of people in the business.

When we were alone and talked over some coke, Richard told me the back-story to Jennifer Lee.

After the fiasco with Deboragh, Richard said he decided to turn over a new leaf. He hired somebody to redecorate his house. Her name was Lucy Saroyan, the daughter of writer William Saroyan, the Armenian-American writer.

As a boy of twelve or so, I first encountered William Saroyan's short stories about a boy named Homer in the school library. Every story was short, funny, and so human. When I learned that he sometimes made as much as ten thousand dollars for a story in Life magazine, I vowed to be a writer.

So I would ask Richard, "What's Lucy like?"

"She's crazy," he would say.

"And?"

But all he would say was that she was a crazy white woman. I was disappointed that he didn't realize her pedigree.

I regret that I didn't meet Lucy. I knew that she was living with him for a few months while she was decorating the house.

Lucy's mother, Carol, divorced Saroyan when Lucy was quite young and married Water Matthau. Lucy appeared in several of Matthau's movies, such as *The Sunshine Boys*. Jennifer had met Lucy when Jennifer played a small part in *The Sunshine Boys*.

Jennifer also had a minor part in that movie: a non-speaking part, Helen Clark. Because of Richard, Lucy had been in *Greased Lightning* (1977) and *Blue Collar* (1978), where she played Harvey Kettle's wife. Jennifer had been in a thriller called *Rape Square: Act of Vengeance* (1974).

Richard would still talk about Lucy. Paul Schrader had promised her twenty five thousand dollars if she could get Richard to agree to be in *Blue Collar*. I know this much, because Richard told me himself about how he promised Lucy $25,000 but never paid her. Schrader did, however, give her a role in the movie playing Harvey Keitel's wife—the best role she ever played, as it turned out.

Richard hired Lucy do the interior designing of his Parthenia mansion. Lucy brought Jennifer along with her. Jennifer did some of the actual house painting and stayed out in the guest cottage.

When Lucy and Richard had a big fight and broke up, Lucy went to the guest cottage to wake Jennifer up to tell her that they were leaving, Jennifer said, "Go, ahead I'm staying."

"Jennifer stayed and never left," Richard would say, amused at how white women betrayed their friendship to each other over him.

It wasn't long after this that Richard announced that somebody was going to give him a hundred thousand dollars to make a film about his stand-up act.

He told me and Paul about Bill Sargent. He came over to Richard and we met him.

Bill was a big southern Texan with red hair. He explained to us how it would work. Richard would go on tour, but at the end of the tour, they would stage a concert. The concert would be filmed and distributed as a feature film. This was the first time Paul and I had ever heard of the film project that became *Richard Pryor, Live in Concert*.

The concert was staged in an auditorium in Long Beach, a half hour's drive outside of LA. The auditorium was in a white section of Long Beach, so lots of black people who came to see him were flooding into the white neighborhood, giving Richard a couple public chuckles over residential segregation that he would share with his hip audience.

Paul and I were in attendance the filming of this live concert. The film made 8 million dollars, more money that any of his other films. When it came out, Paul drew my attention to the fact that the first scene has Richard getting out of the car with Jennifer.

The concert film, which came to be called, *Richard Pryor: Live in Concert* was a recapturing of his social drama of shooting at the car. These social dramas lead to his getting a divorce from Deboragh.

We went to Chinatown to eat some Chinese food one night after the Comedy Store. As we walked to the Chinese restaurant through the parking lot, Richard saw my new red convertible Fiat and asked, "Whose car is that?"

I said, "Mine!"

He laughed, "Damn! You living large!"

That night was memorable too, because Richard later made a comic routine about the experience we had that night in a Chinese restaurant.

"We went to a Chinese restaurant about six months ago," he would say in the routine, "I saw the damnedest thing. A stuttering Chinaman!"

In the *Rolling Stone*, David Felton's insights into Pryor's new film, *Richard Pryor in Concert*, (1979) were great. He recognized that Richard could use the concert performance video format to reach the wide audience he sought his television shows, but was unable to reach because of the censors.

He was the shaman reaching out to his sickos—the masses of white people, black people, and the really rich white Americans who couldn't be reached because the TV censors forbid him from curing them. Now in this kind of genre, he could reach millions.

CHAPTER THIRTY FIVE

AT HOME WITH THE PRYORS

ONE AFTERNOON I went out to the Parthenia, in Northridge, to hang out with Richard.

"Sit down, Partner," he said in a Western cowboy voice, "and rest your feet."

He'd done the voice so well that he rewarded himself with a chuckle.

"What you want to drink?" he asked me as I dropped into the chair adjoining his desk.

I knew he drank vodka, and I asked for it myself. He told this to the maid, who was still standing waiting for her orders, and she went away.

The video was playing the Muhammad Ali Frazier fight. Every time the champ hit Frazier, Richard would jump up and laugh like an excited child.

"Get 'im, Champ! Look at that! Look! The champ's got 'im down. He's knocked the shit out of Frazier! Sonabitch! Is that it? That's it!"

He clicked the television off with a remote control and announced to me, "That's it!" and then said, almost to himself, "I've seen this fight a million times and each time I act just like a damn fool! It fucks me up to see anything that beautiful. I don't know why but it does!"

When he was watching the fight I took the time to take in the room. It was the sort of room that could easily be an office when the occasion arose, and with the carpeting and soft cushioned leather sofas and the video sets and sound systems (large impressive speakers stood ominously in the corners). It could easily be a playpen, a place to kick back in, entertains a half dozen intimate friends.

A long glass window ran along the wall, just behind Richard's desk, and overlooked the courtyard, the guest house, gym, and garage; on the opposite wall a window overlooked Moorish arches, a Spanish styled fountain, and a Moorish plaza.

This gave me an ancient, dark, soothing state of mind, like a bit of fantasy. This fantastic element seemed balanced with the realism everywhere in the room itself. African sculptures, some standing in one corner as tall as an average man, added to this fantastic mood.

Along the walls perpendicular and adjacent to the two walls just described were the many plaques given to him commemorating his genius in comedy, movie posters advertising his cinematic pantomime, pictures and photographs capturing his social life at parties, his personal life in Hawaii, and his family life with his children. Making her entrance and exit as quietly as an unearthly sprite, the Chicano maid brought my vodka. Suddenly, silently, there stood this tall, svelte, attractive woman beside Richard.

"Hi, Jennifer!"

"Hello." She smiled and extended a frail, suntanned hand for me to shake, which I did.

She was wearing a considerable bit more than a Grecian loincloth, dressed as she was in blue shorts and a pink tank top.

"Jennifer has decorated my house," he said.

"It looks great," I said.

"Thank you," she returned.

"We were talking about something," Richard said in a voice that succeeded in both informing her and dismissing her at once.

"I want to be with you, darling," Jennifer said and put her arm around his neck. I made a move in my chair that said, "If you want to be alone I can leave," but Richard made a gesture with his hand that said, "Don't move, I know how to handle this."

"I'm talking to a friend," Richard said with a slight annoyance in his voice.

Jennifer went back downstairs.

"You were asking me about Comedy?"

"Yeah—"

"Comedy," Richard went on, as if Jennifer hadn't interrupted him, "is about trouble. Everybody's in trouble, everybody's got to die. Death makes comedy possible! A comic makes people laugh at their problems and troubles, even though for that particular expression of the trouble, death is not so obvious, but it's always there."

"You don't think living with a white woman is a problem anymore?" I asked suddenly.

"No," he said, "I think we're beyond that now. Everybody feels that a black man and a white woman can have as many problems as anybody else."

A few years ago he told Hollis West that he had the right to date anybody he wanted to.

"And as much happiness as anybody else," I bravely commented.

"That's right," he said.

"But everything you do, records, concerts, films, are all about black people, and yet you don't live like a nigger, like the black people in your records or films. You don't live in a ghetto."

"Don't be naive, Cecil! Don't think like a white boy! You have a lot more at stake than that! And a lot less to lose than you think! Listen, you're about to fall into their trap of making you think that you can be safe in America! You can't, brother!

"If I shit in the street, tomorrow the headlines will say RICHARD PRYOR SHITS IN THE STREET! And on top of that they're making money off it too!"

"Yeah!"

"How about when I shot up my Mercedes? They didn't leave me alone then."

"But the studios will protect you."

"They do protect superstars, but since I'm a black superstar they could just change the rules. You see the situation I'm in?"

I looked at the chess set on his desk: he read my mind.

"You like that chess set?" he asked.

"Where's it from?" I asked, impressed, for each of the pieces had been hand-carved from wood like a miniature tribe of Zulu warriors, each piece representing somebody in the tribal army, with the King and Queen in these little skirts made out of straw and spears made out of toothpicks.

"We picked that up in Africa," be said. "Do you want to play some chess?"

"Sure."

"You have any money? How much do you have in your pocket right now?"

"I got some. Not much."

"How much you got?"

I took out all of my money and put it on the table. It came to something like five dollars and some change.

"Pick up the change," he said. "I'll bet you a thousand dollars against the five I'll beat you."

"Okay," I said, accepting the challenge as if it were fair. My role as ingénue was to pretend that anything he said or did was perfectly normal.

"Hello, baby," Richard said to Jennifer as she came into the room.

"We are playing a game of chess. Would you like some cocaine, dearie?"

She was so pissed that she was trembling. Jennifer shouted, standing right over Richard. "You've ignored me all evening! And I'm fed up with it, goddam it!"

"Baby, I'm sitting here enjoying a game of chess with my friend. Now what's the problem?"

"The problem is that you spend all your goddam time with your fucking friends and I wanna be with you!"

Her eyes were red with anger and it looked as if she'd been crying.

In a calm voice so different from the madman reputation his well-publicized fits of anger had earned him, Richard inquired into the origin of her dissatisfaction.

"All goddam evening, you've ignored me!" Jennifer stammered out, "And I'm sick of it!"

"I have to go!" I stood up.

Richard turned to me and explained they'd had a big party just that afternoon and she was understandably tired. I nodded in agreement. With the same calm voice, he turned to Jennifer.

"Jennifer, we had a party. Many people were here. Now you were downstairs talking with the ladies and I was upstairs."

"That's just it. I hated being downstairs talking with the ladies. You spend all of your goddam time up here enjoying yourself!"

She interrupted herself and picked up a box of cookies that were lying on the table. Holding the box over his head, she spilled the cookies over onto the chessboard.

"Now why did you do that?" Richard asked in a subdued voice. I expected, to be quite honest, for him to hit her upside her head, but he simply nodded his head.

"Because I wanted to! Damn you!"

Richard said, "Listen, I have a friend here and we are playing chess. Now if you wanted to tell me something that I did wrong, why can't you wait until my friend leaves, and then you can cuss me out or kick my ass or whatever. But I think you've gone too far."

"Fuck you, motherfucker, I'm leaving." A cursing white woman! She turned and started for the door.

"Wait a minute," Richard called out, still in that cool voice. "If you want to leave, why don't you do it right?"

He got up and went over to the wall and took down the picture of Jennifer in the role of Antigone, where she had a toga draped over her shoulder in the picture.

He took it down.

"This is the only thing you've given me in all the time we've been together."

He threw it across the room, and the glass shattered at her feet.

"Take that with you, if you want to leave," he said calmly, sitting back down in front of the chess game.

At this point I thought, this is a trick! A joke they both are playing on me! Any minute they'll turn to me and say, "Ha! We caught you, didn't we?" Knowing Richard's reputation as a prankster I pictured some weird put-on. But if this was what was happening, they deserved the Academy Award for their acting, so convincing it was.

Jennifer picked up the picture up and started for the door, but Richard picked up a photo on the desk.

"Oh, I forgot something." He threw it against the wall. "Take all the shit you gave me, okay. And get out of my life. I don't love you anymore. Do you understand?"

Jennifer stood there looking at him, her face red and streaked with tears and anger.

"You've fucked up our chess game, you've poured cookies all over my head. Look, Jennifer, you don't have to abuse me like that. I know how to abuse Richard. I'm very good at self-abuse. After all, I've done that all my life: abuse myself.

"Look," he said. He took a pencil can and knocked it against his head. "Look, I'm very good at self abuse!"

Was this not comedy? I was dying with laughter but I held it in.

"Bastard!" Jennifer spat at him and went out the door again.

He turned his attention back to the chessboard.

All the pieces had been covered with cookies. I started to pick the pieces of crumbs away from the pieces.

"Just look at that? What kind of person would do that?" he asked me.

"I think I should be leaving," I said. But I still wanted that thousand dollars because I knew I could beat him at chess.

"Leaving? Why? Because she's acting a fool? No, man, you're my friend. I want you to stay. I need for you to stay, Cecil. This bitch is trying to make me hit her. If I hit her police will be up here in a minute. I don't want that. If the police come up here I'm going to the penitentiary. She knows this."

Jennifer reappeared in the door. She had been in a film called Act of Vengeance, in 1974. The plot of the melodrama was that a man in a hockey mask rapes a woman named Linda. She finds that a few other women have had the same treatment. Together they form a squad that starts looking for the man and also changes the mind of would-be rapists. Jennifer plays one of the women.

Maybe she was acting out the lines of the movie character she had internalized?

Both Richard and I sat silent and watched her. She came across the room and over to us and swept the chess pieces off the board.

"Bastard!" she announced and started back for the door.

"No. Jennifer, I've had it with you. You took your clothes off in front of my son. My son came to me and he was crying and I said what's wrong but he wouldn't say anything. I made him tell me, Jennifer. He said you came out of your bedroom naked. You showed my son your pussy, woman!"

"And you beat my face in," Jennifer accused him. I realized that they were both showing off right in front of me to embarrass the other one.

"And you spit in my face and called me a nigger!" he shot back.

She came back. "And you beat me up!"

"Well, just leave. I told you to leave. Now leave. I've done all I could for you, just leave. You would never treat Warren Beatty like you treated me. Or any of those other white boys you star-fucked."

He turned to me.

"Man, can you imagine her doing that to Warren Beatty?"

I said, "No!"

That was the first time Warren Beatty's name had come up since I had introduced Richard to him back in San Francisco in 1971. I heard through the grapevine that he and Warren had seen each other. But it wasn't until many years later, in 1992, when Jennifer had published a tell-all book, Tarnished Angel that the full extent to which she and Warren had been lovers was revealed. She told Geraldo Rivera on a TV show that she had been in bed with Warren in 1971. "His girlfriend was Julie Christie at the time. This is in 1971." This would be about the time Richard and I met Warren in San Francisco! She had already been sleeping with Warren - about nine years before Richard had even met her!

She went on to tell Rivera that she was sleeping with Waylon Jennings and Willie Nelson in the same night, even though they were both married. In fact, she was sleeping with Richard while he was still married to Deboragh. "I felt that Richard shot the car so that he would end that relationship and start the one I was waiting and hoping he would start, which was mine-ours."

"What's right, because she doesn't respect me? I'm still a nigger to her. She told me so herself."

"No!" I replied, mouthing incredulous lines I figured my part called for. I was like some weird straight man. "She called you a what? Where?"

"Let's get a drink!" In spite of all this, or perhaps because of it, Richard insisted on a drink. Trailing along behind him, I followed my host into the kitchen, where he took down from the cabinet a fifth of Stolichnaya vodka. No sooner had he poured us out a good portion in two tumblers than Jennifer appeared in the doorway. This time she was carrying a broom. With the broom as a weapon, she attacked us. We fell backwards through the dining room, falling and holding onto the vodka; we managed to make it back to the bedroom, where Richard locked the door.

"That bitch was trying to kill us." He laughed. "But we were trying to be cool, huh? Look," he said as if he'd thought my thoughts, "you're still holding your glass! Ha, ha, ha!" He laughed in that particular way of his. "You didn't even spill a drop!"

He was so busy telling me about my glass that he had forgotten his. He was holding his high over his head like Charlie Chaplin did in his films City Lights, as the waiter with the precariously balanced tray that keeps its equilibrium despite a knock down and drag out fight that takes place in the saloon.

"You know we some funny motherfuckers," he said, laughing deep inside his chest. "We try to be cool out here in Hollywood, but where we come from we've been hurt and abused, man. We never had a lot of liquor to spill. If we'd been white boys, we would've dropped the glasses and poured the liquor out. But we niggers, although we don't want to be, but way down deep in our souls we are still niggers who can't afford to spill the vodka. If Jennifer had a gun and had shot and killed us, we would've fell over each other and died, but when the undertaker came to get our dead asses, he'd have to take the vodka glasses out of our hands and pour the vodka out because there'd still be vodka in them. And some other nigger assistant undertaker would sneak up to our bodies when the white undertaker wasn't looking and steal that vodka. 'That's good vodka,' the nigger'd say. 'Gonna take that vodka home! Sheet, them niggers dead, they don't know no difference.'"

Richard was up, faking the part of the white undertaker, the black assistant undertaker, and the two stiffs (us with the vodka glasses) all at once. 'Mister White Man, hehehe, you think we oughta take dese glasses outa these niggers' hands?' 'Naw, fool, I believe these boys' family gonna pay fo' the vodka, niggers gonna die with liquor on they bref!'"

I laughed hard, briefly feeling relief from the insistent, pounding, urgent knocking at the door. Apparently she'd taken off her shoe and was applying the heel of it to the wooden door. But Richard went on talking as if nobody was there, and I went on pretending that I didn't hear anybody either. His genius for making humor out of any situation, I learned that night, was his protection against hurt; it was his camouflage technique, the yellow and black spots on the butterfly's back that allows him to blend into the yellow leaves and black tree bark and prevents the predator from seeing him and devouring him in one hysterical gulp. His humor was his mimicking device, his cloud of black ink that the octopus uses to hide behind when an enemy attacks.

Boom! Boom! Boom! Jennifer was knocking on the door with something else. We couldn't figure out what it was she was knocking with this time but Richard, momentarily forgetting that he was supposed to be ignoring her ass, tilted his head back into a listening stance like the famous doe deer in one of his bits. *Boom!*

Boom! Boom! Richard looked at me with an expression on his face that said, What the fuck is she hitting the door with now? But he silently let the question drop and took another hit of the coke and passed it to me and I took a hit.

Krack! Krack! Krack!

Jennifer's knocking was gathering momentum now. Boom! Boom! Krack! Now she had picked up something else to hit it with. Richard looked at the door again.

"If I opened that door," he cut himself off. "That door is the door to the penitentiary."

Krack! Krack! Krack!

Richard said, "I had a dream about Jennifer. In this dream she's all in white and leads me with a blindfold on into hell. I take off the blindfold and see I'm in hell. I say to her, 'Why did you lead me here. I've been in hell before, and I'm used to it. I expected better from you.'"

"That was Dante's trip," I said. "Beatrice leads Dante out of hell."

"Dante?"

"The thirteenth century poet. He wrote his dream up as a poem called the *Divine Comedy* in three parts. He had this broad, Beatrice, that led him around through places, except he wasn't blind."

"But a fool like me?"

"Yeah."

"Well, I had the same dream. I'm going to use it in my movie, too."

He got up and went to the door, put his ear to it quietly.

"I think she's gone," he said, opening it just a little.

I expected to see Jennifer dead at the door from having committed suicide. But when be opened it she wasn't even there.

"Let's take a walk," he said.

As we came down the long hallway, Richard peeped into one of the rooms, then another.

He came to one door that was half closed, pushed the door open quietly, and walked in. He turned and beckoned silently for me to come see. I went over to the door and looked in. It was a bedroom and on the bed was Jennifer. She'd curled up in the bed without taking her clothes off. Her face was as quiet, and calm and beautiful as a sleeping child.

Richard reached down and kissed her on the cheek so softly that she didn't wake up. In her clenched hands was the Sukuma African sculpture. Now we knew what she had been using to bang against the door with.

We walked out by the swimming pool and we looked over at the tennis court.

As we passed it, Richard said, "I don't know why I built that tennis court. I can't stand the game now. We walked around the swimming pool. The morning light was beginning to glow, a morning bird chirped, a rooster crowed. Richard looked at his watch. "That rooster," he said laughing, "is never on time."

"I lost the game."

He laughed, "I had to forfeit it."

We walked on toward my car. "Do you realize we stayed up all night?" I asked.

As a reply he suddenly laughed. "I'm laughing at myself," he said. "I'm trying to figure out how to clean up the fact that you've seen my old lady pour cookies on my head." We both laughed.

"I've been wondering how I was going to explain to you, how I could say what I said to her and then say I loved her, but I see I don't need to explain it to you."

He looked at me and gave me a hug. "We're friends," he said.

"I know," I said. "Good morning."

"Good morning to you, Cecil."

I got in the car and pulled out of the yard. He was going into the house. He waved, I waved, and I went out of the gate. The world was just waking up when I pulled out of the gate and onto the highway. A blueness was giving way to a light gray haze. A few more cars hit the road carrying people to work.

I felt exhilarated, not tired. Looking back on this now, I realize that that evening was the first time I'd laughed in a long time. True, I had laughed at my friend's misfortune, but I had laughed at it with my friend; and he had laughed at my misfortune with me. What this meant for me was that I was developing my sense of humor; what it meant for my friend was that he was learning to master his.

I laughed, thinking about him hitting himself across the head with that can. And the way he so sincerely cast himself as more sinned against than sinning!

What Richard did that evening was let me see the inner conflict in his soul. He knew that Jennifer was bad for him, yet he loved her.

Like he did in his spiritual journeys in which he used women to find himself, to be able to take away the male armor that prevented him for realizing his full potential, so Richard had used Jennifer to get to a deeper self.

After Richard told his psychiatrist, Dr. Alfred Cannon that he preferred the world of drugs to reality, because he was disappointed with reality.

"How can you give up on reality, when you haven't been to Africa?" the psychiatrist asked him.

Good question. So Richard took off for Africa, Easter, 1979. He went to Africa with Jennifer, and came back after four weeks.

The psychiatrist was right, the trip did open him up to reality. But it also had another unexpected affect: it opened Richard up again to the disappointing side of reality.

Once Richard began to look around after his trip to Africa, he didn't like what he saw.

For one thing, he and Jennifer began to fall away from each other. He gave up the N word, but still held on the B word. This all-black country in which blackness was not an issue intrigued him, and the trip, according to one friend, moved him profoundly. Whether it affected his subsequent behavior is anybody's guess, but when he returned, things apparently began falling apart. He became depressed, erratic, and volatile. At some point, he and Jennifer broke up. More and more, those close to him feared he was turning his attention to two old friends: cocaine and alcohol.

Most of all, he seemed painfully entrapped by his own guilt, a guilt fed not just by his immediate weaknesses, but by a much more serious and perplexing offense—the crime of being Richard Pryor.

The personal drama took over his interest in movie scripts. He was so much in a movie script, complete with a *dramatis personae* that was a living tableau that he forgot about the actual movie scripts he was suppose to read.

During that week, I left Richard one night, and he followed me in his sports car, an Italian sports car. We both drove down sunset to the Sunset Towers where I was staying with Thelma. I was surprised to learn that he was on his way to see Patricia. Patricia was Richard's old friend from when Richard lived in Berkeley. She was a PAN-Am stewardess at the time, but had since settled in Hollywood. She met Billy Dee Williams through Richard; and despite a falling out with Dee Williams over her, Richard was still seeing her.

One evening, we were all at Richard's- including Billy Dee Williams and Patricia. Paul Mooney must have been there, because when somebody came back in the house and said that Billy had been trying to teach Patricia how to drive the car and had crashed into the ditch, Paul said, "He must have been showing her how to use the stick shift!"

CHAPTER THIRTY SIX

STIR CRAZY

SOCIAL DRAMA NUMBER SEVEN

THE SUCCESS OF *Richard Pryor Live in Concert* (1979) was incredible. Grossing over eight million dollars, it also opened Richard's eyes to the possibility of making a film based entirely on his stand-up act. This was a new genre that didn't involved the expenses of a cast of actors or production costs spend on scenery and locations.

Rolling Stone reporter David Felton loved the concert film, but became more interested in Richard's personal life. He especially liked Richard's change in attitude towards women.

Then Felton announced, "Today Richard has a new woman, actress Jennifer Lee (she's the one with Pryor during the opening credits of the movie), and things are looking better all the time."[35]

He's resolved his problems with the law in the case of the car murder. While there are characters Pryor did before that I prefer to almost anything in the movie—his preachers, drunks and junkies, and a wonderful old man named Mudbone — this film has another dimension; it's as if Pryor, in examining his life during this chaotic years, has grown.[36]

Then, he recites some examples of what he means. You would have thought from his selections that Richard had really made a big change. "At one point he suggests that one should have pussies that lock up,' so they can catch rapists."

That phrase and line of thinking is straight out of the script that Jennifer starred in. It was called *Act of Vengeance* (1974).

One day we were sitting in his office and the phone rang. It turned out to be Miles Davis.

"It's Miles!"

He cupped his hand and said to me. "He thinks I have Cecily Tyson up here!"

That October, He had finally started *Bustin Loose,* a comedy.

Richard plays Joe Braxton, an ex-con who has to drive a bus-load of kids across the country, under the supervision of Vivian Perry, played by Cecily Tyson.

Richard had told me this story when we were back in Berkeley, when he first called it *Family Dreams.*

He hired Oz Scott, a young black director, from New York. The studio was reluctant to give him a chance, but Richard stood up for him.

The problem was that as soon as Oz got into trouble, the studio turned to Richard and blamed him.

The movie *Busting Loose* was on hold for months now. Some of the film had been shot already in Montana. He told me he had ad-libbed through the script and it had exhausted him. He said that Cecily Tyson was nervous at first, because he improvised so much. But then she had gotten used to it and he liked that.

Then, he went back to the phone, "Naw, Miles, Cecily ain't here! What? Okay? Okay, good day to you too!"

He put the phone down and rolled with laughter. That was Miles Davis!

He would be sitting in his bed with his base pipe. He was fighting with Jennifer, calling her on the phone. She would come over for a while, and then they would fight, and he would go back to the base pipe.

Richard had just gotten the part of Harry Monroe in a movie with Gene Wilder.

We were celebrating. I was thumbing through the Stir Crazy script.

Meanwhile, the competition was gaining ground. Hannah Weinstein, always with a literary bend, hired Bruce Jay Friedman to write a film based on an article he had published in *Esquire*, about a rodeo and a bunch of New York guys who tried to be cowboys.

You would consider yourself a smart guy or gal, if you knew who Bruce Jay Friedman was. His first novel, *Stern* (1962), was a literary sensation and introduced the comic type, the *schlemiel*, into the American Literary scene. Albert Goldman had profiled him for the New York magazines.

I remember Jay Bruce Friedman very well from the days when I frequently Elaine's, the literary hangout on the upper Eastside. Bruce was a running buddy with Norman Mailer's and Frank Conroy. Conroy, the author of the brilliant autobiography *Stop-Time*, and I became friends and he introduced me to the other guys.

With an over-sized head of curly hair, Bruce was always funny, and a smart writer. Hannah Weinstein purchased his Esquire story about these city dudes who wanted to be cowboys. Then she wisely hired him to turn it into a screenplay called Stir Crazy for Gene Wilder and Richard.

In writing it for the screen, Bruce made one of the characters, Skip Donahue, into a writer; and he turned the other character (Richard's character), Harry Monroe, into a waiter. On their way out West, he has them get stuck in some western town, broke.

In order to get money to continue the trip, they perform as two chickens for a bank promotion. After they take off their costumes for a lunch break, two men steal them and rob a bank. They are accused of a crime and sentenced to 125 years in jail. They find a way out of the prison, and manage to tickle the funny bone in what turned out to be a likable light-hearted comedy.

At the time, Richard had the script. He was excited that Sidney Poitier was going to direct it.

"Man, I'm going to be working with Sidney!"

I was excited, too. Because that meant I would get to meet Sidney Poitier.

In terms of writing, Richard had told the studios that he was writing a film all by himself. But after a few months, he called Paul Mooney and me back in.

Two or three times a week we would have a conference with Richard. The whole movie set of *Stir Crazy* was in Arizona, but some of the interiors were shot on Columbia Studio lots. When I went out to the studio see Richard on the set, he told me about the watermelon seed incident.

On the *Stir Crazy* set, one of the guys threw a watermelon seed on Richard by mistake.

Apparently, the crew was bored and wanted to get back to LA, where most of them were from. They blamed the delay on finishing the movie on because Richard was late to show up a few times.

One of the crewmembers was eating a watermelon as Richard was approaching him. He spit the seeds out at Richard's feet.

"I left and came back," Richard told me, laughing, "with two forty-fives!" When it was reported that he had had shown up with two guns, the production was closed down until Richard could be brought under control.

Richard was a good actor, and equally brilliant off the set, too. They gave him a million dollars to come back and finish the movie.

He told Rashon, "That's what I wanted to happen. I knew them motherfuckers would pay."

It was an act.

But David Felton, *Rolling Stone* reporter, put it differently. [37]

During the shooting of the film by Sidney Poitier, there had been a series of disturbing incidents, culminating when some cameraman apparently dropped a piece of watermelon at his feet.

Whatever way it was reported, the message was the same: Richard got an extra million dollars for being insulted by the cameraman.

One day Richard invited me to meet Sidney Poitier.

After we were introduced, we sat at a table.

"How does Baldwin do it?" he asked me after Richard told him that I had met James Baldwin.

Sidney said he couldn't do what Baldwin did.

"What was that?" I asked.

"I couldn't live the life of an expatriate."

We were puzzled by this.

Poitier looked at me.

"I could never understand why Baldwin left this country," he said.

"I could," Richard said.

I joined in with Richard.

"Well, you leave your country," Sidney went on, "and all the family you have, just to live in another country!"

The bohemian life did not appeal to him, even though he had made a film about it with Paul Newman called *Paris Blues* (1961).

How different Sidney was from us! Although America was his adopted country, he seemed to feel more at home than Richard or I did, to say nothing of Baldwin.

I asked Sidney Poitier for an interview. I called him on the phone. My first question was, "Why have you failed to be a male superstar. Does it seem that Richard Roundtree has taken that role?"

"Listen, I only gave you the interview because I thought you were intelligent." He was very offended. He didn't agree with me that the new black hero had change and that this change centered around new faces like Richard Roundtree, Billy Dee Williams, and Richard Pryor.

Not long after this interview, the filming of *Stir Crazy* finally stumbled to completion; and Richard was exhausted. He played a couple quick roles in succession, though, because he was on a roll. He played "God" in a cameos in *Wholly Moses.* Then he put away his grievances towards Mel Brooks and performed another cameo in Brooks' *A History of the World, Part One* as God.

He didn't know which way was up in June of that year, right after all these great activities on the sets.

But all his plans were going to be put on hold, for a few weeks later; he had the big fire and almost burned himself to death.

Chapter Thirty Seven

Freebase Inferno

Social Drama Number Eight

I T WAS THE night when I left Richard and Rashon watching television. As I remember from seeing him during our writing sessions, he was depressed mainly over his relationship with Jennifer. I would sit with him, too. Richard's "sessions," as we called them, lasted months. When he was in one of his sessions that is when he would be zonked out on freebase and would think that these dolls were alive.

I got a phone call from Rashon that Richard had been taken to the hospital because of an accident "with fire." I drove out to Richard's house in North ridge. Roshan opened the gate and the place was empty. We stood on the back steps that lead up to the house.

"We were watching a television show," Rashon explained to me.

They were watching a show on television about monks who set themselves on fire. Richard was sitting on his bed. He was wearing a polyester shirt and khaki pants.

Rashon told me he had mentioned to Richard how hard that must be to endure. Richard said, "Yeah, especially the first part, when you first strike the fire to you!"

Thinking nothing of it, Rashon went to the kitchen to get something. Not long after that, not more than five minutes, he saw a ball of fire coming after him. He sidestepped the flaming ball and realized it was Richard. By that time, Aunt Dee, Richard's Aunt who was living with him at the time, ran out and put a blanket over her nephew to damp out the flames.

Throwing the blanket off, Richard ran down the street, with his aunt Dee after him. He ran down the streets, as somebody called the police.

Before police came, Rashon took out any incriminating evidence that he had been freebasing. He found a half-gram of cocaine and took it to a friend so that the only thing left a bottle of 151 rum. When I arrived, Rashon wanted to show me what happened. He took me to the back of the house. We stood in the driveway, looking south towards the gate and beyond to Parthenia street.

"A patrol car spotted him running down Parthenia Street," Rashon said pointing down the driveway to the gate.

When the police Officers Richard Zielinski and Officer Carl Helm arrived on the scene, they saw a man running down the street in flames.

"Hey—isn't that Richard Pryor?" Officer Helm asked his partner.

They drove up alongside Richard and asked him to slow down.

While Helms went to the police car to call for more help, his partner Zielinski went running after Richard. Not to shoot him, as might have been the case if he was not famous, but to engaged him in a dialogue that would be the envy of a Hollywood screenwriter.

"I think you ought to stop," he told Richard. "We've got to get you to a hospital." He took him by the wrist.

"I'm going to the hospital," Richard answered. "Just show me where the hospital is. I'll get there."

"You can't walk there. Why don't you just stop and wait for the ambulance?"

"If I stop, I'll die," he said, and kept running.

Richard was running along the street loudly shouting, "God, please give me another chance!"

He pleaded publicly for forgiveness. "Lord, please give me another chance."

The L.A. police officer Zielinski seem to agree that Pryor got what he deserved. Stripped of his pride, and his skin, he told Zielinski "This is the way the Lord is paying me back."

Richard carried on a conversation with the policeman about God. He kept saying that he had "really screwed up." He addressed God directly, "God, I really screwed up, Man. I fucked up. Please give me a second chance. I know I did wrong, but there's a lot of good in me. Haven't I brought happiness to anyone in this world?"

Instead of an answer from God, it was the cop who spoke up and tried to reassure him. "Sure you have brought happiness to people in the world," Zielinski said, "We all love your stuff."

Although, Richard claimed that he set himself on fire by accident, he later confessed the truth, but only on-stage. While he concocted a story about rum exploding, it was only when he was recreating the incident On-Stage that he told the truth, "My bitch [Jennifer] left me and I went crazy freebasing for eight months straight."

In social dramas, there are no scriptwriters. Unlike the on stage drama, where Richard can assign roles and create characters, in the social drama, society creates the characters and assigns roles.

When I left Rashon that day, I was depressed. I had no idea if Richard would be announced dead in the next hours or days. This was the second time I experienced having him leave me forever. The first time was when I was flying back to Oakland after the release of *Which Way Is Up?* And somebody had read the article in the *Rolling Stone*, and told me that Pryor was dead. Now that old dreaded feeling came back. Would Richard survive this time? I was nervous when I dove back to Hollywood to await the news of his fate.

CHAPTER THIRTY EIGHT

CONTROLLING THE CRISIS

THAT TUESDAY MORNING, David Franklin took the first flight out of Atlanta. I was depressed and went home. There was no way to find out what condition Richard was in.

They searched the house. Rashon had taken the half-kilo of cocaine to a friend who lived not too far away. Narcs were looking for any evidence.

That next day, Wednesday, David organized a press conference and news story based on the fact that the police did find rum and broken glass, but no drugs.

With that out of the way, Franklin and I sat down late Friday night in the sumptuous living room of Richard's overlooking the San Fernando Valley, and discussed Richard Pryor. David Franklin glanced back at the room of journalists. David Felton, Jim Brown, and some other black actors were there.

"Richard is doing well," David Franklin told us, "But he wants me to give a true account of what happened." His condition was still serious and he was not out of the water yet.

This was a lie, but it was as much you could get of the truth in a social drama (Real Life).

David Felton asked me what I thought. I was so depressed that I could only shake my head. What bothered me was that nobody mentioned that he was freebasing and had an accident. To light the cocaine in the glass, you had to heat it. First, people would use a lighter, and then they got into bigger lighters, and then bigger ones. Finally, they were using torches, the kind for soldering model airplanes. Richard had a lighter that was more like a flamethrower and I was always very careful when I used it. I could imagine that if his hand was shaky, as it usually was, he might have ignited the rum that way.

"I don't believe it." Felton chuckled.

Franklin went on to give a startling personal view of Richard. I hated to hear how he was going to psychoanalyze Richard. But David was his spokesman. He was careful how he handled this situation because Richard's career was on the line (if he survived).

"Richard is a supremely gifted and talented person," he began, choosing his words carefully, "who does not believe he should be. Know what I mean? He does not believe he should be, and that, I think, is the root cause of a lot of his problems.

"He's obviously had several relationships with women that have turned out badly because, I believe, he does not believe that a 'good' women, whatever that means, will put up with him. That's what he wants, but he's scared to seek that.

"He's a person of supreme intelligence—you can see that by his material, by his insights. But because he formally has only a ninth grade education, he believes he's not bright."[38]

And these misgivings, Franklin indicated, are magnified because Richard is a visibly successful member of an oppressed race.

"I mean, Richard is the greatest comedian in this country, in terms of modern comedians, black or white, name 'em all. They know it and he knows it. And yet—it's a guilt thing. He does not believe that he should have so much, and so he will try to give it away, to reject it. He will constantly try to prove to people who he should cut loose from the vultures, the hangers-on that he's one to them. And he's not. And the only thing they can do is bring him down." [39]

What he seemed to be getting at was a pattern of self-destructiveness. "Still, didn't the shit around him," I asked Franklin, "justifiably precipitate many of Richard's actions?

"I have found," he said, "that generally when Richard has gone off, some big thing preeminently reported in the news or at some type of social setting where there're people, and they say, 'Oh my God, he's crazy, he's gone off"—on ninety percent of those occasions, there was cause for him to go off. But as I told Richard, what he has to watch is *where* he takes it."

"How far," I asked, "can Richard take it, though? And how many chances does he get to find out? Will the cycle be unbroken, despite the flames of that Monday night?"

"If this doesn't do it," he said, "if this doesn't do it." Franklin leaned forward and whispered, "Will anything do it?"

Like the policemen, David Franklin, the lawyer, was suddenly a member of the star-groupers.

No sooner than David had sat down, Jim Brown stood up.

"Richard is a genius," he started. There was another member of the star-groupers. "His childhood is another thing to consider."

He said that he and Richard had much in common. Both come from broken homes, both know the transitory illusion of celebrity and more importantly, both are black. The difference between them is that Richard is a little fragile.

"Those of us who are from broken homes, we want love without conditions. If you grow up without that [kind of] love, then you have to fortify yourself. Because if you don't, you are not going to survive. Pryor has proven himself in the professional world, because that's satisfying in a great way, but it doesn't satisfy the basic needs."

Felton asked him if Richard loved himself.

"Well, you get broken down, man." Jim said.

"At birth, you come into insecurities in your family. You come into a hypocritical society. They praise the chumps and kill the real heroes. They killed Malcolm X, they killed Paul Robeson, and they killed Nat Turner, and they make heroes out of cats that don't do shit. I mean, you don't come into that shit brilliantly and fortified; you come into it fragile. And every day, you're fighting your way out of that shit to get to some level of truth. Warriors have a difficult time. And basically, Richard is a warrior who was never shaped properly."[40]

Jim described Pryor's fight to recover as "the battle of his life," and many people seemed to see it as more than just a physical one.

CHAPTER THIRTY NINE

STAR-GROUPERS

THE NEXT DAY, I went to the Sherman Oaks Burn Center to see Richard. The lobby was full of people. Many of them were fellow actors who had been in films with Richard, like actor Stan Shaw. And Gene Wilder. There were family members. Two of his ex-wives came with their children. Then, there was his most recent ex-wife, Deboragh McGuire. But Jennifer Lee was noticeably absent.

Jim Brown, standing in the center of the room, told us that nobody was allowed to see him. He stood like a giant at the hospital door, not allowing any of Richard's friends to see him. He jealously guarded Richard as if he were his pet, or his own court fool. Since Richard entered the hospital, Jim had been heaping it on him, standing guard at his bed night and day, dealing with the press and the doctors, supporting and sometimes prodding Richard in the exhausting and agonizing work of recovery, seeing to it that his few rare moments of peace were not intruded upon by well meaning friends and fans.

While Richard was in the hospital, other members of the Star Groupers became imminent. Jennifer was largely kept in the background. Richard didn't want to see her. He knew that she had been the cause of his long funk that had resulted in his accident.

Instead of seeing her, Richard admitted his ex-wives, particular Deboragh, who reconciled with him.

I was in the waiting room one time when Jennifer showed up. She had been slipping notes to Richard on the trays that the nurses took in to him.

I came to the hospital with my cousin from North Carolina, Kimba. Kimba had recently arrived and I was his contact until he got himself settled. He had recently graduated from Morehouse and was inspired to be a comedian. Yet he was very country, and would often say things that would cause people to turn around and look at him.

We went into Richard's waiting room, where we joined Rashon, Gene Wilder, and Jim Brown.

Jim Brown was, as usual, in control. Richard wasn't seeing anybody because they didn't want him to get an infection.

My cousin Kimba saw a backgammon set on the table and looked up at Jim.

"Can you play that?"

Jim looked at him like he was crazy. "What do you mean? Can I play?"

"I mean, do you know the rules and enjoy the game is all."

They sat down and played backgammon for a straight hour. When it was over, Kimba had beaten him. Jim got up an said that Kimba didn't know the rules of the game.

Then Kimba asked him if he knew how to play chess. He saw that they had a chess set there too. The ex-football star gave Kimba a withering stare, and then sat down in front of the chess set.

They played chess until Kimba checkmated Jim. Jim was getting pretty steamed up, so I was happy to get my cousin away from the hospital.

Just then, before we could leave, a doctor entered and addressed us.

"My name is Dr. Jack Grossman," he said. "Richard is my patient. The explosion burned half of his body. He has undergone a second operation to graft skin over the burned areas. He is in critical conditions." We were encouraged that the news was not worse. We were given hope that he would survive. The next star-grouper was Larry Murphy, the assistant at the Sherman Oaks Burn Center.

As the weeks went on, it was apparent that Richard would live and that he owed his life to this incredible doctor.

He saved Richard's life. He was on duty when they brought Richard in. He said, "I just happened to be in the hospital room when he came in, and I just couldn't believe it. He was pretty cooked but he was sittin' up. I said to a coworker, 'Wow—that looks like brother Richard Pryor."

He examined Richard and discovered that he had suffered third degree burns over much of his body above the waist.

Later, On-Stage (OS) in his Sunset Strip comedy concert, he would joke about this moment. "The doctor said I was so burned up that he said, 'Why don't we just get some cole slaw and serve this up?"

Murphy devoted all of his time to seeing that Richard was saved. While Richard was still in the burn clinic, celebrities all over Hollywood visited him:

Sidney Poitier, Elliott Gould, Rosalind Cash, and Marlon Brando came by.

"White people never came to see me," Richard was able to laugh now, "until I got burned up."

One of the people that called was Ted Kennedy. A nurse brought him the phone and said that Teddy wanted to talk to him.

Teddy and Richard had a nice talk, Richard later told me. Because he had called him a few days before the Democratic National Convention, the telephone call meant a lot to Richard.

I was impressed, too. The attention that Richard got off the screen demonstrated how important social drama was to his career.

If he had not been a *negative exemplar,* a object lesson, nobody would have given a hoot. Because he was able to use his marginality as a spokesman he was able to garnish the status of a culture hero. That was why Teddy called him; not just because he was a famous comedian.

On July 23, 1980, Richard was released from the hospital, a few days earlier so his fans would be there. It had been about seven weeks since he was admitted. His cure was miraculous and ahead of schedule.

I called Reverend Banks and found out that Richard was coming out.

It was announced that he was coming out on the 19th but this was to keep people from gathering to see him.

I drove out to Northridge, but I had to take my cousin with me. I had to stop and use a pay phone to call Rashon to see if Richard was there. He said he was.

I drove up to the gate and announced my name over the intercom to Rashon. I drove into the driveway, with my excitement rising. I parked at the back of the house and told my cousin to wait in the car.

I went up the stairs, hoping to see Richard but expecting not to be surprise if I didn't. I climbed the carpeted steps to his study, and just as I was coming up to the head's level, I saw Richard's feet.

When I got up he was looking at me laughing.

We grabbed each other and hugged.

"Man, you look great!"

He did.

"Man, I just didn't want you to see me like that!"

"But you look good!"

"Damn, man, it was a bitch!"

My cousin, instead of staying in the car, had gotten out of the car as soon as I went up the stairs.

Now he came up the stairs.

"Hey, man!"

When Richard saw him, he jumped back. "Who is the fuck are you?"

Kimba laughed. "I'm Cecil's cousin!"

"I don't give a fuck! You can't just walk in my fucking house like that!"

"Yeah, man, I'm sorry. That's my cousin. You know he was a little kid when I was growing up."

Richard went off.

"I don't give a fuck, Cecil. Man, long as I been known you, you never pulled no crazy shit like this. I don't know this motherfucker. He could be wanting to do me harm."

"Man, I'm sorry…" I had told him to stay in the car, I probably explained.

"Do you want me to leave?" Kimba asked.

Richard thought about it for a second. "Yes. I want you to leave."

Kimba started across the room to the door.

As he walked away Richard turned to me.

"Who in the fuck is he?"

"He wants to be a comic."

"A comic?" By this time, Kimba had got to the door, but Richard called out to him.

"Say, man? You really gonna leave?"

"Well, you told me you wanted me to leave. I mean, it's yo' house."

Richard fell out laughing. "You are funny. You got heart. Come on, man."

Kimba came back up the stairs to us.

"You really were going to leave, huh?"

We all laughed again.

"I'm going to call Mitzi at the Comedy Store and get you on."

"No, no, no!" Kimba protested. "I'm not ready yet."

"Yes you are!" Richard insisted. "Just don't tell Paul Mooney your jokes, or he'll steal them."

I was so glad to see he was his old self. He was funny and upbeat, as if the tragedy could only be dealt with through humor.

"Do you guys want to drink something?"

We said, "Yeah!"

"What do you want? Orange juice?"

"Yeah!"

After we put our orders in, Richard just looked at us.

"You seriously don't think, I'm going to go downstairs and get this shit for you, do you?"

We burst out laughing. "There ain't no servants working today!"

Kimba went down stairs and got the juices from the refrigerator, giving me time with Richard. I went over to him. He looked thinner, but well tanned.

"I'm alright, man," he said.

He had his shirt opened. I saw his scars. They were brown and shiny.

We started talking and laughing right away.

"I'm sorry, Richard, that I wasn't there."

"It's not your fault, man."

"I just didn't know."

Was it the mixing the rum with the scraped coke? Richard and I had developed a little technique of mixing the scraping of the coke left in the bottom of the pipe that gave the best hit. (Roshan later claimed it was he who taught this to Richard.) The bottom was scrapped up and placed with a taste of rum on the top of the pipe. When Richard hit that he would say, "Home run!" When he mixed the rum with the coke with the torch there was always a danger, especially if you have been doing it for a long time when your hand is shaking. Richard let me know with a look that that was what had happened.

"I wasn't trying to kill myself" he said, "I was just fucked up ."But I'm gonna learn from this shit."

"You've learned how important life is."

"Yeah, the fire taught me a lot."

"Now, you'll have a chance to grow."

He said Jim Brown helped him survive. When he woke up in the morning, Jim was there, and when he went to sleep, Jim was there. So he decided that he couldn't disappoint Jim.

Kimba came back into the room. "So you are the one who was talking to Jim Brown, like that?" Apparently Richard had overheard the conversation between Jim and Kimba when they were playing dominoes and chess.

"You picked the right place to have a fight with Jim Brown," Richard laughed, "In the Sherman Oaks Hospital. 'Cause they won't have far to take your ass!"

Kimba was amazed at the sophistication of the topics that Richard and I engaged in, he later told me. "You were talking about things that were going on in Europe and the theater scene in New York."

The phone rang. "Excuse me." Richard talked to somebody for about a few minutes and came back.

"Now see that was a woman friend of mine," he told us, "She wants me to give her fifteen thousand dollars. Before the fire, I would have given it to her. But now, I'm not doing that shit no mo'. No, I'm finished with that."

"What she wants fifteen thousand for?"

"I don't know," he laughed. "But I told her where she can get a loan."

He said he found that people in his own family was dividing up his wealth because they thought he was going to die.

"I'm missing 75 thousand dollars cash I left in a boot. Uncle Dicky spent every day of his waken life," he laughed, "trying to steal my shit."

"Yeah?"

"He stole 75, thousand dollars out of my boot!"

"Really?"

He told me that everybody in his family tried to steal it from him.

"They thought I was going to die, man."

He said for the first few hours, he was so out of it he didn't know where he was or who he was.

Then the topic was on movies.

"Do you guys want to see *Sleuth?*"

Sleuth was in the current cinema.

"Yeah!" Kimba said.

He thought we were going to go to a cinema. But Richard led us to his screening room down in the basement.

Kimba would remember this as his first experience of seeing a screening of a current film that was still in the theaters.

As we watched the film, Richard and I analyzed it, and marveled at the ingenious method of story telling. What is so remarkable, Richard said, was that the whole film was made with just two actors.

At the end of the film, Deboragh walked into the room. I looked at Richard and he at me. We were cut-buddies and we knew what was up.

Kimba and I took our leave.

Richard told me he was working on *Busting Loose* and that I should come by the set.

He said goodbye and took off for his home in Maui, Hawaii. There he recuperated for the rest of the summer and fall in his house overlooking thousand miles of Pacific Ocean. Jennifer Lee was out of his life, he told me. Deboragh was back with him. "I do love her, man," he would say.

While he was in Maui, *Stir Crazy* was released. Although it didn't get high marks from the critics, it made over 30 million dollars. Richard was still hot.

As he was getting health, some of the star groupers began to change because it was clear that Richard was back.

Instead of looking for another movie, he turned to his standup routine.

He wanted to deal with using his social drama of being burned nearly to death as the material for a new act.

"You need to have pain to be funny," he would tell the press. He had told me this many times, so I wasn't surprised to hear it.

Richard felt that he had "really fucked up." He had tried to blunt the story of how much he had "fucked up" by telling the rum story.

It was his realization that if he wanted to change his life and become a new person, he would have to do it on the stage.

But the major reintegration was Richard himself. After the fire, he was no more the old Richard. He was now the "New Richard," who would stay off drugs.

CHAPTER FORTY

RECUPERATION IN MAUI

WHILE HE WAS in Maui, we waited. Paul and I had nothing to write. The news I got was that he was lying back in a hammock, sipping a coconut.

That was actually true. Richard had built a wooden house near the beach away from everybody. His nearest neighbor was the film actor Burt Reynolds. Further down the road were Kris Kristofferson, Carol Burnett, and George Harrison.

"Man, I love Hawaii," he would say to me, "and everything about it."

He also loved being alone. He would later tell me that all he did all day was get up. After he got up, he would drink a glass of fruit juice laced with protein powder, eggs, and yogurt. Then he would put on his straw hat, and get his fishing pole and go fishing. As the summer drifted on, he would ride his moped.

But as he began to heal, he got really bored and wanted to come back home. The movies he had been in *Wholly Moses* and *Stir Crazy* were about to be released. *Wholly Moses* had been rushed to be released to take advantage of his accident, but it wasn't good enough to do that, a reported wrote in the trades.

Universal was having problems with *Busting Loose* and they wanted Richard to come back and redo some scenes. But, as he would later tell me, he wasn't even thinking about movies. He was thinking about a new act. He wanted to go back on the stage and tell his story of the freebasing incident, of how he ended up nearly taking his life. He felt that he had to tell his story on the stage and then to put it on vinyl. The demons he wanted to talk about were the word "nigger," his trip to Africa, his broken love affairs, and prison injustice. But more than anything, he wanted the world to know that he had fucked up when he set himself on fire.

"The only way to exorcise that [demon] was to seal it in Vinyl," he would say.

At the end of the summer, Richard was back in Northridge. I went out to see him.

When I walked into his study, the decor was the same. Behind his desk, Richard sat.

"Hey, partner."

That was the way he always started.

"Hey, man!"

Whenever we met, I would ask him about the Charlie Parker story. Were we ever going to make it?

"Yes, we working on that," he would say. He had a two-picture deal with Columbia and Rastar productions. One of he two films was *The Charlie Parker Story* and the other one was *Nobody*, the Bert Williams story.

First, he had to deal with Universal and *Busting Loose*. He said he was going to reshoot some scenes.

Meanwhile he started doing publicity for *Stir Crazy*. He gave a combination birthday party and publicity party on his birthday, December 1, which Warren Beatty came to. Jennifer was definitely not there. Richard was in great sprits because as he told everybody, he was a "new" Richard Pryor.

Columbia Pictures was ecstatic about the box office, and everybody noticed the chemistry between Richard and Gene Wilder. Sidney Poitier had predicted that this spark between these two would become ignited with the public, and he was right.

That week I went to the set of *Busting Loose*.

When I got to Richard's dressing room, he grabbed me in an embrace.

"Where's Kimba?"

It was funny that he would remember Kimba. We went to the lot where they were preparing Richard for a scene that he had to be re-shoot..

I saw my old friend Michael Schultz again. Although Oz Scott was scheduled to direct the film, there had been a dispute and Michael was brought in to finish the film.

"Before the fire," Michel Schultz explained to me, "he was pretty bloated up from a life of partying!"

He glanced at Richard.

"I looked like shit," Richard concurred. Now there were tears in his eyes.

He said be began to see the beauty of things, instead of trying to destroy it.

There is an excellent example when the two dramas collide and must be reshot to make a seamless transition from one to the other. The movie had to be redone to accommodate the results of a real social drama. To maintain the ritual and rite of Richard Pryor, a few details had to be tucked away.

Cecily Tyson said that after the fire incident, Richard was not the same to work with. She said that it took a lot for him to come back. Before the fire, he was "loose and funny, after the fire, he was not." Now he would just shoot his scenes and then go back into his dressing room.

The fire incident had made him realize how much beauty he had wasted.

The set was closed because they didn't want Richard around too many people for fear that he might be exposed to a disease. He had to wear extra paddings to match the weight he had in the film footage. He had to wear a kerchief around his neck to conceal the scars.

Yet despite these minor set backs, Richard was excited about the money his films were making. As we sat back in his office, he would often exclaim his own mystery of his financial success.

"I can't believe this," Richard would say when I visited, talking about the incredible money his films were making.

"*Stir Crazy* made about 100 million and *Busting Loose* made over 40," he would say, "and I just burned my ass up!"

Another thing Richard had to deal with when he got back from Maui was his management, David Franklin. Before the Fire social drama, Franklin's place was secure. After the fire, Richard began to rethink his role in his life and business.

David Franklin told Richard that he had to fire Rashon, because Rashon couldn't read. Richard called Rashon to talk to him about it, saying that he couldn't have anybody working for him who couldn't read. Rashon told him he had a library of books and that he read all the time. After Rashon demonstrated to Richard that he could read by reading to him from a number of books, Richard said he would not fire him. But Rashon turned his worksheet in and quit anyway. This was after he realized that it was David Franklin who had turned him in to Richard for not being literate.

CHAPTER FORTY ONE

THE NEW PRYOR RETURNS
TO NORTHRIDGE

WHEN RICHARD CAME back to Hollywood from Maui, he heard that David Franklin had been saying in private that Richard had indeed been freebasing, not drinking rum.

This was a breach of lawyer client confidentiality, according to Howard Moore, the eminent lawyer. Franklin had no right to disclose what his client had told him. According to Mr. Moore, who ran the law offices in Oakland, California that Michael Ashburne worked out of, Franklin had made a big mistake.

In fact, Richard was very upset about what he felt to be Franklin's betrayal. Every time I met with him around this time, he expressed his depression and disappointment in what David Franklin done.

Out of the window went Richard's faith in black leaders like Franklin. He had believed that the "talented tenth" had an obligation to help black people in show business. The "talented tenth" was Du Bois dictum that ten percent of the educated black population should be responsible for uplifting the black race.

Yet Pryor contemplated a slander suit, but soon after this breach, another breach was discovered. According to his new lawyers, Franklin had been cheating Richard out of money.

He had diverted more than $215,000 from Columbia Pictures for the movie *Stir Crazy* and $800,000 from Warner Bros. Records. He was ordered to return more than $750,000 that he was paid by Mr. Pryor during the five years when he acted as Mr. Pryor's agent and manager. He was also ordered to return the $75,000 fee he had received from Universal Pictures for acting as executive producer of Mr. Pryor's film, *Busting Loose,* a job that the judgment said he had not fulfilled.

Two of the scripts that Franklin diverted were *Nobody* and *The Charlie Parker Story,* scripts I had suggested to Richard and for which I had written treatments.

On August 21, 1982, hearing commissioner, Carl G. Joseph, called David Franklin, who had been with Richard since 1975, "guilty of serious moral turpitude "and said that he had misappropriated 3.5 million dollars from Richard over the past seven years. The judgment was that Franklin had to pay Richard back for all those deals he made after *Greased Lightning.*

This was the biggest blow of Richard's career. He had been disappointed with his agents, starting back in Berkeley with Don Pruitt, and he was disappointed with Don Debasio, who didn't understand where Richard wanted to go with his humor. Now this with Franklin was the unkindest cut of them all. Why?

Because Franklin, being a black man, was like Richard: somebody who was honest and who wouldn't steal from his own people!

He would now deal with his demons on stage. As he had dealt with the ills of the counter-cultural audience, now he is turning the focus on himself.

Richard had already begun his come back album, *Richard Pryor On Sunset.* First, he would do a tour of the new show, which would give the world the first glimpse of the "new" Richard Pryor; the new phoenix that rose from the flames of the fire. With David Franklin out of his life, Richard took more control over his life after the emergency of the "new" Richard Pryor.

He accepted to do a role called *Some Kind of Hero*, a story about army life and Vietnam, co-starring Margo Kidder. Since the Berkeley days, Richard had toyed with the idea of a story about Vietnam, where he had had some experience. One of the first things he ever published was *Nigger, Uncle Sam Wants You Dead.*

Richard liked the story because it was a serious story. He plays Corporal Eddie Keller, who had served in Vietnam. Coming back home, he is broke and lonely. In a bar, he meets a white hooker, Toni, who takes pity on him and shacks up with him for the night.

Keller loses his nerve in a bank robbery attempt, and ends with him and Toni driving off into the night filled with possibilities.

During this shooting, Richard had an affair with Margo Kidder who played his love interest in the film. He introduced me to her; I had met her when she was shooting a film with Peter Fonda in Florida. Just as he had taken the black actresses under his protection while filming *California Suite*, so on this film, he took Margo Kidder under his wing, when the director of the film mistreated her. Richard always wanted to show that he was a defender of women no matter what their color.

All that spring and summer, I would see Richard as he went back from North ridge to Maui. That summer, Richard spent a lot of time in Maui with Jennifer. While he was in Maui, he and Jennifer got married. They were married in August, 1981. I was surprised that Richard had married Jennifer, because I had the impression that he was back with Deboragh.

This time when he married his lawyers saw to it that he signed a prenuptial agreement. For a while he and Jennifer were happy. She accepted that he was an actor with a lot on his plate.

Then he was ready to stage the big comeback, the concert film that came to be known as Richard Pryor: Live On Sunset Strip (1982).

Paul Mooney and I were hired to work with Richard again. But when we met up out at his place, we were mostly sounding boards for Richard's ideas for the new show. Columbia Pictures selected the site for the concert to be filmed. The new project was a concert film like *Richard Pryor Live In Concert* (1979). The first night for the performance was at the Comedy Store and the second night was at the Palladium, which was also in Hollywood.

Columbia Pictures selected the site of the new concert film. But instead of Bill Steward, the producer from Texas, who had been able scrap up a mere $750,000, this time the producer was Ray Stark, who started with a budget of 4, million (3 million would go right off the top into Richard's bank account.) This time instead of just fairly competent editors and cameramen and directors, top names like Haskell Wexter and Joe Layton were brought in. This was being produced with the same professionalism of a feature film.

The problem was that Richard was not up to speed. The first attempt at the concert film was a failure because for some reason he and the audience didn't sync.

Richard wanted to talk about his new self. He was nervous and talked about that a lot, mainly because he had been off the stage for a long time now.

We arrived at the Palladium. The first night of the comeback at the Comedy Store didn't go well. Everybody in Hollywood was there. Limousines pulled up and Warren Beatty got out. Another limousine arrived and Dustin Hoffman got out.

As Richard walked on to the stage that night at the Palladium, thousands of fans jumped to their feet, clapping and cheering and showing support in every way.

"We love you, Richard!"

I went back into the dressing room. Roshan was standing at the door. When he saw me, he waved me into the room, where Richard sat hunched over smoking a cigarette. He was dressed in his fire-red suit and black shirt, with an orange handkerchief in his jacket pocket.

"A lot of people out there," I said.

"Yeah."

He was silent. Now he looked at me with a worried look. "I'm just so nervous…"

"Talk about that," I suggested, "on stage."

"Yeah, that's what I'm going to do!"

"Okay, I'll let you be by yourself."

"Thanks."

He always liked to have that moment just before he went on all alone, with nobody standing over or around him. He wanted to exercise his demons in public, so that he had to call them up first of all.

I looked over at the audience just before he came on stage. There was Jesse Jackson, John Belushi, Robin Williams, Lily Tomlin, Stevie Wonder, and Sugar Ray Leonard. I was surprised to see so many white people who were themselves famous. It had become a status symbol among the Hollywood celebrities to be seen at a Richard Pryor concert. Just as Richard had appealed to the counterculture in Berkeley in the 70s, and just as he had appealed to the blacks during the Watts Riots, so now he appealed to the white and black celebrities in Hollywood.

These white celebrities came to see Richard for an entirely different reasons than the counter-cultural. He was really one of them. They felt his pain and identified with him as some one who was rich and famous yet was not happy; someone they could relate to.

After the laughter and shouting and screaming of joy had subsided, he took on he voice of the Reverend.

"We are gathered here today, to eat—"he clowned. They were laughing even before he finished the sentence.

"—to eat—"

They were giggling before the punch line was delivered.

"If not each other," he said, capping the punch line, "then, at least some food…"

That gave him some license to admit his fear of not being funny. "No, y'all don't understand. I came out to do the last show and I wasn't funny. I mean, I was so damn nervous! I couldn't remember what I was suppose to do!"

The audience liked his being so honest and rewarded him with immediate encouragement in the form of generous applauses. He told them that he was so scared that they wouldn't like him.

They had so much in the past. He was self-deprecating. "I fucked up!" And he would tell them how. Because he had fucked up so badly, he would not be surprised if they rejected him too. He reenacted his anxiety so thoroughly and completely that he moved on to his routine with confidence.

"It takes a lot to get back up on the stage," he pined. "A lot and I appreciate your welcoming me back…"

When it finally settled down, he said, "Let's talk about something serious—*fucking!*"

They went crazy—and he was on his way. "The first time I jacked off—"

They loved that. "The first time I came, I was like, 'Hey, this is something! I got something here!'"

Then he looked out at the white faces. "Now wait a minute! Is there anybody here that don't know what I'm talking about?"

This was his way of cleaning out the hecklers, the sealing of the agreement between him and the audience that they want to have some fun.

"Cause if you don't know, raise your hand so we can see what you look like as you are leaving—"

He had them laughing because (he said) women really do like sex even more than men, but they don't want to talk about it.

They never masturbate, he contented, but they do have "all this electrical equipment."

He admitted that one of the greatest perks of show business is the sex. Before he came to California, he lived in Peoria during the "pussy drought" of the 1950s.

When he started in show business, he rose to the top when he went home with a playboy bunny. The playboy bunny had an apartment so luscious and hip that he thought that if he didn't score with her, he could make love to her couch.

She seduced him by making him pretend to talk in baby babble. At the end of the routine, he is reduced to a small child, and by the time they had sex, he had been reduced to the size of a newborn infant. The sex theme brought another concern to him: his personal life with women.

In the real social drama, he found it hard to express his hurt, especially to Jennifer. But in the show that night, he told and re-enacted his feelings for all to see and hear.

"Women, they don't know how they hurt us—"

He twisted his body to show that it was a physical effect, too.

"Women don't know how we feel when you fuck up our hearts. You don't know how we feel when you fuck up our hearts." Imitating a guy at some bar, he asks for a fifth of "anything."

He impersonates a lonely guy, glancing at his watch. "I want to call he but she's not at home!"

He tries to call her. "Why, isn't she at home?"

He describes the fight to get equilibrium in a relationship as *a rite of passage*: "If you come through that shit, you're a man!"

"I am married now," he confessed, "But I find it hard to live with one person. My wife, it took her 6 years before she landed me. Because I ain't no picnic at the park. When I get mad, I can't talk!" He begins miming a mute saying in non-verbal gesture, Fuck You!

"You women can be so cool. You can't wait to get somebody in love with you, so you are so cool. 'Richard, are you calling again? Don't do this to yourself. Oh, just a minute, John!'"

In imitating the woman on the phone with him, he reminded me of that time when I would be sitting with him and he would be calling Jennifer. But it was only on the stage in front of thousands of people who formed a distant public could he really reenact the feelings that went along with his rejection.

These were missing scenes from his life in the social world.

"And why do women look so good after you don't see them for a long time? Why do we become bored with any other person than the one we are going through shit with?"

Then he talked about the black men he met in prison. Drawing verbal portraits of these men, he then turned to his experience of going to Africa. In these two bits, which lasted six and ten minutes, respectively, he reenacted his experience in going to prison himself and traveling to Africa recently.

These artistic reenactments of his social life experience were meant to show that one way to let go of the misery of losing our identity in a boring life is to reenact it, putting in the emotions and reflection.

Richard has a special oral technique of telling stories with in stories, a series in which stories are inserted into other stories, as in Chinese boxes. The next bit was called "The Mafia Club" illustrates that device brilliantly.

Somebody yelled out, "Do Mudbone!"

Richard paused. Should he do Mudbone? He wanted to give them something new and he had done Mudbone almost to death. Yet, what if he could do Mudbone in a different way? Somebody else yelled up demanding Mudbone.

"Okay," he said, finally, "I'm going to do Mudbone, but after this Mudbone is going into retirement!"

They shouted back their excitement.

He slipped into the Mudbone accent, and disguised his voice as if he were a ventriloquist speaking through a dummy. Then he put on the mask of Mudbone and criticized himself.

Mudbone admits to the audience that he knew Richard Pryor.

"But he fucked up," Mudbone told them, "That fire got on his ass and fired up what little sense he had. 'Cause I remember—he could make a motherfucker laugh at a funeral on Sunday, Christmas day. But he got some money and went all the way crazy."

I looked at the audience again. They loved him!

He was so unlucky that they felt great pity for him.

Using the persona of Mudbone, Richard could speak the truth about the connection between his wealth and his cocaine habits. This was his way of criticizing himself in a positive way, a way of creating an art form.

After the Mudbone skit had been so well received, Richard paused and looked long at the audience.

Before he got to the main event of the evening, which was talking about his freebasing incident, he had something else on his chest that he wanted to get off.

He had recently been in a legal battle with David Franklin. One of the elements of the social drama is the last phase, which is the reintegration of opposite qualities. In this case, Franklin was the force behind Richard and it had all been based on what has been missing in the black community: trust. Black people had the reputation of deceiving each other and being untrustworthy.

"I got a black lawyer—a brother! He wanted 40,000 dollars the first day we meet. I said, 'I just met you!' My lawyer took me line, hook, and sinker—on dry land!"

It was this joke that Michael Ashburne, who was David Franklin's assistant, would use as his case to sue Richard for character defamation when the film was released in 1982.

Then he switched to the topic everybody wanted to hear about: his freebasing incident.

"You know, I've been talking to my friends about what I should do? Should I talk about freebasing?—Or should I just leave it alone?"

The audience cried out, *"Talk about it!"*

"Yeah—I got to talk about freebasing!" he declared, agreeing with heckler.

"Well, I'll tell you the truth! The bottom line is my bitch left me. And I freebased for eight months!"

The audience went crazy with that honest confession. As I have said, Richard had lost his confidence with Jennifer. She would make him jealous by flirting and being so cool about his getting upset. In addition, Richard loved the fantasy of being a rich famous sugar daddy to Jennifer's poor white girl who had been brought up in a trailer in a small town in New York State.

"I fell in love with the base pipe," he said. "The Pipe would say to me, 'Richard, don't answer the phone!' I wouldn't answer the phone. The pipe would say, 'don't knock me over and break me! It's hard to replace me at 3 in the morning!'"

Becoming addicted was a slow process. He recalled (for the audience) how he first noticed that he was addicted when he wanted to always rush home from other social activities. He noticed that he was hooked when the dope dealers begin feeling sorry for him, suggesting that he stop smoking cocaine and go back to snorting it.

"When you are a junkie," he joked publicly on himself, "You will not admit it. You become defensive. 'I don't like the way you said that!'"

Pacing the stage, he said, "And your friends can't talk you out of it!"

Then he added another swipe at the people who never came to see him until he burned up.

"I recently went up to Oakland and was talking to one of my old friends, an old dope dealer. I always paid him and I didn't stay at his house. He was acting like I was one of his bitches. He got mad because I fired on his ass (criticized him). He started signifying. I had my shirt off. He looked at my scars and said, 'what about those rings around your neck? Nigger, you burnt up!' I realized that nobody say anything about my scars."

Somebody in the audience, "Say fuck all that! Nigger, tell us about how you got burnt up!"

"So I got to tell you about the night of the fire!"

The audience screamed back, "Yes!"

They howled with anticipation.

"—Have you ever heard of a motherfucker getting burned up from freebasing—other than me?"

They laughed with raucous laughter. Having established his marginality status even among the lowest of social dregs of the most fringed groups, the free basers, he goes on to apply his license of spokesman.

"Nobody gets burned up freebasing but me! I didn't burn up because I was freebasing! I burned up because I had given up freebasing. I lit my own arm accidentally."

Then he pretended that was not true.

"My friends really know how I did it. They know that one night I had some cookies and milk before I go to bed. This time, I had some of that low fat milk. When I put the low fat with the cookie, it exploded! I dropped my cookie and it blew up. It caused a fire. Every thing caught on fire. Have you ever caught on fire? It's inspirational. I ran a 100 yard dash in 46 seconds."

Then he redid his experience of being in the Sherman Oaks Burn Center.

He praised Larry Murphy, a black man, who was responsible for cleaning off the scabs that would result in a painful experience.

Recalling that it's better to think about the experience now than it was when it actually happened five months ago, Richard reenacted the scene between him and Larry as he was being prepared for the bath.

"Every day, Larry would say, 'we gonna give you a bath!' and I'd say, 'Okay, let's do it!'"

Then when the day for the bath arrived, Richard had to undergo excruciating aching pain. To the audience's delight, he twisted and turned, recreating the experience safely while distanced from the actual act.

After reliving this dreadful experience, he pivoted to the audience for a farewell.

"I want to thank you for all the love you sent me. I love you!"

He took out a match and struck it. "What's that? Richard Pryor running down the street!"

After the show was over, Richard was exhausted but ecstatic. This joke of his taking the match and lighting it he had used to start the first concert. Now he switched it to end the show. He had used it judiciously, because it wasn't strong enough to open the show but had the right grace note to end it.

He walked off the stage amidst a large canopy of applauses and laughter. He was the walking symbol and image of sincerity. He was spontaneous in public.

Richard won the battle that night, but how long could he maintain his dominance?

"I did it," he said to Paul and me as he came off the stage. "I showed them my new self."

This was, indeed, a new Richard Pryor. In those days, Richard was always threatening to be "new." Richard Pryor's name was a brand for something "new." Yet, this did seem authentic to me. This was a new Richard.

Everybody knew it, and after the show Richard was out on the sidewalk talking and laughing with his fans just like the old days.

But astute observer Rob Cohen, who had produced *The Wiz* in which Richard played "Oz," made a comment that summarized the general feeling we all had about Richard's return.

"The difference between Pryor before and after the fire is not that he is less funny," he said, "but that his anger had been redirected."

He went on to say that Richard's audience used to "laugh at themselves," but no longer. In the days of the counter culture, Richard made the audience laugh at *their* shortcomings. Now it was different.

"Instead, now they laugh at Richard as this quasi-pathetic figure on the stage. He use to be angry at the "white establishment but now he had changed because he saw how all people rallied around him and gave him a new perspective on life.

Yet, finally, he was back, he was strong, and he had cleansed his demons in view of the public.[41]

I agree with that. The fire really taught Richard that famous white people genuinely loved him as much as poor black ghetto people did. You could hardly go anywhere in West Hollywood and not hear somebody talking about how sad Richard Pryor's life was, and how he had become a new man. The fire had expanded Richard's audience to include the rich, famous white celebrities as well as the rest of us.

CHAPTER FORTY TWO

THE LAW SUIT

A S *RICHARD PRYOR Live on Sunset Strip* was waiting to be edited and released, Richard and Jennifer went for another vacation. There were some rumors, too, that they were getting a divorce.

In March 1982, Jennifer did sued him for a divorce. When I saw Richard about a week later, he said, "Man, I don't understand this shit."

In her suit against him, Jennifer asked for "spousal support property rights, and attorney's fees." She cited "irreconcilable differences."

In the spring of 1982, *Richard Pryor Live on the Sunset Strip* was released and earned eight million the first week and ended up making thirty million dollars. Since his return from the fire, four of his films had been successful in the box office.

But he still would not do the Charlie Parker story or the Bert Williams story.

"Encouraged by the staggering fees he could collect for his performances," one journalist wrote, "Pryor did not follow his heart and 'take charge' of his artistic destiny. Indicative of his turmoil is the fate of the Charlie Parker Story, a picture he'd wanted to make for some time."

Michael Ashburne, a black lawyer who worked for David Franklin, was offended by Richard's reference to "black lawyer" and sued him. Michael had been away on an extended vacation that lasted 18 months after his boss had split with Richard.

When Michael came back into the country, he was picked up at the airport by his friend, Stan Lathan. Lathan was, and still is, a black television director who had worked as an assistant to Richard in the past and would be his assistant on *Here and Now* (1983).

He told him that Richard made a recording that could be a reference to him.

"I wasn't in the county for 5 minutes," Michael told me, before he was hearing about Richard's joke about him and David in the concert film.

In any case, Michael had seen the *Richard Pryor Live On Sunset Strip* (1982) video in London and realized that he had a case to sue Richard on.

"I started thinking about it in a different light," he told me," I did the research." Michael said, "I found out that Stan knew that he was talking about David Franklin, but others might have talking about me. That was the hypothesis."

Based on this fraction of the law, Michael decided to sue Richard.

"In Richard's mind," Michael reasoned, "he is telling the story about what somebody did to him. He was talking about David. It was the only black attorney he was talking about. But it could have been misconstrued to think he was talking about me."

David couldn't sue Richard, because there was already bad blood between them, since Richard had already sued David. "I wanted$50,000," Michael told me, "which is not much money and I wanted them to drop the lawsuit against me which is baseless. So Richard paid me $50,000 and I was left to sue Columbia Pictures who registered the sale, and they paid me $500,000."

One reason why the jury awarded the Ashburne the victory was that the official censor hired by Columbia Pictures testified that Mr. Pryor had instructed her not to take anything out of the film. In a normal release of a film, she was instructed to take out anything that might cause somebody to sue them, but because Richard was so much against censorship, he personally instructed her to leave everything in. Richard helped Michael by allowing the offending material to appear in the film that had been distributed by Columbia Pictures. They had to pay Michael.

After this negative hit by yet another black lawyer, Richard turned more to the personal world of chaos that Franklin and Ashburne had been hired to quell. Now Richard turned more and more to the social drama to occupy himself. When Franklin was in control, he made all the script decisions for Richard. Now that Franklin was gone, Richard had to turn to somebody for the script consulting. He turned to Ray Stark, the producer of his next disastrous films, *The Toy*.

The Toy was remake of 1979 French film *Le Jouet*, directed by Francis Verber. Richard was offered *The Toy* for a lot of money, about five million dollars. He plays Jack Brown, and out of work journalist who takes a job as a "cleaning woman" in a department store.

I went down to Baton Rouge to hang out with Richard on the set. He was glad to see me, but there was little time to talk about our projects. Richard was not so excited any longer to talk about working for black cinema.

He was more bent on having fun. Working with Jackie Gleason was a thrill for him. Richard had grown up with *The Honeymooners*. He wanted to work with Gleason because he admired him.

There were a few incidences that I remember which are worth mentioning. One of the actors was in a scene with Richard and made the mistake of ad-libbing. In the ad-lib, the actor called Richard a "cockroach." "Without missing a beat," one reporter wrote, "Pryor allegedly walked off the set and returned to his hotel room. Neither the crew nor the actor could understand why Pryor took offense.

When the producer's representatives tried to speak with him, he refused to let them into his room or take their phone calls. The next morning, he showed up on the set, as if it nothing had happened, and just went on working.

While the crew would be waiting and the director going crazy, Richard would be relaxing with his close hangout buddies as if there was no movie set to go to.

When he got back to the set the next day, we stood around while they set up a shot for the swimming pool scene.

"Action!" the Director Richard Donner called.

Richard Donner, the director, called action and Richard's character walked over to the swimming pool.

"Cut!"

Richard stopped and the crew dissolved into a huddle, leaving Richard on his own.

As he was walking over to the hairdresser, Robert Stevenson, who was waiting to fix up his hair between takes, Richard slipped and fell into the pool.

Richard went under the water quickly. Robert noticed that he had gone under, handed his make-up kit to the woman next to him, and jumped into the pool.

I watched as Robert pushed a thrashing Richard to the edge of the pool. Somebody threw a towel over him.

Richard was very grateful, of course.

Richard hired Robert as a hair stylist back when they were doing Car Wash and Robert had become part of his inner circle.

Yet on the next film, *Superman III,* Robert flew with Richard to London for the premier. Richard asked Robert to come downstairs with him to meet the English press, but Robert was busy on another error for Richard and couldn't come downstairs with him. Richard became irate and fired Robert. Robert told me how he sat there not knowing what to do.

Richard had told him to take the next plane back to LA.

Then Rashon went to Richard and said, "Listen, Richard, how are you going to fire Robert. He's the dude that saved you when you fell in the swimming pool on *The Toy* set."

Richard recalled the incident and said, "Oh yeah," and reversed himself and rehired Robert.

Richard Donner, who directed *The Toy,* also directed *The Omen* and Superman. He said he enjoyed working with Richard.

But for me, *The Toy* was the first indication that Richard was beginning to lose interest in making black films. Another journalist asked, "Had Pryor sold out?"

Richard had begun to say in public that he was taking roles that they paid him enough money." The journalist went on to say, "Watching him on the set of *The Toy* and on his next film, one might take Pryor at face value."

In an interview in late 1982, Richard said himself that "I don't know what I want to do anymore. I don't think about movies that much. I don't have that performing urge anymore. I don't want to work myself to death," he emphasized, "I want to take some time for Richard and just enjoy myself a little bit."

In June 1982, when he played a part in *Superman III*, he was paid more money than the leading actor Christopher Reeves. Richard got 5 million and Reeves got two million.

The pattern they showed me that night was repeated again and again. Again like Jodorowsky, he tried to use a negative relationship to purify himself in his struggle to reach a higher consciousness.

PART FOUR:

WHICH WAY IS DOWN?

"Being a good medicine man means being right in the midst of the turmoil, not shielding yourself from it. It means experiencing life in all of its phases. It means not being afraid of cutting and playing the fool now and then. That's sacred, too."

-John (Fire) Lame Deer Sioux Medicine Man of the Lakota Tribe) Quoted in Jodorowsky's Spiritual Journey

CHAPTER FORTY THREE

JO JO DANCER, YOUR LIFE
IS CALLING YOU

S INCE THE BERKELEY days, Richard talked about directing films. He had starred in many films, but he had yet to direct one. *Jo Jo Dancer, Your Life is Calling* is unique in that it is the only film that he ever directed. Furthermore, it presented a problem for the critics when it appeared in 1986. With the exception of Vincent Canby of the *New York Times* and Roger Ebert of the *Chicago Tribune* (both of whom gave it reserved praise), most critics panned the film and left it to die.

But the one complaint they all had was Richard's denial that this was an autobiographical film. Even though he shot most of it in his hometown, Peoria, Illinois, Richard insisted that the film was not autobiographical. He even changed the name Peoria to Madison in the film to establish the illusion that this was not shot in his hometown.

None of the critics went for the ploy. Canby insisted on the film as being "autobiographical," and Roger Ebert said that it "is unmistakable based on his life." Nathan Kamal, a critic who reviewed the film fifteen years later, calls it "a bio pic...It's not exactly a movie about Pryor's life, but also, it completely is." [42]

Then Kamal goes on to compare the similarities between Jo Jo Dancer and Richard Pryor. "They are both African-American standup comedians who grew up with equally powerful positive and negative female figures in brothels in a tiny mid western town. The similarities between Richard and Jo Jo Dancer were so obvious as to ask the question, why did he make such a denial? Why not admit that the film was autobiographical?

The film critic who liked the film did so because it was auto-biographical. Even when the critic Kamal who wails against the film for being "mawkishly sentimental," and being "clumsy" cin-ematically, will forgive the film if it is seen and "framed through Pryor's own life." Even the clumsy flashbacks make sense when you see it as Richard's perspective.

So why the denial?

Here is the answer: He saw the value of using his social dra-mas as the basis of reflection and recreation of art, but he had been so disappointed with his lawyers. He had laid out his concerns about trusting his black lawyers and he had voiced his complaint in public. "I found a way to talk about my life," he told me, "with-out getting sued."

"It doesn't matter if the incident happened or not," he told me, referring to the different version of the story, "what matters is if it works!" Remember what happened to him as a result of being so honest? Not only did he discover that the lawyer was stealing from him, but his lawyer's partner sued him for even making the accusation.

In order to avoid lawsuits, he fictionalized the social dramas surrounding this childhood, his business, and his personal life.

While most critics did not go deeper, they did recognize that the film is about the separation of the soul from the body. By us-ing this technique of fictionalizing, he was able to go beyond the petty clutches of lawyers and ex-wives and embrace the theme of body and soul.

"After he sets himself on fire," Roger Ebert wrote, "Jo Jo is raced into an emergency room with burns over most of his body." Jo Jo faces a decision. "Jo Jo's alter ego separates from his body, looks down at the bandages, and says 'Jo Jo, what have you done to us this time!'" Similarly, Vince Canby wrote, "While hovering between life and death, Jo Jo Dancer flashes back to his childhood, where he grew up in a brothel." Another critic Nathan Kamal noted that "Jo Jo's spirit pulls itself from his wrecked body, then starts cursing his burned body out."

The plot of *Jo Jo Dancer* is based on a myth that when one is dying the soul wanders off on a journey. A variant of the same myth is that just before you die, your life flashes before you. This myth is in two parts: One is the soul "wandering off" and the other is "your life flashing before you." This was another story I heard from Richard.

What these critics missed was the story behind the plot of the film. The story of a wandering soul had fascinated Richard for a long time.

The first time I heard the myth from Richard was in 1971 in Berkley on his radio show, "Opening Up." He recited it to a person who had called in and was relating a story. He mentioned it again in a hotel in St. Carlos just before he was to open that night with Patti LaBelle. He carried this idea around with him the way a bluesman might carry a ballad about a man who killed another man. It was his story too. It was his story in a way that a written story is not his story.

Richard was working a script back in 1971. He gave it to me to read. It included many of the scenes later appeared in *Jo Jo Dancer*. Some of the scenes in the movie could have been lifted right out of the script he showed me back in Berkeley in 1971:

```
FADE TO:
INT.ROOM IN A WHOREHOUSE - DAY
Richard, His Mother, and Trick.
This is a hallucination of Richard as he is lying in
a casket. He goes to see his mother, (who is a pros-
titute) in her room while she is turning a trick. A
white dude is on top of her.
MOTHER AND TRICK—ANGLE FROM CORNER OF ROOM -NIGHT
```

```
RICHARD (OS)
Why is it happening to me?
MOTHER
Life is like that, Richard.
That's the way life is.
```

The script (1971) switched back and forth from his casket to the bordello. Just like in *Jo Jo Dancer,* the scenes switch back and forth from the bandaged Pryor and the scene of his life as a young boy growing up in the bordello.

If we compare our contemporary society to that of a tribal society before writing, back when the shaman was the center of the tribe, we see some stark connection between what the shaman did and what Richard was doing in this film.

The task of the guardian spirit's journey is to find medicine to heal the sick person. If he doesn't get back before the person wakes up, the person will die. It is a widespread folklore motif in the world of folklore and mythology. But African-Americans have their own variant, especially in the South. In the shaman societies (according to the research of specialists like Professor Geza Roheim), the clan gathers around the shaman for any sickness that it recognizes among their group.

I wanted a description of the shaman's journey and went to the library, remembering the discussions with my own professors Alan Dundes and Albert Goldman. I wanted to see if there was a shared pattern in *Jo Jo Dancer's* structure and a shaman's journey. Dr. Roheim's most famous book is the *Gates of the Dream*, a study of shamans among the natives of Australia.

I lugged all 550 pages of that big book into my study one afternoon, and started reading. I became so engrossed in the book that it was midnight before I closed it, so fascinating were the stories of the shamans that Dr. Roheim had witnessed.

Here I will give you a sample from the *Gates of the Dream:*
The shaman sits surrounded by the clan members who are sick.
The shaman takes a drug and goes into a trance.

The shaman's soul becomes a guardian spirit that takes a journey to find the cure for the clan.

According to Roheim, "A receptacle for the guardian spirit (his soul) is made...Then the shaman sends out the guardian spirit (the soul) to take a journey to the lower world."

If Richard is the shaman, then his clan is the people sitting in the nightclub or on the sofa in television land.

The shaman evokes a guardian spirit to take the clan to the underworld where they will find the cure to what is ailing them. In Richard's story (film) the Alter Ego (guardian spirit) takes the film viewer back to his hometown.

Let's compare the shaman journey with the Alter Ego's journey in *Jo Jo dancer*. This is a description of the typical journey of the shaman as collected by Dr. Roheim.

Richard had discovered that the world of the shaman was not so far from Hollywood's dream of itself. In fact, Paul Mooney and I were working with Richard on an autobiographical screenplay in 1979 about Richard's life. We had come up with the concept of Alter Ego who would take him and us (viewers) back to Richard's hometown.

What was missing in our version was an incident that would put Richard, the character, in the hospital. We were not prescient enough to come up with the freebase incident, which was a few years off.

When he would burn himself in a freebase accident a few years later, he provided the element that was missing in our script. His life (real Life) provided a canvas upon which to paint his art.

In a significant scene in *Jo Jo Dancer,* Richard gets into an argument with his "Alter Ego," as his soul is called in the film.

In the traditional tale, the soul is lost and wanders around, but in this version, it is Richard (in Real Life) who is the lost soul. The reasonable soul tries to talk sense into him.

The script calls for Richard to be scrounging around for cocaine rocks hidden in the thick expensive rug. He finds a sack of cocaine in his jacket pocket. He goes back to the fireplace and retrieves a pipe, which he had thrown there in accordance with his determination to quit freebase. But Richard tricks his soul. We see him put his arms around him in an embrace; but we also see how he, with lighter in one hand and the rum in the other, ignites a flame. Cut to: big explosion outside the mansion. Next cut: In the next scene, Richard mummified in white gauze is being pushed down hospital corridor.

Just as the guardian sprit encounters helpers, so Jo Jo meets Satin Doll, a maternal figure that helps him when his own mother (the prostitute) does not.

On this spiritual journey to the past, Jo Jo is a grown man, but his parents treat him as if he were a child. In his interview with his mother, Jo Jo's spirit is not able to forgive her.

Just as the guardian spirit returns to the clan through the shaman, so Jo Jo's Alter Ego returns to his charred body, to bring a message. It is up to him, Jo Jo Dancer, to decide if he wants to live.

The guardian spirit returns with a positive message for the clan. In the same way, Jo Jo Dancer's spirit reunites with him physically. His soul says, "I thought you'd never ask "and goes over and gets into Richard's sick body.

Reaching out his hand, Richard says, "Yes!" In the film, after the victim (Richard) says yes to his soul, and the soul goes back into him, a new Richard Pryor emerges. This parallels the return of the guardian spirit back into the body of the shaman. Just as the shaman is the conduit in which the clan has been revived again, so the audience is allowed to feel renewed by Richard's artistic resurrection?

When the Shaman's consciousness returns, the clan lifts him up. They express their joy that he has returned from the underworld. The moment that Richard's Alter Ego goes back into the burn victim's body the transformation is complete. The next cut is of Richard Pryor on stage, announcing the "New" Richard Pryor has been reborn.

In the next scene, Richard is doing a standup routine. The next cut is to Richard, the comedian, on stage.

"I am going to bury the old Richard Pryor," he tells the staged audience. He proceeds to treat his old Richard as a joke. Richard as a joke is Jo Jo becoming his alter ego, and now he becomes the "real" Richard Pryor. A resurrected Richard Pryor! A new Richard Pryor ! Pryor Lives!

The scene structures the real life images of Richard's transformation from the Old Richard Before The Fire to the New Richard After The Fire. Just as he had used the stage performance or the concert movie *Richard Pryor Live on Sunset Strip* (1982), so now he was using the film as a way to reenact his physical transformation from the ill Richard to a renewed one when he was recuperating in Maui.

This was the first time a director had used the dream form to control a narrative about black life. Because his life is flashing in front of him (as he lies in the hospital covered in gauze from head to toe), the director is able to skip around, non-linearly, non-sequentially, like a dream.

In fact, Jo Jo Dancers's real ancestry is not in films but in theater. The father of the memory play, August Strindberg, who in writing *Dream Play* (1898) introduced dreams as a structure in drama. Like Strindberg, Richard uses the dream structure as a way to recall emotional experiences—emotional experiences seen through the eyes of the main character.

In *Our Town*, Thornton Wilder used the character Stagemanager, as a narrator. Richard's Alter Ego has some of the omniscience of Wilder's character. Tom in Tennessee Williams' *The Glass Menagerie*, the classic example of a dream play, is related to Jo Jo Dancer.

Jo Jo Dancer was an important film. Richard has proved that he was a mature director. He had told me that in putting in his social drama on stage or in film, he had found a way to talk about his life without being sued.

This was a great accomplishment, for it meant he found out how to use his art to express his art. There was another important reason why he became the subject of his art.

The film was not successful financially, earning only about four million dollars. This may have been because he had dealt with the material about freebasing already in his *Richard Pryor Live On Sunset Strip*, and because the topic was not new. Artistically, the film was panned because few critics were prepared for the non-lineal structure, the interplaying of motifs, and the sophisticated narrative levels. He was just ahead of his time.

CHAPTER FORTY FOUR

RICHARD'S LAST
PERFORMANCE - 1994

I N 1987, THE next year, after making *Jo Jo Dancer*, Richard starred in his last feature film, *Critical Condition* (1987), playing Eddie Lenahan, a con man who is framed for a jewel robbery. He fakes insanity in order to escape custody. To escape he impersonates a doctor and runs the hospital. The film received bad reviews and was not a commercial success.

The most significant event for Richard was that he discovered that he had multiple sclerosis (MS). When the director of the film, Michael Apted, asked him to carry out an action, he discovered that he could not move his limbs. After being tested at the Mayo Clinic, he was diagnosed with multiple sclerosis in 1986. By the early 1990s, he was using a motor powered scooter for the remainder of his life to get around as the disease took its toll on his body.

By the time, I met him again, he had moved out of the Parthenia address, which had been razed to the ground. He had a house in Sherman Oaks. He had not been confined to a wheel chair yet and had been doing small parts in films starring his friend Wilder.

We were happy to see each other.

But while he was in New Orleans, he did a show called "Here and Now."

The significance of the show was that Richard was at his best, and it was in this show that retired "Mudbone."

In 1984, Paul Mooney emceed the Black Filmmakers Hall of Fame at the Hyatt Regency, Oakland Hall of Fame. Both Stepin Fetchit and Richard Pryor were presented awards. Ninety two year old Lincoln Theodore Perry, the famous Stepin Fetchit, was there at the Gala Diner and Celebrity ball .

Meeting Stepin Fetchit made an impression on Richard, and he wanted to talk about it. We did.

Richard was there with his girlfriend Flynn Blaine. A few days before they arrived in Oakland, Flynn had told Richard she was pregnant. Richard freaked out and only reluctantly agreed to have the baby. Still, he refused to marry her. But when he won $600,000 from a gambling excursion, he gave the money to her for the new baby.

He had a son, Steven, and then married Flynn Blaine in October 1986.

They divorced that next year in July. They got married a second time on April Fool's day in 1990, but divorced again in July, 1991.

While Richard was dealing with his MS and Flynn Blaine, Jennifer had been living in New York. She had missed his films *The Toy, Superman III, Jo Jo Dancer,* and *Critical Conditions.*

But she had been busy publishing her own book, a book about her life in Hollywood, a tell-all called *Tarnished Angel* in 1992. She sold the idea of the book by relating it to Richard Pryor, but a negative image of how violent and brutal and misogynistic he was in his private life.

When Richard had gotten burned, he was in the middle of finishing the movie Busting Loose. Michel Schultz, who directed it, said that when Richard came to watch the film, he saw the person on screening that he was before the fire." Jennifer went on the airwaves with her book.

When she appeared on the Rivera show, she told about another revealing incident, involving her, Richard, and a black German girl.

Jennifer and Richard had a *ménage à trois* with a black German girl, she told Rivera and during the sexual act, Richard "just went off. He just went over the top and stated smashing the house. He went berserk. The 10,000 dollar Tiffany lamp that I had just bought for his house, he smashed, and everything he could get his hands on, crying, sobbing, really, you know, primal sobs. He blamed me for arranging the threesome."

Given what I experienced that night, I take what Jennifer reported with a grain of salt.

She talked about Richard's violence towards her, but didn't seem fazed by the circumstances that produced the violence. For example, she explained that Richard gave her a "really huge beating, when she had to wake him up" to go to court for the New Year's Eve incident with Deboragh. To wake him up, she "kicked him in his butt." Instead of awakening him as one would expect, "I kicked him in his butt, and he just...rose up out of the bed like a raging demon and came after me and caught me in the dressing room and just, you know, lit into me with his fists."

If you think about it, this is not unlike her role of Nancy in *Act of Vengeance*, a film about women being violated and taking revenge on their perpetrators.

Another fight occurred on her birthday, when, after showering her with gifts, Richard laid down to rest, and asked her not bother him. "He was very generous with me. And it was very sweet. He had things sort of tucked in every nook and cranny of the house.... I wanted to tweak his toe. He said, 'Don't do that or else I'm going to show you why you shouldn't do that.' So I called his bluff."

Jennifer couldn't resist the opportunity to tweak his toes. She annoyed him, she bragged, until "he came after me, grabbed a Cognac bottle and started whacking me over the head with it.... It was horrible."

I could see that she provoked him. Just as she had that night when I was playing chess with Richard.

When Rivera complained that he didn't see much "angel" in her autobiography, that her "first sexual encounter was with your sister's boyfriend," he might have added that her relationship with Richard extended his pattern - after all, Richard was going with her best friend, Lucy Saroyan, when Jennifer met him.

Not long after the publication of *Tarnished Angel*, Richard invited Jennifer to come back and help him.

Jennifer got Richard to appear on some of the television talk shows to discuss his misogyny. But now Richard was frail and the power of his former self was missing. I thought he looked pathetic as he sat beside Jennifer, who was constantly berating him publicly for his treatment of her.

When Jennifer Lee came back, she arrived like the cavalry, according to one reporter. Richard was happy to have Jennifer back to take care of his affair. He had to marry her, but this was to facilitate business. They had no sexual relations then. Richard nevertheless went on live network television in August, and called her a Nazi. "I said that because she gives me a hard time sometimes. I appreciate Jennifer more than ever. I just wish she'd lighten up. She is a strong woman. I want to say: 'you don't have to be strong with me, Jenny. Because if I want to fight now, I can't.'"

He was too sick. Before Jenny came back, the only kind of women who visited him, he said, "Are the kind I gotta pay."

Rashon would tell me about those kind of women that he had to pay. "What I hated was the way the white women use to exploit Richard."

When he would have a girl over, he would ask them to take as much as they thought they were worth. He would always have a stack of money by the bed, hundreds, thousands dollar bills.

"The black hoes would take about two hundred; the white hoes would take up to 5 thousand dollars. It would piss me off. I was tempted to say, 'Bitch, you know you didn't deserve that. I should rob your ass!'

"But the sisters would take only two hundred. They wanted to come back and get close to Richard. But even if they came back a few more times, they would never get next to Richard."

One night in August 1992, he went to the Comedy Store on Sunset Strip and announced that he was going back on stage. He started coming every night and sitting in his limousine, while the crowd outside shouted, "Richard is back!" and "We love you, Richard." One of the people waiting outside to wish his return to comedy was none other than his old running buddy, Warren Beatty.

He did go back on stage, briefly. When he appeared at the Comedy Store, the crowd went silent when he sputtered and rambled incoherently. When he couldn't take anymore, they yelled, "We love you, Richard!"

He traveled across the country, making his first live performances since 1986. He was doing six shows in ten nights. However, at this point he had joked about his heart attacks, his shooting his car, and his nearly burning himself to death. Sometimes, M.S. interrupted his act. Why not joke about M.S.?

From time to time, he became confused and finished the act before his time was up. He was ill, but he was able to appear in public. Eventually, he entered a stage during which he could not carry on a routine for more than twenty minutes. He was nearing his last performance.

Chapter Forty Five

No Longer The Fool – 1995

I T WAS APPROPRIATE that Pryor's last stand up performance would take place at the Comedy Store on Sunset Boulevard. This was to be Pryor's last performance. It was also appropriate that it would take place at the Comedy Store, where he had his beginning in the early 70s.

On the way to the event at the Comedy Store, as the van went passed a narrow bend in Coldwater Canyon, Jennifer began to ridicule Pryor in front of Robert Chalmers, the reporter who was recording the incident.

"All the time that Richard beat me up I never dialed 911." Pryor, his baseball cap set at an unsuitably jaunty angle, said nothing. [43]

I wondered what he was really thinking. Jennifer was running the show. Had Richard ever seen Jennifer's film *Act of Avengers* (1974), in which she is a member of the "Rape Squad," a group of women who go out to kill men who raped women.[44]

When they arrived at the Comedy Store, his wheelchair was put on a hydraulic hoist. It carried him to the stage door. Then two big fellows carried him in. Once inside, they took him by his shoulders and walked him on stage, in such a way that it appeared he was walking himself.

The capacity audience in the small room gave him an astounding round of applauds. He looked at the audience.

"I haven't been on stage in a long time," he said. "I don't have a rehearsed act. I'm winged it. That is real hard for me. And getting up here was hard," he added.

He looked to the stagehands who helped him get on the stage.

"I wish you guys would stop helping me. I can get up here with canes. I'm gonna do that. I'm going to get a cane."

He was up on the stage for 20 minutes and was well received by a highly sympathetic audience. His voice was so weak as to be sometimes barely audible, and he occasionally repeated himself.

Then he began a dialogue with God. "God told me to slow down," he said. "Take your time, smell the roses. I never did stop to smell the roses. He said, 'take five' He can *make* you take five," he told the audience. They jumped up with applause.

"God got mad at me," he went on, "because I tried to kill myself. God said, 'No. You're not going to die. But I'm going to fuck you up.' I said, 'Wait, God. I don't understand.' He said, 'Oh. You will.' He told me: 'it's part of my plan." I said, "Fuck your plan!"

He glared over at Jennifer.

"That's Jennifer," he said. "She's in charge of me now. I was married to the bitch, man. And I dogged her awful when we were married. I beat her up and shit. Now its payback time. I wake up every morning and I say 'God, please. Don't let her remember.'"

He makes a gesture. It is familiar and yet classic, like the old days, when he was at the top of his game.

Richard's persona is a stage fool. A man in the front let out a high-pitched squeal. "Yeah, man," Pryor wheezed. "That' the way I laugh too!" A champagne glass fell to the floor. "What's that? White people rioting?"

He talked about his suicide attempt, his impotence and his tendency to urinate involuntarily. "The dog says: 'Rich, man. That's my spot. I have been pissing that geranium for two years.'"

His will was changed, Rashon told me. They forced him to have a vasectomy. He was fine, Rashon told me. "He was fucking and as long as Richard's fucking he is going to survive."

Good point, there.

"Why the vasectomy?" I asked Rashon.

"One of the wives said we couldn't have him having no more babies. He is going to take all the inheritance from the rest of the children. So they had his dick tied off. After that, he lost interest in life.

Richard was asked if he had the vasectomy willingly. He said, "No," and when asked if it had any affect on him, he replied, "My dick won't get hard."

Back on the stage at the Comedy Store, in his last act to thrill the public, he is taking the audience with him on a ride to the hospital.

"I was going to the hospital to have open heart surgery," he said, "One of my ex-wives wanted me to buy her a dress. I said, 'Can't it wait?'"

Big applause on that one.

"What do you need a dress for? For my *funeral?*"

This got big laughs too. They thought it was really funny that his ex-wife was getting ready for his funeral.

"Can't you wait until after the operation?"

The audience encouraged him to drag out the big demon, the one that showed they really identified with his ex-wife.

"Why can't you wait?" he asked his ex-wife.

Then he brings out the real issue.

"There is a law in California, that says if you get married, you will have to pay—one way or another!"

They liked that admission.

"I said, I want to get married, but why bring the lawyers into it. Once the lawyers start talking to the judges, you are finished.

"There are those of you out there who will never break up. Good luck on that. But for the rest of us—"

Big chuckles on that one too.

"My wife wrote a book about me," he said, referring to Jennifer's book, *Tarnished Angels* (1993). The book is not, technically about Richard, but his point is that she got it published because it had a lot of scenes in it about how Richard beat her up.

"I thought, 'Ah, well, it's okay.' I just dismissed it," he joked. This was a mistake on his part, he suggests; in retrospect, he should have read it. The moral here is that, if somebody writes a book about you beating them up, read it.

"We got back together," he grinned. "For three days, it was great!"

He looked over at Jennifer, who is also grinning. "Then on the fourth day! She became *Kathy Bates*!"

It was a derisive, and decisive, cut, but it was funny. They all stood up.

"Thank you!"

That was it. He bowed his head, slightly. It was the last public joke he told.

In some measure, Richard was rejecting the role of public fool. He tried to disavow himself of the public fool, and tried to make light of her control by pretending that he was in his ex-wife's hands. When he left the Comedy Store that night, which was his last farewell to the world he had inhabited for the last three decades.

This was the end of his career. But it was not the end of Richard.

Now in thinking over that meeting, I can see his lingering bitterness with Jennifer. In referring to Clint Eastwood's marital problem, he equated his own problems with Eastwood's. "You can never win with a woman!"

His father, Buckey, was cruel to him—yet helpful. In some ways, his father was like Mudbone. Like Mudbone he is sagacious and embarrassing at the same time.

On March 3, 2000, Richard kicked his son Richard Pryor, Jr. out of the house. About three years before, Richard Pryor's two-year-old grandson was in a critical condition after suffering smoke inhalation in a house fire that also injured Pryor's son, authorities said. Richard Pryor Jr., 34, fled the house. The cause of the fire was under investigation.

On March 6 his son sued to take over the household. Richard is quoted as saying that he "hates him." How much like this incident was to Richard's own life? I would say very close to the same. Richard was forced to look through his father's armor and see his sympathetic heart. Perhaps his sons will have to do that for him.

In a six-month period of time, Rashon informed me, when the wills were getting changed, Richard went down suddenly. He would defecate on himself. He asked Rashon and his wife to change his diaper, and wipe him. At that time, he was out of here. The spirit was gone. It was worse than comatose. Richard was gone.

The most disgusting thing was the funeral. It should have been bigger, bigger recognition. And that was because of Jennifer Lee. "I don't hate Jennifer," Rashon went on, "but if there were a reason to hate her, this would have been it."

She let Richard go out like that," he lamented. "So many people loved him. It should have been like James Brown's funeral."

But Richard's funeral was nothing like James Brown's funeral. Rashon would tell me how disappointed he was that it looked so ordinary, and the only big star that came was Dinah Ross. Rashon doesn't believe that Jennifer got in touch with Eddie Murphy or Red Foxx or Quincy Jones.

There was no music. Diana Ross sang "Amazing Grace" and it filled the whole chapel like her voice was a symphony.

And yet, Rashon had to thank Jennifer for what she did in giving Richard's last days the dignity that he deserved. She stood by him and made the calls that brought people to the house to wash and bathe him and feed him. Unfortunately, Richard's ex-wives didn't do that.

In the end, though, Rashon gave Jennifer respect. "What she went through with Richard." he said, "I can't comment on. That's their business. I can't get to that." Then, he said, "But there is a point in which Richard belongs, not to Jennifer, but to all of us. Because he shared it with all of us. You can't take his humor personal, and it should be shared like that. The last moment should have been shared like that. The real people wanted to see Richard. The opportunity was not there."

CHAPTER FORTY SIX

TEACHING RICHARD- PRYOR LIVES!

I TAUGHT A CLASS on Richard at UC Santa Barbara in 2005. I took a position in the African American studies department. I decided to teach a course on Richard Pryor, because I wanted to see where his place was in the next generation. It turned out to be a great way to make that discovery about the new generation's view of Richard's life in comedy and films. Since my students were in their twenties, I had to provide a context to explain Pryor's humor - contexts that no longer existed. There was a generation gap.

The class was almost equally divided by gender - ten men and twelve women. There were three black men and seven whites. There were twelve women, five white and five black. There was one Asian female and one Chicano female. Most students started the class with little knowledge of Pryor's work. About five of them had seen a movie. My task was to introduce them to a cult figure whose significance had depended on the times he lived in. The world that produced Pryor no longer existed. None of them were born when Pryor was at his peak (1977), or even when his powers began to wane in 1980s.

With Pryor's fans today, it is no longer a question of censorship. What makes people continue to laugh at him? How does one explain to young people Pryor without the political context of the 60s, 70s, 80s, and 90s?

Every session we began with a dose of Richard Pryor, beginning with his earliest recordings, when he was imitating Bill Cosby's "clean" humor, up to his last film.

In writing this book, *Pryor Lives!* I have tried to stay away from analyzing Richard's humor. To do so would stop the flow of the narrative. But not to analyze Richard's humor and joke strategy is to miss the real fun with Richard.

This chapter, then, is where I will analyze Richard's comedy and its relationship to joke structure. In discussing the social dramas against the on-stage dramas, I have purposely ignored a large part of the equation, and that is the joke itself.

Jokes are really about groups and group identification. In order to get this point across to my class, I gave them an introduction to a few terms and a few concepts about comedy that guided Richard's genius.

I began the class with a definition of the terms "esoteric" and "exoteric," as they are known in anthropology. In order to explain the exoteric/esoteric factor in folklore, I began the class with a joke. "What is the first thing a sorority girl does in the morning? Answer: Gets up and goes home."

The class laughs. Then I explain that these jokes were collected from a member of a sorority, and are what folklorist calls esoteric humor, meaning humor collected by a member of the group about that group. When frat boys tell jokes about sorority girls, it is called *exoteric* humor. We then go into black humor, pointing out how Pryor mined his point of view from black people themselves. Most of what passes as black culture is filtered through the eyes of whites, and this is exoteric.

I had them read Enid Welsford's, *The Fool; his social and literary history.* I gave them an essay, "Jokes," by Mary Douglass, the British anthropologist. I wanted them to see that the role Richard played in society had ancient roots in the court jester and fools. Mrs. Douglass studied the Joke and its rituals and rites in African tribal societies. The ritual and rites of everyday in these societies are balanced by private and public joking. In some of same ways, Richard's daily life became a part of his joking career.

I told them about Dick Tarlton, who was the court jester (during Shakespeare's time) for Queen Elizabeth. In plays like "King Lear," Shakespeare used Tarlton for a model, it is said. I had them realize that the Queen of England regularly employed professional fools to help her make good decisions. I also introduced them to University of Maryland Professor Lawrence E. Mintz, the wonderful scholar on the art of stand-up comedy, in "Standup Comedy As Social and Cultural Mediation."

I did not give them any number of books on the theory of comedy - from Aristotle to Bergson. I gave them only one book to read. In a slim volume, entitled *Wit and It's Relation to the Unconscious*, Sigmund Freud laid out the best theory of comedy technique I have ever read. To write the book, he collected over two hundred Jewish jokes, which he uses as the basis of his analysis.

"The central ideas in Freud's treaties on jokes," wrote Elliott Oring, professor of Anthropology at UCLA, in his book, *The Jokes of Sigmund Freud: A study in Humor and Jewish Identity*, "are easily grasped and understood." He is right that Freud's ideas on humor can be easily understood; my students, after some hard reading and class discussions, seem to have understood them. The problem is that the rest of the world has not; Freud's ideas on comedy are not generally known as well as his theories on dreams and psychoanalysis; they are certainly not known in relation to Richard Pryor.

"Freud carefully distinguishes between technique of the joke, which constitutes the joke's envelope or façade, and the substance of the joke," Professor Oring explained, "that is, the joke's *underlying thought*."[45]

As soon as Richard began to tell "dirty jokes," making allusion to black folklore, he came to use this facade for humor to highlight the underlying thoughts of his comedy. Professor Oring explains the structure of Richard's jokes this way: "These two aspects (the facade and the underlying thought) of the joke are theoretically independent of one another."

What Richard learned in Berkeley was that the joke's façade was only that—a façade for the underlying thought, the forbidden idea. One never told jokes for the fun of telling jokes. Freud divides jokes into two types: The Innocent Joke and the Tendentious Joke.

The innocent jokes are told just for amusement, for a demonstration of the joke teller's wit. But it is the tendentious jokes that are of psychological interest to the joke teller and his audience. The tendentious jokes always have a purpose- usually hostile or obscene, two of its main forms.

The Innocent joke

I want to tell you I'm really excited to be in San Francisco, I've never performed here before, I really love it a lot. I'm from Peoria? Where? [Addressing the audience] Illinois! [Audience reaction is dumbfounded, like who cares] Oh? Yeah? Usually, that's the reaction that I usually get. Or people throw up. But I'm from an average family—you know, eleven kids. My grandmother use to wash us. Some times, we could get washed three or four times, because somebody didn't show up. They all looked alike to her. 'Gimme a kid,' [imitates her] Once she hadn't had a bath in a month.

This is the innocent joke, because it has no purpose other than the laughter. Richard does get a lot of laughs on this cut. The underlying thought: black people have so many children that they can't tell one from the other—even if he is a white kid down the street.

The fact that Pryor says he is from an "average" neighborhood I saw façade for the joke, but it's a façade that doesn't contain any hidden substance, or deeper meaning.

Tendentious joke

According to Freud, a 'tendentious' joke is one that can be reduced to an underlying inhibited thought, and it is such jokes that prove to be the greatest psychological significance to a joke teller and the teller's audience."

He goes further to explain why the tendentious joke is more pleasurable than the innocent joke - "The joke technique comes to the aide of the inhibited thought by circumventing the inhibition. The technique diverts the attention and allows the censorship function to relax."[46]

When the censor is relaxed, then the joke happens. "Then, as is characteristic of jokes, the forgiven thought is suddenly and abruptly expressed. It is too late for the censorship to react."

When whites heard Pryor in the Berkeley days in Mandrake's, they laughed heartily; the least of the reasons was that they were not holding on to their old prejudices about blacks. In letting go they turned their energy from repression to liberation.

"The energy that had been directed to censoring the forbidden thoughts," Oring wrote, "has suddenly become superfluous and is discharged in the behavior of laughter."

He then gets to the real source of the joke's pleasure. "Although the technique of the jokes may in themselves be enjoyable and pleasurable, it is through the circumvention of the censorship and the expression of inhibited thoughts that the joke makes available its deepest source of pleasure."

Remember the Playboy Innocent Joke? Here is the same joke as a tendentious joke:

Tendentious

I use to get upset waiting for a taxi. I thought it was because I was black. Then I saw that Whitey had a problem getting a taxi too. [Imitates the white guy yelling for cab] I'm white! [Laughter] but cabs never stop!

Even in this joke, it is a joke for itself. There is a denial of race in the joke. The comic reverses himself, seeing race was not the reason he wasn't getting a cab: even white guys don't get taxi. He calls the white guy "whitey," which is a neutral term.

Later as he transformed his comedy, he uses the same reference to whites as "honkey" in a meaner and leaner way. But this is because he now wants to attach a "purpose" to his humor—making it more "tendentious."

The source of pleasure for the white audience is that they were relieved of their racism. They were awakened by the way Richard used the "magic" words—nigger and motherfucker.

The tendentious joke has three forms, as Freud wrote, they are either "jokes that strip naked, or obscene jokes, aggressive (hostile) jokes, and cynical (critical, blasphemous) jokes."

It was Richard's hostile jokes, obscene jokes, and skeptical jokes that made my class laugh the hardest. So why was that?

Both innocent jokes and tendentious jokes work with displacement and condensation of double meanings; however, the tendentious jokes are aimed at insulting, ridiculing, satirizing others.

It was easy to see that the reason Bill Cosby was called a "clean comic," was because he told "innocent" jokes. His jokes about his childhood rarely alluded to white racism.

Most critics agree that Pryor's comic career can be divided between his first attempt at comedy—in which Bill Cosby influenced him— and his transformation in Berkeley in 1968-71.

Richard tried clean comedy, too, or what he liked to call "white bread" humor. But it was not for him. It took a long time coming, and it didn't come until 1967, when he was performing at the Aladdin Hotel in Las Vegas. Another important comparison with these two categories are the categories introduced by Mrs. Douglass, the standard joke and the spontaneous joke. The standard joke is, of course, like the white bread humor, or Freud's innocent joke. The spontaneous joke is closer to Freud's tendentious joke, or what we know from Richard as "crazy."

Instead of improvisations, Richard came on the stage at the Hungry i in San Francisco and performed with "mostly prepared pieces that often resembled the stuff Bill Cosby was doing," David Felton, *Rolling Stone* reporter, wrote. He went on to say:

On the very first track, "Peoria," his performance is as much like a traditional stands up, as you're likely to hear him sound. His voice is surprisingly young (he's 25) and amiable. He tells some contrived, sanitized jokes about his childhood in Peoria, Illinois, where he was born to a prostitute in 1940. And his language is clean! He doesn't use any four-letter words in fact, he doesn't use an obscenity until track seven, and he doesn't use one of his favorite terms of endearment, motherfucker, until track 20, when, as we will, see has a tremendously liberating effect.[47]

Felton thinks that the two words—'motherfucker' and 'nigger'—"magically free him to fall in love with his characters," make them sweeter and more human—something the censors could never understand."

As we listened to Richard's "clean" period, his Bill Cosby period, I noticed that the class rarely belly laughed. Usually, the class would only smile.

"The pleasurable effect of an innocuous joke," Freud wrote, "is mostly a moderate one; a distinctly agreeable feeling, slight smile, is usually all it is able to provoke in the listener."

Here is the seed of the hostile joke, the kind of joke that Freud calls tendentious, the kind that made Pryor's reputation as a comic genius. In this joke is a façade, but here there is also an "inhibited" thought: that white racism is wrong and that it is based on sexual envy. The white audience is liberated by the black humor.

But with the tendentious jokes there is "a sudden outburst of laugher." Since the technique is the same for both forms, Freud suspects that a "tendentious joke has a source of pleasure at its disposal—by virtue of its tendency- to which innocuous jokes have no access."

Freud's essay turned out to be a way to introduce the class to Pryor's humor. The late Professor Alan Dundes introduced me (and others) to Freudian interpretation of folklore. I found many of the theories of comedy to be abstract or dated. But Freud's essay was instructive and oddly relevant.

What was different after the Berkeley revolution was that Richard began to relate his jokes to a personal motivation. Although jokes are usually passed down, and are not the creation of the people who tell them, the true meaning of them can be traced to the joke teller's personality.[48]

As Oring wrote "…even when jokes are borrowed from an established social tradition and retold, they should not be exempted automatically from questions concerning personal motivation."

Why, he asked, does the teller choose this particular joke to tell at this particular time? More and more, experiment after experiment with a white audience, convinced Richard that what people wanted to hear was jokes that were rooted in his personality, jokes that had as their façade the life of a man who had been reared in a whore house, one who rooted his humor in the personality cult.[49] For Freud, words like 'motherfucker' and ' nigger' would have a liberating effect because they elude the censors and allowed the forbidden meaning to slip through.

Freud's categories of two types of jokes corresponded neatly with Richard's two types: White Bread humor (innocent) of the Bill Cosby variety and the "Good Shit" (tendentious).

Yet in his first album, *Richard Pryor,* the tendentious jokes are rare, as most of them are clean. After the Prison Play cut, he returns to the clean type of joke, as in the next one.

Here is a brilliant portrait of a white mid western white hick. No purpose is intended other than Richard's gift of showing off the wit and brilliance of a comic figure.

In his bit, "Movie Stars in the bathroom," Richard continues with the joke that the president (and other officials) don't go to the bathroom. While he does mention President Johnson, he doesn't go as political as he does in Craps, where he says that Nixon was a lesbian and vice president Agnew is his woman.

In the next cut, "Hank's Place,"(1968) is a clean version of the Craps, where he really gets dirty and uses the joke as a façade for more important inhibited thoughts.

He ends the album with "Mankind," which he recorded at the Troubadour, April. 1968. This ended Richard's career as a clean comic, and when I met him, he was beginning to see his comedy from the point of view of the black community. This was the esoteric view of black comedy, but after meeting Cosby in San Francisco, he went even further.

This is shown by turning, as we did, to the jokes Richard told after his transformation in Berkeley.

For the class, I began to play the dirty stuff from *Craps: After Hours.* There Pryor started with words like "fuck," "bitch," "nigger," and "motherfucker.")

They laughed in loud, outbursts of pleasure. Their reaction was a stark contrast to their reaction to the "clean" humor. Did black students laugh differently from the white students? Did the women laugh differently from the men?

The young white males laughed along with the black males more than I expected but what I didn't expect was to see all of the females laughing along with them.

What had happened between 1966 and 1971? For one thing, we changed presidents from Johnson to Nixon. We saw the rise of Black Power, the explosion of African American literature, the rise of the Black Panthers, and the white resistance to black Americans throwing off the cloak of shame and humiliations that the segregated America brought on. In 1971, the Vietnam War was coming to a close and African Americans had seen how empty white people's promises had become.

The number one song from 1968 was James Brown's "Say It Loud, I'm Black and I'm Proud." In 1971, they were still proud, but their pride had been tarnished by broken promises of the Civil rights movement.

After we examined Pryor's obscenity as a ventilation of oppressed feelings, we breathed freer. But when students discussed other comedians, such as Martin Lawrence, the vulgarity returned. It seems that only Pryor could make the most obscene humor elegant and insightful. How did he do that?

But let's see. Like most of her classmates, Gaylord, a female student, sees the connection between satire and oppressed cultures. "Through characters such as Mudbone, anecdotes, one liners," she goes on, "Pryor conveyed the shared experience of black people in America."

Students tend to look at stereotypes as all negative. But the work of Alan Dundes shows that stereotypes are actually helpful. In his study of stereotypes and joke cycles, he shows how stereotypes can be used profitably in thinking about how society works in general. For him, jokes "perform a defensive function" in allowing members of society to let off steam about issues that produce anxiety. If there is no anxiety in the society, there are no jokes. He expands on this insight:

Joke telling brings about ego satisfaction for the joke teller, he claims:

"[Jokes] and wit allow certain topics to emerge that are otherwise taboo. However, under some circumstances.... anxiety may become all pervasive. In such cases, jokes arise to counter offer a threatening situation, and thus to prove a release of anxiety. The joke becomes a "harmless aggression- an aggression that hurts no one but that provides a transitory gain for the joker's ego."[50]

One cannot underestimate the good that joke telling did for Richard's own ego. I remember how he would tell me that he got more out of his routines than his audience did, that his comedy "helped" him. Larry Murphy said that he was not sure Richard would have surveyed his ordeal without his sense of humor. "It was his comedy that took the upper hand when it was needed, when he was suffering and refused medication...the jokes gave him the strength to deal with his ordeal." After the freebase accident, Richard said he used "self love" to heal himself. This love of self may have begun with his ego ideal from telling jokes.

CHAPTER FORTY SEVEN

RICHARD PRYOR AND MISOGYNY

ONE OF THE surprises I got from the Pryor class was the attitude that my female students had towards humor about women. I had expected that they would object to his raunchy comedy as offensive misogyny. On the contrary, they found his jokes to be – not just funny – with a positive, healthy attitude towards women. Richard would have loved the reception given to him by the young students, especially the women who agreed with his slant on women. For example, I was apprehensive when I played this joke:

"A lot of people never masturbate, especially girls. 'Oh, no, no, I never touch myself. That vibrator is for my back.'"

One student—a white female—compared Freud's idea of women with Pryor. Freud was limited in believing that women couldn't laugh at sexual jokes unless they were "disguised." Women, Pryor believed, could laugh at undisguised jokes. For young women, Pryor was liberating.

Contrary to the popular view of Pryor as having a negative view of women, most of my students thought his view were healthy. His comedy viewed women as active participants in -not passive victims - in Richard's life.

When we discussed why they laughed as much as the men, I began to understand why. Kathleen Matlock, 20, wrote, "Pryor took [white] women off the pedestal that white hegemony had historically placed them." She defended Pryor against attacks of being anti-white, and said that in his interviews, "he mixes comedy and social commentary."

After describing the raunchiest scene in Pryor's early recordings, two students explained how these scenes liberate women.

After quoting from the routine in which Pryor says, "The bitch was so fine, I wanted to suck her daddy's dick," she writes, "This term symbolizes the power that women hold in society."

But Lauren Alexander, a senior, gave the most complete, detailed analysis of why Pryor is better on sex than Freud.

Historically, white women were outside the pale of humor, Miss Alexander claims. "Cultural ideologies excluded women from humor." It was not until the 20th century that women began to free themselves from the shackles of public laughter as being male. So far, so good. Like Pryor's humor which "exposes the absurdity inherent in American gender hierarchy."

This student had certainly hit on an important trait in Richard's genius: absurdity. "The nonsense in the joke," Freud wrote in *The Joke and Its Relation to The Unconscious*, "serves to expose and demonstrate another instance of nonsense."

For Richard, like Freud, absurdity is countered with another absurdity to show the "sense in non-sense."

As a kind of introduction to Richard's "Super Nigger," a seminal example of absurdity, I would like to give you one of Freud's own example of absurdity as an element in the joker.

There is this guy who takes his daughter to stay with a friend of his. He's a close friend, so he tells him to look out that his daughter doesn't get pregnant. He has already seen this guy had a young son. So he comes back after his trip, which lasted a few months, to find his daughter pregnant. So he goes to the guy, and he says, "Man, I told you that I wanted you to watch my daughter's virtue while I was away."

His friend couldn't explain the misfortune.

"Where did she sleep then?" he asked. She slept in the same room as my son."

"But how can you let her sleep in the same room with your son, when I begged you to look after her?'

"But there was her bed and then his bed, with a screen between them."

""And what if he'd gone round the screen?"

"Oh, I didn't think of that."

What is important is Freud's comment: "You have no right to blame me. How can you be so foolish as to hand your daughter over to a house where she had to lie in the company of a young man? As if it were possible for a stranger to be responsible for a girl's virtue under such circumstances!"

"I'm correlating women's humor with the black humor because both groups utilize the expression of humor to make collective integrity, and group solidarity."

Miss Alexander claims that in Pryor's *That Nigger's Crazy*, "woman's laughter satirizes the expectations that woman are innocent and pure."

After quoting the routine in which Richard says, 'I never got no pussy as a legal teenager (in a female voice) 'Ahhnn you can't even sing.'" Miss Alexander comments that "here, he satirizes the standard by choosing an absurd criterion such as singing." Although she may not know this, singing still plays a part in African American courtship.

In the same way, Pryor's routine about menstruation – in which the girl is on her period, and elicits the one-liner, 'Damn, bitch, you going to bleed to death! "This shows the absurdity in avoiding sexual intercourse."

"Here, in this joke, Pryor is mocking their practices, providing laughter and alleviating the pressure, imposed on them by culture and society," Miss Alexander wrote. In other words, the women laugh at the joke but for different reasons than a man does. Richard's humor is esoteric, even from the female's point of view.

And Freud? Freud believed that women need to have their sexual jokes "disguised." But, Richard Pryor's male/female performance calls attention to women and social conditions. "His exoteric humor arouses laughter because it alleviates them from structural oppression."

Because of women's "voicelessness," Pryor's humor "allows them to transcend gender barriers."

Sarah Zoucha, 20, wrote persuasively about this special world of the comedian's early life. "To be a comic," she wrote, "is to heal people." She gave examples of how Pryor's life-long belief in honesty stemmed from his early childhood. She places high standards on such a person who is destined to "attack existing standards."

Indeed, according to this student, the comic's role is to "deprecate others, to achieve a unique status in life." A comic is someone, she says, "with special powers."

She connects this transformation from clean comic to the dirty comic of the oral tradition to his stay in Berkeley from 1968 to the 1971. After Berkeley, "he reemerged …he spoke the truth, captured the absurdity of black people."

"It was in Pryor's genius to weave social commentary, blatant truth, and human nature that changed comedy forever," wrote Jennifer Gaylord. "This paper will discuss Pryor's ability to expose audiences to issues such as systemic and internalized racism, social class oppression, addiction, and feminism through satire." That's a lot, but it represented most of what students have come to appreciate about Richard Pryor's significance as a major American culture icon.

Other students explored the careers and talents of Bert Williams and Lenny Bruce on Pryor. Others studied his art of satiric impersonation. Starting with Aristophanes, Antonio Lewis, 20, explained the ancient art of impersonating political figures like Cleon, who was in the audience when Aristophanes lambasted him with an imitation. Most of the characters that Pryor played in such movies as *Harlem Nights*, *Silver Streak*, and *Stir Crazy* are impostors, Mr. Lewis told the class. One of the most brilliant skits of a political satire is Pryor playing - or impersonating- the president of the United States.

We had many heated discussions, but the most memorable one was when the members of a panel on psychological interpretation of Pryor's humor meandered off into a discussion of comedians versus hip-hop performers.

One student, after reviewing *Jo Jo Dancer*, saw the film as a fictional autobiography that allowed his unconscious to speak for him.

One day I played *Which Way Is Up?* I had intended to play only half an hour, but the film was so good, so fascinating, and so nostalgic, I played the whole film. Most of my students thought that *Which Way is Up?* was his best film, because it was closer to the early comic routines that established Pryor as different from other comedians. They may have also thought that it was his best film because their teacher had co-authored the screenplay.

The class showed me that Richard's life and humor will become a part of the learning experience of all young people in this country. For them, and for future generations, Richard Pryor lives.

CHAPTER FORTY EIGHT

EPILOGUE

THE LAST TIME I saw Richard was on Sunset Boulevard, Hollywood, in 1995, at the book signing of his autobiography *Pryor Convictions*.

After the event, he invited me back to is home in Sherman Oaks. I remembered the path to his house and the garden around it. I still see him in his wheel chair and see his smile and dignity.

He and I met alone for an hour or so. We just sat and talked as if we were back in Berkeley in the 1970s. I felt he had done what he sat out to do. He was relaxed, and seemed satisfied with his life.

As we sat there, talking about this and that, I realized how much Richard changed my life, and I suspect I had some small effect on his; if I did, it gives me great pleasure.

That was the last time I saw him.

This is my last view of richard.

Since that time I have had the opportunity to be in Los Angles, I often drive through Sherman Oaks where I last saw him, and I think of the 1970s and black revolutionaries at Laney College in Oakland, California where he joked publicly about racial mistreatment of black people in prison and out of prison. I think of another group of people, the new age, alternative group, at the Hollywood Bowl, in 1977. You have done wonderful things, he told the mostly gay crowd. He praised them when it was not a popular thing to do. I think of the Hollywood Celebrity crowd in the 90s—the rich, famous people like Burt Reynolds, and Warren Beatty and other celebrities who celebrated him as a spokesman for the tired, the rich, and the still unhappy group.

I think of my college students at U C Berkeley and Santa Barbara, and how they are embracing a new Pryor, free of rancor and insult, as a pure comedian.

Now, in 2013, a new audience of young people is finding that Pryor is still alive.

I think about how he took the traditional standup form and used it to become America's most important social satirist and cultural hero. It is Richard's comic laughter that unites all of us, that "flawed species," and it is his laughter that we take shelter from the blistering rays of reality. We laugh and in the laughter we hear and see and feel that Richard is, indeed, alive.

Cecil Brown,
Berkeley
July 15, 2013.

SCREENING OF RICHARD PRYOR:

OMIT LOGIC.

I ATTENDED A SCREENING of the film, *Richard Pryor: Omit Logic*, where I met some old friends, (like Rashon) and new friends like Sara Hutchinson and Marie Zenovich, who directed it.

There was Tom Mount, the one producer that Richard got along with. Mount had produced about eleven of Richard's films ("Carwash," for example) when Mount worked for (and later became President of) Universal Pictures.

APPENDIX

The social drama number	Social Drama (Real Life) RL	Breach	Crisis	Redress (Art: films)	Reintegration (Back into Real Life)
Social drama One	The Government	IRS Tax	10 days in Jail	Performance with Flip Wilson	Stir Crazy,
Social drama Two	Gays at the Hollywood Bowl	The word "faggot"	He challenged the gay community	He found the courage	He helped the gay community to unify
Social drama Three	Blue Collar	Hit actor with a chair		Great film, *Blue Collar*	Awareness and consciousness of acting
Social drama Four	How to shoot a car	Domestic violence and ménage a trios. The word "faggot"	Censorship	Comedy album & *JoJo Dancer*	Open up comedy to descendants
Social drama Five	*California Suite*	Defend actress	Fight with Ray Stark	Ray Stark helped with actress	Worked well with Ray Stark
Social drama Six	*Stir Crazy*	Watermelon seeds	He challenges the film community	He learns how to risk it all.	He got a million dollars more
Social drama Seven	Burning with Freebase incident	Flames were too long	He is in the hospital, Jim Brown	Here and Now Concert films Mudbone	Spiritual rewards as Cultural Hero

NOTE ON SOURCES

FOR THE MCCONNELL essay, see "Commonweal, New York Oct. 23, 1992. For the comparison to Lenny Bruce, see Albert Goldman, in *Freakshow,* New York, 1971 "The Comedy of Lenny Bruce."

Lawrence E. Mintz, "Standup Comedy as Social and Cultural Mediation, *American Quarterly.* 78.

My account is similar to what Pryor told David Felton, see David Felton, "Jive Times: Richard Pryor Lily Tomlin & The Theater of the Routine, *Rolling Stone,* Oct.10, 1974, p. 44. Also, see Richard's own account published in *Pryor Convictions,* 1995. p. 59-60.

Mr. Elwood gave the unpublished letter to me a few months before his death.

Personal interviews with David Reverend Banks, Elaine Brown, Michael Campus, Melvin Van Peebles, and Robin Williams were conducted on May, 9, 12, 13, 14, and 24 respectively, 2008. The Dave Chappell interview took place on June 9,2008. The interview with Michael Ashburne took place in December 2012, in Berkeley.

BIBLIOGRAPHY

Billington, Sandra. *A Social History of the Fool*. The Harvester Press, 1984.sh

Brown, Cecil. "Blacks On the Hollywood Plantation: Richard Pryor," *Mother Jones*, (cover story), 1981.

Dundes, Alan. *Cracking Jokes: Studies of Sick Humor Cycles and Stereotypes*. Ten Speed Press, Berkeley, Ca. 1987.

Douglass, Mary. "Jokes," in *Implicit Meanings. Oxford*, 1976.

Freud, Sigmund. *Wit and its Relation to the Unconscious*, 1910.

Goldman, Albert. *Freakshow*, New York, Athenaeum, 1971.

Jodorowsky, A. *Psychomagic: The transformative Powers of Shamans Psychotherapy* (2010). Park Street Press.

—————. *The Spiritual Journey of Alejandro Jodorowsky*. Park Street Press.

Klapp, Orrin E. "The Fool as a Social Type," *The American Journal of Sociology*, Vol. 55, No.2 (Sept., 1949) pp. 157-162.

Mintz, Lawrence. *American Quarterly*. Vol.37. Mp 1. American Humor (Spring, 1995), pp. 71-80. The Johns Hopkins University Press.

Roheim, Ezra. *The Gates of the Dream*. International Universities Press, New York, 1952.

Roheim, Geza. *The Eternal Ones of the Dream: A Psychoanalytic Interpretation of Australian Myth and Ritual.* International Universities Press, New York,1971.

Thompson, Robert Farris. *Flash of the Spirit.* Vintage,1984.

Rovin, Jeff. *Richard Pryor: black and Blue.* Bantam Books, 1983.

Williams, John. *If I Stop, I'll Die.* Thundermouth Press, 2006.

Welsford, Enid. *The Fool: His Social and Literary History.* Peter Smith, 1966.

Zijderveld, Anton C. *Reality in a Looking-Glass: Rationality Through an Analysis of Traditional Folly.* University of Tilburg, 1982.

(ENDNOTES)

Endnotes

1   *San Francisco Examiner,* Sat. Feb 20, 1971.

2   Goldman, Albert. *Freakshow,* New York, Athenaeum, 1971. p. 194.

3   Ibid.. p. 93

4   http://en.wikipedia.org/wiki/Main_Page, Attica

5   Hollie I. West, "Comic Pryor," *The Washington Post,* July 28, 1969, p. 65.

6   Ibid.

7   Reported in *Rolling Stone* by David Felton, Oct. 10, 1974, p. .65

8   David Felton, "Richard Pryor's New Film Attacks the Heart, casts Out Past Demons and Foils the Censors," May 3, 1979.

9   *Los Angeles Times,* June 14, 1974, pg D3.

10   Ibid.

11   Lawrence E. Mintz, "Standup Comedy as Social Mediation," *American Quarterly, p. 76.*

12   *Ibid.*

13   Ibid.

14   Ibid.

15   Sardi Vancocur, "A Sparkling Car Wash," *Washington Post* Sept 3, 1976.

17   Hollie I. West, "Comic Pryor," *The Washington Post*, July 28, 1969. p. 75.

18   Ibid.

19   West, p. 81.

20   *Jet Magazine*, Sept. 1976.

21   See, Victor Turner, *From Ritual to Theater*, Amazon edition.

22   Lee Grant, "A Night for Rights' at the Bowl," *LA Times*, September 20 1977.

23   *LA times*, Sept. 25, 1977. Correspondence.

24   Ibid.

25   *LA times*, Sept. 25, 1977. Correspondence.

26   Lee Grant, *LA Times*, Dec 18, 2005.

27   Lee Grant, *LA Times*, Mar 5, 1977.

28   David Felton, "Richard Pryor's New Film Attacks the Heart, casts Out Past Demons and Foils the Censors," *Rolling Stone*, May 3, 1979.

29   Gene Siskel, *Chicago Tribune*, Nov 9, 1977, pg A9

30   Robert Chalmers, "No Joke," *The Observer life*, September 3, 1995, p. 27

31   "Nobody Move! It's Richard Pryor," Sunday, April 10, 2000. *Ask Jeeves*.

32   Rovin, *Black and Blue, p. 153*

33   Mary Douglass, "Jokes," p. 107.

34   Aljean Harmetz, *New York Times*, Aug 21, 1982.

36   David Felton, *Rolling Stone*, July 24, 1980, p. 14.

37   David Felton, "Richard Pryor's New Film Attacks the Heart, casts Out Past Demons and Foils the Censors," *Rolling Stone, May 3, 1979.*

38   Ibid.

39   Ibid.

40   Ibid.

41   Aljean Harmetz, *New York Times* Aug 21, 1982.

42   Ibid.

43   Robert Chambers, p. 3.

44   *Act of Vengeances: Rape Squad* (1974). See Internet search.
45   Elliot Oring, *The Jokes of Sigmund Freud: A study in Humor and Jewish Identity,* University of Pennsylvania Press, (1984), p. 10.
46   Ibid
47   Joel Dreyfuss, *Washington Post,* Sept 2 1975, "Some black Humor from Richard Pryor."
48   Alan Dundes, *Cracking Jokes,* p. 43
49   Ibid.
50   Ibid.,, p.78.

59488111R00204

Made in the USA
Charleston, SC
05 August 2016